The Legend of John Dietz

Pioneer Vigilante

Gunnard Landers

Badger Books Inc.
P.O. Box 192
Oregon, WI 53575

To my sisters, Jean, Betty, Sonya, Anita and Yvonne, family and friends.

Introduction

Pioneer Vigilante: The Legend of John Dietz is a true story. The confrontations between the Dietz family and the law are well documented in newspaper stories and court transcripts of the time. As is normal, the exact details of confrontations are less clear and are dependent upon the participants' interests and point of view. For the most part the story has been aligned with the version that had corroborating testimony or seemed most objective and least self-serving.

The day-to-day frontier routine and the personalities of the participants have been interpreted based on available information. In addition to recorded court testimony, John Dietz wrote a number of letters to the press. Additionally, reporters throughout the Midwest, from Milwaukee and from St. Paul, made the long journey to the Dietz homestead in order to report his story. These news articles relate what Dietz or family members reportedly said or did. As much as possible this information has been incorporated into the story, for instance, using portions of John's letters or testimony in his dialogue.

The headlines and advertisements at the beginning of each chapter were taken from newspapers of the time.

The story of John Dietz initially was of local interest, but in time spread to become nationwide. A headline in the *Phila-*

delphia Public Ledger of October 16, 1910 read: WHY JOHN DIETZ DEFIED A STATE AND AN ARMED POSSE. Another newspaper called Dietz one of the greatest heroes the state of Wisconsin ever had. Others called him a bloodthirsty outlaw.

The early 1900s were times of virulent muckrakers, violent union organization and outraged socialist politicking against the monopolistic practises of Rockefeller and the oil trusts, Vanderbilt and the railroads, Morgan and the banks, and Hines and the lumber mills. One man's stand against the big mills became a symbol of justified defiance.

The socialist elements of the press agreed, John Dietz would not have a chance against the "monied interests' in a court of law.

In time John Dietz's impact would help defeat a candidate running for U.S. senator, help prevent a governor from seeking re-election, and could gather 40,000 names on a petition in his support. Visiting reporters for the Milwaukee Journal, city fellas, were blithely informed by North Woods residents John Dietz could hit 198 out of 200 reporters at 300 yards and that he often salted his victims and ate them during the off-season for deer. The Wisconsin Supreme Court said the details of the final fight with Dietz "sounded like an extract from the annals of a Mexican revolution."

John Dietz's move to the isolation of Cameron Dam had all the appearances of the desperate move of a failed 43-year-old man. Only belatedly did he discover a company-owned logging dam sat partially astride his land. He took a stand and as a result became a cause célèbre, culminating with a posse of 73 men surrounding his farm. In the process he took his family, wife Hattie and six children with him, even refusing during, the final stand to let them walk out with the State Attorney General.

For more than six years, one man held off the power of the trusts, hired posses from Milwaukee and Chicago, the numerous sheriffs from Sawyer County, and the legal weight of the State of Wisconsin. The press and the public built John into a legend. Men trembled at his mere presence. Large armed posses abandoned wounded comrades and fled from a single man. When word passed through the tiny town of Winter that John Dietz was coming to town to rescue his wounded daughter and son, the town of more than 300 people panicked and did not sleep that night.

During the long years of fighting, Hattie tried to hold the family together. It was a monumental task. John was a force unto himself — a man who became so taken with his own cause he was heard to remark, "They can kill me as they did John Brown and then I suppose there will be another revolution."

Meanwhile one of his children died of disease. The family was ostracized. Two other children were shot. In the end, it was the family who paid the price.

— Gunnard Landers
March 1998

TORRENTS OF BLOOD FLOW ON THE BANKS OF THE YALU

Russia Loses 4,000 Men Killed in First Great Land Battle of the War with Japan

---

HOLDS UP DRIVE WITH A SHOTGUN

Determined Man at Cameron Dam Holds Big Log Drive Until Company Settles Vexations Delay and Much Expense Caused

---

Ask any "Jap" that you
may see,
"Why the Czar, with
Bear behind,"
had to climb a tree.
The Yanks, God Bless
the Yanks, says he,
They gave us Rocky
Mountain Tea.

CHAPTER I

He moved his family, wife Hattie and six children deep into the wilderness during the middle of the winter of 1901.

The announcement of the move had all but knocked Hattie on the floor. She read the hard look on John's face and knew his mind was set. Nevertheless she voiced her protest. Could John possibly comprehend what he was asking of them?

They argued. John naturally triumphed. Hattie's desires simmered without redress. John was the man, her husband. She had her say and then held silence: For the man is not of the woman, but the woman of the man. She recalled the passage well.

The family carried most of their worldly possessions with them in one wagon, meager results from years of toil, Hattie thought. She quashed her bitterness. They'd have to make do the best they could with what they had, she lectured her brood.

The Dietz family traveled east of Rice Lake. The first night they stayed with a homesteader, the eight of them crowded together on the cold living room floor with blankets, quilts and winter coats for warmth. The morning temperature hung at ten below. The sun gleamed a pale yellow through snow and frost-covered trees. The family ate the hosts' offered porridge for breakfast then heated rocks and gathered marsh grass to keep their feet warm. They loaded into the wagon and set out on their way.

Late that evening the frozen family stopped at a dilapidated cabin next to Bishop's Bridge. Hattie, fearing frostbite with the children, immediately started a fire and put snow in a kettle to melt. The unlit cabin was dark and gloomy and mounds of windblown snow had leaked through rotting logs. Johnny Ginger, less than a year old, cried for his meal. Young Helen and Stanley, ages four and five, whimpered over the pain of thawing fingers and toes. The oldest girl, Myra, 11, was still in a sulk over being moved far way from school and friends. The oldest boy, Clarence, grumbled his opposition. Only Leslie, 10, seemed to accept the move as a matter of course.

"This place isn't fit for an animal," Clarence muttered as he carried in a box filled with pots and pans.

"We haven't seen a house for miles," Myra added in support of her older brother.

"If you kids want the strap, I have it. " The speaker was their father, John F. Dietz. He was a solid man, a farmer, a woodsman, five feet ten, one hundred and ninety pounds. His brother, William, was the sheriff in nearby Barron county, one of the best lawmen the county ever had by some accounts.

People said the Dietz brothers were principled men, proud, honest. Their word was their bond.

"You kids don't understand," John said in his lecturing voice. He seemed amused at their distress. "I'm giving you opportunity here. We're the last of the pioneers. That's something for which you kids ought to be proud. When a man lives in the wilderness, a man learns what life is all about. In the wilderness the fruit of a man's toils are his and his alone. No man, no trust can take that away."

His brood stared silently, six pairs of wary eyes that laughed when he laughed but they knew better than to provoke his wrath.

The Dietz family lived only briefly at Bishop's Bridge before moving into another abandoned shanty owned by the Chippewa Lumber and Boom Company and located next to

the Price Dam on the Brunet River. John had talked to a foreman named Mulligan. "Could be the mill will need someone
to tend the sluice gates to the dam, come spring," Mulligan
said.

"There'll be some income there," John promised Hattie.

Hattie had simply nodded. The shack at Bishop's Bridge
was rotting and caving in. Anything would be better than that.
Besides, John had visited, promised the cabin was in good
condition, a nice place to live.

"There it is," young Helen cried.

Hope blossomed. Their necks craned. The log cabin was
grey with age. The door stood ajar. The only window was
broke. The center ridgepole sagged as if about to collapse.

Shoulders sagged. No one spoke.

"Well, what did you expect?" John shouted at Hattie's tight-
lipped disapproval. "A mansion? Our kind don't live in mansions. We're not part of the gilded crop."

Hattie ignored John and put herself to work, giving orders
and jumping to do things herself if the children were too slow.
It was one way to keep from thinking, keep busy, keep active.

John trailed her like a dog, arguing in her ear, trying to convince her he was right. "Do you think I want to be here?"
John's jaw flexed with tension. "Did I not try? I farmed. I
worked for the mills, for Stinsen. Frank Stinsen. Remember
that time I told you I was a road monkey? Barely Clarence's
age over there. Mucking horse and oxen manure out of the icy
sleigh ruts. There comes Stinsen, just as high and mighty as
you please riding in his cutter. Blanket over his lap like a girl.
Looks down at me and says, 'Get back up the hill; my horse
shit in the tracks.'"

"That was twenty years ago," Hattie pointed out.

"Do you think I'd forget!" John roared in a voice that shook
the rafters. "You think I'm stupid just like the mills do? Stinsen
cut me out. I was supposed to become a skidder, get an increase in pay. He said no."

Hattie did not respond. When John was like this it was best
to let him vent his spleen, give it relief and in a few minutes
he'd be as tame as a deer. But try to reason and he'd be ranting

all evening long.

* * *

The next morning Hattie lay awake and listened to a fierce wind pummel the small cabin. A cold chill emphasized the comfort and warmth of her and John's body heat under the pile of quilts. It had to be well below zero and the wind made it that much worse. John snored softly, still deep in sleep. Hattie stared at his balding head and wondered at the course of life that had brought her to the isolation of the deep Wisconsin forest.

She'd married John on February 9, 1882. She had been but sixteen, the daughter of Rufus L. Young from Winneconne, Wisconsin. She'd bore nine children during the past nineteen years. The oldest son Harry and the middle daughter Leanna were already dead, Harry from smallpox, Leanna from reaction to what they thought was a spider bite. Her oldest daughter, Florence May, had married as young as Hattie and lived on a farm near Rice Lake. John, of solid German ancestry, worked a farm those early years and also worked for the big lumber mills, cutting timber winters and assisting in the wet and grueling spring logging drives.

John had always been hard-working. Hattie could appreciate that; after all, she'd struggled side by side. He did not drink. He did not gamble. Nevertheless, their gains had been few. Hattie, in addition to raising the children, taking care of the house and working on the farm, briefly took a position school teaching. It was a way to make ends meet.

In April of 1899 John went into the real estate business with his brother, William. They had even been written up in the local paper, Hattie recalled: J.F. and W.W. Dietz are distributing 5,000 circular folders descriptive of Barron County and Rice Lake that cannot fail to bring new settlers and good results.

The move brought anything but good results. The few listings of rural property the Dietz brothers obtained were isolated, near swamps with ramshackle log homes and stripped clean of valuable timber. In truth the properties were a class removed from the richer mansions owned by the logger barons. Even if he wanted to sell mansions, those properties were

Photo courtesy of Malcolm Rosholt

The Dietz family in 1905. From left, back row: Leslie, Clarence. Front row: Helen, John, Myra, Stanley, Hattie and John Jr.

located on a side of town John could not penetrate.

The real estate men who handled that side of town were relatives and friends of the mill executives and owners. An outsider did not have a chance.

Eight months after going into the real estate business, John, ignoring Hattie's protest, sold the home farm. The selling price was $1,800.00, but their equity was far less than half. In a year's time John had fewer than half a dozen sales.

The money obtained from the sale of their farm was all but spent. The big purchase was in October, 1900 when John purchased a quarter section of land, 160 acres located miles from civilization in the isolated wilds of southern Sawyer County. Investment property, he claimed.

Yet in February of 1901 the Dietz family departed Rice Lake for the wilderness, first Bishop's Bridge and now this abandoned logging camp at Price Dam. In truth, after what had just happened up in Hayward, they were escaping political refugees, John had angrily complained.

In the long tradition of German citizens, John was a political man, indeed a passionate man. In fact Teutons outnumbered all others of the Socialist Labor Party that was born in 1876 and founded upon the theoretical literature of socialism. Those German-originated beliefs held that the small, independent self-employer deserves the full product of his toil. That it is the duty of the working classes to conquer political power and to make use of the machinery of the state to promote their interests. Early on John had learned from his immigrant father: compromise was not an easy part of his being.

John was a self-taught man, self-read. As if in an effort to gain recognition, John had served on the local township level as treasurer of the local school district.

He'd always been willing to speak his mind. America was a democracy, capitalism the engine that moved them ahead. He had been heard to remark on how the corporations had corrupted that trust. He had lived through the Granger Wars, when monopolistic railroads charged farmers three acres of production to move one acre of their produce back east.

He'd been a young man during those days, and he'd witnessed farmers driven from their fields. He knew of some farmers who had died.

During the years he lived in Rice Lake John began to avoid the Company Store.

As were working men throughout the nation, John became discontent with the order of the day. He knew of the efforts to organize unions, of the riots, bombings and police killings. John had his own personal doings with the monied trusts at the county seat in Hayward, the place some people referred to as "Robber's Roost." In later days Socialist-leaning newspapers printed his story:

BEARDING THE LION IN HIS DEN

John F. Dietz Quells an Angry Mob and Proves
Himself Friend of Law and Order
Aftermath of Hayward Election

The hostile gathering was an aftermath of an election in Hayward. The better class of citizens, long denied a voice in the affairs of the town and county government, succeeded, by a united front at the polls, in electing a full set of town officers from among Hayward's best men. Notwithstanding the overwhelming majorities given to every man on this ticket, the old officials doggedly hung on to their offices. Not even waiting for a complete counting of the ballots, each of them hastened to the town clerk's office to checkmate by that move any contemplated action on the part of the victors to take the office contested for.

...Slowly but surely that anger that is the only successful agency against a leech-like body of political grafters who carry gang rule beyond all forbearance, began to rise in the breasts of all Hayward, and in the early part of the evening plans for the strike began to take shape.

Dietz Takes a Hand

The town hall was the point to which all men wended their way .... From 8 o'clock until 11 the parties to the meeting labored for their points, each hanging on doggedly, as if to life itself; and then, thru the crowds in the hall and the street, the watchers in the alley, the news flashed along..."John Dietz has won!" ... It was John Dietz and John Dietz alone who pre- vented bloodshed. In the right always, whether it afforded him a seat in the band wagon or a march to the tune of a funeral dirge, Dietz was in this instance interested in seeing the newly-elected town officers given their rights. The defeated candidates, representing what was worst in Hayward, politically and otherwise — who had so openly carried on corruption in public once that today and for years past the town has been known throughout the length and breadth of the state as "Robber's Roost" — refused absolutely to give up their offices.

Sheriff Calls for Troops

The excitement that prevailed the night of election and throughout the following day was intense. The then Sheriff William Giblin, as fierce as an eagle foraging for her young, and ignorant of his social duties and their limitations, was still at sea and took to drinking heavily in his inability to otherwise generate wisdom. He cried for blood, and he would have heard more than the echo but for the cool heads of John Dietz and other men of his stamp.

Sheriff Would Use Gun

Dietz kept himself within arm's length of the sheriff for emergency sakc... The sheriff's hand reached for his hip pistol

but once, when a lightning-like slap brought him to his
senses. As quick as a cat, and being able to read the lawman's
every thought of action, Dietz had the man floored even
while the brawny sheriff was busy recalling the admonition
of people who live in glass houses and dress in the dark.

The article went on to describe how John faced down the
band of slinking cowards backing up the sheriff by telling a
wry joke. New elections were scheduled for the fall. For a
time John was a candidate with the reform party. The gang
learned the "farmer from the lower Chippewa" was a man to
be reckoned with.

Then John's troubles began. Promises made in good faith
were quickly forgotten. Stories derogatory to his character
were circulated. Eventually John withdrew from the ticket.
He did not have the stomach for the subterfuge, nor the money
to campaign against representatives of the mills. He could not
walk in and buy a saloon full of men a round of drinks. He
could not promise them jobs.

New elections were held that fall. When all was said and
done, what John and many others viewed as the grafters and
corrupters, still held their places of power and influence.

The vote, the popular will of the people had been denied.
The attempt, as one reporter called it, "to remove the pig from
the parlor," had failed. The old order of things had been re-
stored.

The long fight ground at John. Hayward had been John's
last real effort to fit into the community of man. "Born of the
wrong class, I expect some presume," he told a sympathetic
Hattie. Fight on, Hattie argued. No, John said. He dropped
out then, took nature as his priest. They'd remain in the wilderness, pioneers, clean, hardworking, unsullied by the filth
of the corporations or the imprint of civilization. Naturally
the family would be there as well.

Hattie's bones ached with the memory of these past years.
The sagging logging shanty was drafty, the logs warped and
twisted. They caulked the holes with manure and mud dug out
of a frozen marsh. They were short of beds and blankets and
every night Hattie would crawl out and stoke up the flames in

the potbellied wood stove that also served as a cook stove. They subsisted on potatoes, rutabagas, oatmeal and the occasional isolated deer John and the boys shot.

They'd even eaten muskrat and once the stringy carcass of a wolf. Yes, they were pioneers, Hattie thought as she listened to John's snoring. Pioneering was the history of her life.

Always the first to rise, Hattie slid from under the covers into the grey, frigid air. She pulled on moccasins and stepped into the outer room where all the children, except for Johnny, slept under their mounds of quilts and coats. Here and there lay small white carpets of snow that had leaked through holes between the cold-shrunk logs. More caulking, she thought and mentally marked the spots. She bent to the potbellied stove with wood chips, kindling and larger sticks of oak.

"Morning, Ma," Myra said from where she lay with Helen.

"Morning dear," Hattie said and was suddenly seized by a deep sense of desolation, of where she'd brought her children.

As soon as the fire was crackling, she put on larger chunks of wood and returned to bed to wait for the cabin to warm. She spoke without looking at her husband. "John, I think we should move back to Rice Lake. There'd be more there for the children. Except for oatmeal and baggies, we're getting low on food. We have no meat. I think it would be better all the way around."

John turned on his side, his back to his wife. He had that mood, Hattie saw. Nevertheless she found herself continuing to push. "We can't go on like this, John. Where is it going to end?"

With a powerful heave, John tossed the quilts from the bed. He clambered to his feet in his red long underwear. His voice boomed like the crack of thunder throughout the small cabin. "You'd turn against me, Hattie? You'd turn against your own husband after what I faced?"

"I'm not turning against you." Hattie tried to be reasonable. "I'm only thinking of what's best for the children."

"Has one of them complained?" John bellowed. "They didn't come to me."

"No one complained," Hattie said.

"Then what are you nagging about? You want meat, Hattie?

I'll get you meat." John pulled on his clothes and stormed out of the house.

It was the winter of 1904. They'd been living in the drafty mill shack almost three years. From time to time John and the boys had made the journey to their 160 acres and worked on the farm fixing up the old horse barn and replacing the cabin roof with scooped logs split down the middle and laid like tile. John had seen the logging dam, didn't seem to realize it lay on his land. The first step of the long fight began when he wrote the mills a letter demanding compensation because their dam was flooding part of his land.

He received no reply.

A few months later John again wrote the mills, this time demanding wages for watching and tending the Price dam for three years. This time the mills had replied; he should take the matter up with whoever hired him.

Well, damn them, he would, John thought. He ground his teeth as he snowshoed through the deep snow. If Hattie wanted meat, he'd give her meat.

He approached the driving camp and sought out the foreman, John "Red" Mulligan. That Mulligan, a man who loved to fight, was considered one of the roughest loggers in the North Woods, John paid no heed. He waved the company letter at Mulligan and demanded his wages.

"What do you think you're trying to pull here, Dietz?"

Mulligan growled for the benefit of his audience. "You think we're as dumb as a partridge? We don't hire men to watch those dams year-round. Never have. I put you on the pay roll last spring out of sympathy for your family. That's why we let you stay on the mill property. And now you pull this pile of manure up and throw it in my face. Well, you're nothing but a no-account, goddamn squatter."

"Your language is abusive." John's voice was deadly calm, his eyes as direct and unwavering as those of a hawk. "Is this what it has come down to in this country? The trusts take and take and a workingman has no say." John looked to the gathering loggers, workingmen just like himself. He shouted, "And you men go along with this? Let yourselves be used like oxen."

"You're wasting my time," Mulligan growled. "You've got

two minutes and I don't want you in my sight." He grinned at his audience, winked playfully and advanced on John.

Mulligan swung, but for all the impact he might as well have punched a tree. His knuckles screamed as if split wide open.

For a brief moment the two large men traded blows, cursing and bellowing like two raging behemoths. Mulligan had imagined Dietz angered the minute before, but not like this. Dietz bore in, oblivious to blows his way. For the first time ever in a fight a sense of dread gripped Mulligan's entrails. Dietz was relentless, unfearing. Mulligan experienced doubts. He saw the blow and tried to fend it off. But the force was terrific. He reeled sideways and crashed to the floor.

A scaler named Brown seized a stick of stove wood and made a rush at John but was quickly knocked to the floor.

"Anyone else?" John defiantly asked the remaining loggers. He glared at the two on the floor. "You men satisfied?"

"This is still mill property, Dietz," Mulligan growled in an effort to salve his ego. But he did not rise to the fight. "You can't beat the mills. They'll get you. I know. I'll live on the Thornapple longer than you."

"Not even the mills can kill a man before his time," John said and walked outside and past as many as seventy-five loggers. The men were quiet, watchful of this man who'd so soundly thrashed two men, including one of their best. Already the stories would start. John Dietz was some man.

John returned to the mill shack at Price Dam. "Hattie, we're packing up. It's time we moved on our own land."

"It's the middle of February," Hattie protested. "I thought we were waiting until spring."

"Spring came early," John said with grim irony. His eyes sought Hattie's. "It doesn't matter how far a man moves. The mills will get you, take everything a man owns." He pressed Hattie's hand then strode to the door. "Clarence! Leslie!"

His bellow carried for a quarter mile.

Myra stood over a wicker basket of frozen laundry she'd just carried in from the hanging line. She exchanged glances with her mother. She was fourteen now, starting to blossom.

In town she could socialize, talk to girls her own age.

Every week there was a dance. Out here ...

Hattie shook her head, warning Myra. Myra blamed her just as much as John. It was the middle of winter and they were moving again, to their own property this time, more isolated and removed from other people than ever before.

* * *

The logs jammed the man-made flowage for half a mile back. They were prime virgin white pine, some with a base forty inches across. They'd been felled with axe and crosscut saw and skidded with oxen and draft horses to the Thornapple River. Now they lay quiet, jammed side by side and pushed one mounting another until they formed a treacherous carpet across the flowage upstream of the dam. The logs were like fenced cattle waiting on the opening of the sluice gates and the long and dangerous log drive down the Thornapple to the Flambeau and Chippewa rivers and down to the big sawmills of the Chippewa Lumber and Boom Company in Eau Claire and Chippewa Falls. Six and a half million board feet of timber, two hundred years in the making; and this was the day they would start their final journey — but for one man, John F.

Photo courtesy of Malcolm Rosholt

The Dietz homestead looking across the Thornapple River and the flowage created by the Cameron Dam. The barn is on the left; the cabin is the low building in the center. In the distance at right center are the two shanties of the log driving camp.

Dietz.

It was mid-April, 1904. Daylight in the swamp, the cocks cried to rise and take to the woods. The clear, cold spring morning had bite through the wool and flannel of loggers' clothes. Thin sheets of ice had formed on puddles and back in the marshes. The last vestiges of winter lay in scattered snow mounds protected by the shade of the forest. Buds were springing on nearby willow and alder.

The crisp spring air pumped through John's blood like an elixir. He watched as the driving crew, peaveys and pike poles in hand, straggled down on caulked boots toward the holding pond. He felt a kinship with these men, working men beside whom he had toiled from dawn until dusk for a paltry thirty-five dollars a month. While the company made millions!

Blood throbbed hotly through John's temples. All up the marsh, much of it created by the dam and flooding as much as twenty acres of his land, lumber mill logs were floating over his property. All his life he'd slaved, given of his sweat and blood, service in the name of the Lord. He could feel the stiffness of age, the passage of too much time. The mills followed the Rob Roy theory: "The good old way, the simple plan, that he shall take who has the power and he shall keep who can."

Yes, John knew the philosophy well. An ordinary property owner had no say. Down below three men walked out on the dam, once known as Leavitt Dam, by the man who had built it in 1874, and now named Cameron Dam for the man from whom John had purchased the land. The men waved at Dietz. John did not wave back.

That he carried a rifle they paid no mind.

The loggers knew John. Some days he'd stopped by to take a cup of coffee and chat. He'd spoke on how he'd written the lumber company to get a little money for using his dam and flooding his land. "I've offered a number of deals but they won't answer my letters. I'm just a common stick along the river here. A few crumbs that fall to the floor ought to be mine. The trusts have to learn, the rest of us count just as much as do they."

The loggers had shrugged. Dietz was a working man as were they. Everyone complained. It didn't mean that much.

No one had really listened.

Thus the three men calmly passed the "No Trespass" sign Dietz had nailed to the dam. They inserted crowbars in the wheels to the sluice gates and began to crank up the gates.

John's blue eyes peered through narrow slits. A knot, like a heavy weight, formed between his shoulder blades. He was forty-three and this farm, this dam were all he had to show, a tiny piece of clearing isolated in a corner of a vast wilderness. He'd moved as far as he could. He swallowed. He was a law-abiding man, had always been a law-abiding man. But a man had his rights. He raised the rifle for emphasis.

"Don't raise those gates," he yelled.

The loggers looked at Dietz and then at one another as if to examine how they should respond. "He ain't going to go against the old C. L. and B.," the foreman remarked. "They own this country. They'll get the law out here so fast Dietz will think he got run over by a train." The man used the crowbar for leverage to turn the wheel another notch and raise the gate.

A single shot rang out. The angry whine of a bullet buzzed just over the men's heads.

The men crouched, staring at one another to see who would be the first to bolt. "If he wants to hit us, he can," one said. He couldn't conceal his tension. "Dietz used to put on sharp shooting exhibitions at the fairs in Rice Lake. I saw him shoot potatoes out of the air. If he wants to hit something, he can."

"...or someone," the other man said.

"He ain't our business," the first man said. "Let the company take care of this. We aren't being paid to get shot at. They can send out the sheriff." The men straightened and slowly walked from the wooden dam.

"The sheriff will be out, Dietz," the foreman shouted.

"You're costing these men work. You're just one man. The logging industry keeps this state alive. Don't think you can possibly win."

"Oh, I'll win," John Dietz said quietly. "Either that or I'll die." It was a simple statement of fact, an acknowledgment there could be no turning back. He stood still, in the open where all men could clearly see. He watching until the driving crew departed. He hadn't wanted this, bringing Hattie and the children along. But the mills left no choice.

The haunting cry of a flock of northbound geese passed overhead. For a moment he envied their freedom, their community with well-defined codes of natural behavior. Geese mated for life. In truth, he thought they were superior to man.

John slowly turned for home. The family could watch the driving camp from there. Hattie and the six children would be waiting. They would want to know why the shot.

PITY POOR OLD JOHN D (ROCKEFELLER)

Business Representative Says That he Hasn't Got Much Money After All Draws Only $59,523.00 Per Day

By Exercising Frugality He Manages to Keep The Wolf From the Door

---

DIETZ HAS NOT BEEN ARRESTED All is Apparently Peaceful at Cameron Dam and if Anyone is Looking for Dietz They are Careful Not to Find Him - Something About the Man

---

CHEATED DEATH

Kidney trouble often ends fatally, but by choosing the right medicine, E.H. Wolfe of Bear Grove, Iowa, cheated death. He says: "Two years ago I had Kidney Trouble, which caused me great pain, suffering and anxiety, but I took Electric Bitters, which effected a complete cure. I have also found them of great benefit in general debility and nerve trouble, and keep them constantly on hand since, as I find they have no equal." Druggist guarantees them at 50 cents.

CHAPTER II

A few days after the shooting at the dam, one Thomas Sargent, a timber cruiser and surveyor for the Chippewa Lumber & Boom Company, journeyed out to the Dietz farm.

Sargent was a slight, keen-eyed man who always had a chaw of tobacco planted firmly in his cheek. He'd been apprised of the situation and had been hurriedly dispatched to run a survey line and determine the exact location of the dam before spring runoff.

Sargent crossed the large clearing towards the Dietz farm. He was unarmed, his hands held where any watching soul could clearly see. After all Dietz had already thrashed two loggers in a fist fight and put a bullet into the air over the heads of two dozen loggers. Sargent understood, Dietz was not a man you could push.

A stocky and balding man stepped out on the porch to greet the visitor. John appeared unarmed. He shook hands. In truth, the atmosphere at the Dietz cabin was polite.

Mrs. Dietz and the oldest girl were cooking over the wood stove and invited him to stay for supper. John was friendly and talkative as if starved for conversation. Despite his isolation, John seemed well-versed on affairs of the world.

"I've awarded you an extra rod on your south end, John," Sargent said. "Just to be certain there's no mistake. Half the dam appears to lie on your property. What do you need to be satisfied?"

That opened the floodgates, Sargent later said. Dietz wanted to be paid for logs that had been sluiced through his dam for the previous three years, plus ten cents per thousand feet for the current drive. Plus the flooding of his crop land. He wanted fifteen thousand dollars, a veritable fortune.

"Small payment for use of what is mine," John said. He leaned back in a chair, his feet propped up on a trunk like a big executive. "The lumber trusts should study the law. Even little trees such as myself have a right to our place."

He spoke quietly, but with such subtle force Sargent found his arguments in opposition strangely stilled.

"The mills owe me back wages. I have the telegrams to prove it. They owe me for flooding my crop land. Look outside there."

"I cannot speak to any of that, Mr. Dietz. I just came to check the location of the dam."

As soon as he thought it reasonable, Sargent departed.

He returned a few days later with a counter offer of five hundred dollars, more than a logger's wages for a year. Nevertheless Dietz howled as if he was being robbed. "For five hundred dollars the company would make me a prostitute?" Hattie looked askance, but John paid her no mind. "This is my land, Sargent. You tell your trust that they can use it on my terms or not at all." He moved in close on Sargent, a force and a power that struck nerves like the electric warning buzz from a rattlesnake. "It's long past time someone stood up and put the mills in their place. You watch, the workingmen are going to rise as one. The wealth of this country should be spread according to how much a man works, not how much the mills can take."

Sargent stood to depart. He had no authority to offer more. "I hope you know what you're doing, Mr. Dietz. The company has a great deal of money tied up in those logs.

"They have political connections and monetary clout from

the courthouse in Hayward to the capital in Madison. If you think you can fight them, I must say you're making a serious mistake."

The words had been a mistake, Sargent confessed. He thought Dietz might strike him. As it was the man went into a long diatribe about the excesses and abuses of the lumber trust, for whom he accused Sargent was a spy.

"I'm just a surveyor. I made you their offer. What happens now is between you and the company," Sargent said.

He was a slight, wiry man, not given to fisticuffs but not given to backing away either. He'd been taken by the entire family, Sargent said. They were miles from the nearest town. The children appeared clean and properly instructed in principles of etiquette. They were disciplined, respectful of their elders. Mrs. Dietz had basically listened, although she had, from time to time, spoken her mind. She seemed to feel the lumber trust should pay something for the use of their land. A clear statement in support of her husband, Sargent claimed.

If the company had more offers they could send someone else, Sargent said. Dietz was the problem. The man had been hospitable, conversant, religious and totally without fear or hint of compromise. One minute there was irony, the next minute rage. With John Dietz a man never knew.

* * *

"Will they shoot Pa?" young Myra asked her mother. The question smacked like a bullet into Hattie's heart. That one of her own children could ask a question such as that. Her flour-covered hands paused on a large roll of bread dough. The question was innocent enough, seemingly more a matter of a child's curiosity rather than a feeling of dread. Nevertheless the pain of failure cut deeper than she imagined possible. "Why would you ask a question like that?"

"Yesterday that surveyor, Mr. Sargent said they'd be sending out the sheriff and that he just hoped no one got hurt." Myra looked up from a Montgomery Ward Catalog, their wish book, their contact with fashions of the outside world.

"You shouldn't listen to others," Hattie snapped. "And get your nose out of that book. It's time you did some work. This is your father's and my land. All we want is fair payment for use of what is ours."

Hattie observed Myra stiffen at the sharp tone. The girl began to pout as she greased the bread pans with lard. That was Myra; if you pushed her, she rebelled. She was getting to that age. Hattie relented in her tone. "The logging companies will pay. They offered once because they know they are wrong. They'll be back." Her voice took on a wistful air. "Then we'll have a little money. We can buy some nice things."

"Will we stay out here in the woods then?"

For several seconds Hattie was silent. She turned the dough over, kneading it with her fingers, rolling it over and over and working in the flour, yeast and water. Life passed so quickly. Married at sixteen, frightened, her firstborn at seventeen. Before that she'd cared for her brothers and sisters and worked on the farm. She'd always hoped there would be more for her children. At least some economic gain, some greater social standing, more opportunity. Perhaps with this dam ...

Hattie shook her head angrily. Such nonsense. "Your pa doesn't like to live in town, Myra. He has his beliefs. In town he runs into people who don't always see his way. That's hard for John to accept."

"So we do whatever Pa wants?" Myra said.

Hattie whirled. "You know better than to talk like that. Put more wood in the stove." She turned from her daughter and wiped her hands on a towel beside the stove. It was a warm spring day. But Saturday was baking day so she and Myra would have more free time for Sunday. Wisps of hair clung to a thin sheen of perspiration on her temples. She watched as Myra added some dried birch wood to the flames of the cast iron Monarch cookstove. Hattie pulled three hot loaves from the oven and added three more. The fresh baked aroma brought water to the mouth. Her practiced eye judged the rust brown crust to be exactly right. "Why don't you fetch a pail of water, and tell the boys there's hot bread."

"Then can I play?" Myra asked.

"Sure," Hattie said. "I'll do the pots and pans. You can go and play."

"Oh dear Lord, please give me strength," Hattie mumbled. She began to hymn *Rock of Ages*. The music filled her being, giving strength, salvation. She watched Myra trudge up the hill to where spring water seeped out of the ground. At times the water was sweet, pure. Other times, after hard rains, it tasted hard as if tinged with iron ore. There were times it gave them the runs. But it was what they had, Hattie thought. John had promised her a well, some day.

On her way back with the heavy pail, Myra paused where Clarence and Leslie were making fence rails by splitting small maple trees with wedges and a sledgehammer. Leslie, always ready to take a break from his toils, reached for a dipper of water. He said something and laughed, as did Myra. That was Leslie, Hattie thought, carefree and always clowning around. Despite his shiftless ways he was John's favorite. John would get mad and Leslie would disarm him with a joke, even when he was getting a whipping. "This is one cowboy leaving home," he'd said through tears once when he was six. He was gone half the day until darkness and an empty stomach drove him home.

Myra had to interrupt Clarence's splitting to get him to drink. That was Clarence, steady, serious. He was more quiet, introspective. He liked to tinker with mechanical things, to figure how they worked.

With the exception of those months in Rice Lake when John tried to sell real estate, the children had lived all their lives in the country. They were close and seldom fought. Which was a blessing, Hattie thought. For they'd never lived in such an isolated place as this.

At that moment John stepped from the barn. Clarence immediately picked up the sledgehammer and set to work. Leslie lay indolently, staring up at his father. "First break I took all day, Pa," he called.

"Well don't make it any longer," John yelled back. "One five-hour break doesn't make up for two hours of work."

Leslie still sat and stared. A smile played at his lips.

John stepped towards the hill. "If you want I can make it less comfortable to sit," he yelled.

Clarence slammed the sledge at a steel wedge. A maple split lengthwise. The clang rang out through the bright spring day and across the open fields and into the grey willow catkins in the marshes of the Thornapple where geese and ducks cackled and scarlet-winged blackbirds trilled.

Around the clearing of stumps and fields, birch and poplar were budding, and grouse and snipe scurried through thickets where arbutus covered the greening forest floor. The sweet, fresh wood-and-sap smell of the maple filled the air. "You better get up, Leslie," Clarence warned. "You know how Pa has been these days." Clarence peeked at his father. The mere sight of the man generated a familiar rage and fear. As the oldest he felt it was his responsibility to stand up to John. But he never knew how far he could go, argue in friendly fashion one day, be the butt of a tirade the next.

"Ma said the first loaf of bread is done," Myra called to her father. They waited for his response.

"Well let's get to it then," John said. He was amiable, in a favorable mood. The children relaxed and started down the hill. Clarence called and young Helen and Stanley came running from the barn, racing each other headlong down the hill.

Hattie noted John trailing after his children like a sheep dog herding his flock, her heart caught in a confused mixture of love, loyalty and surprising irritation. There were times, when John got to politicking, that he seemed to lose sight of the children and her. As if they did not count. Then Hattie could feel the rage. But also her confusion. For she knew of work and grinding poverty, the years she and John had endured side by side. She'd seen ill-distributed wealth, those trust women with their silk gowns and huge bonnets and smooth white hands. She felt the ache of her muscles and the stiffness of her joints. If the mills could charge others for the use of their dam, surely a common landowner deserved the same right, Hattie thought, something for all their years of toil. On that point John was right.

Even now she could see his amusement as he chased after his children, as if possessed of a unique insight only he could see. "The crust is mine," he called goodnaturedly. It was one of the family rules, they could always stop work for the first loaf of fresh hot bread topped with melting, home-churned butter. It was a family free-for-all, pushing and shouting and laughing and everyone grabbing for the crust.

"The crust is mine," John said and pushed ineffectually from outside his milling children. By the time he reached the small plank dining table both ends of the loaf had been seized. John growled, "You'd think a pack of scavengers had paid the mortgage on this land and think they can pick it clean." He glowered. They all laughed, even Hattie.

A watch dog barked furiously. Helen and Stanley raced each other to the window. "Pa, there's a man coming," they both shouted in unison.

"That's probably Charlie Peterson," John said.

Hattie's head snapped around. "Sheriff Peterson! How do you know?" The raw edge of fear raised the tone of her voice.

"Now, Hattie, don't fret, dear. I've known Charlie for a long time. Valentine was over earlier and said word had been passed Peterson left Hayward yesterday." John spoke of their nearest neighbor, Valentine Weisenbach, a German immigrant woodsman who lived in a ten-foot by twelve-foot rough plank and tarpaper shack three miles down the narrow, dirt tote road.

"What are you going to do?" Hattie asked. "I won't stand for guns, John."

John's blue eyes switched from squinting furiously to twinkling amusement. "I don't need guns. I'll just feed him some of your hot bread. That will ease the pain of his journey, build the yeast in his belly for the two-day wagon ride back to Hayward."

"I'm serious," Hattie snapped at her husband. She would not be pushed. "He's the law. And we don't break the law in this family."

"No one's breaking any law," John shouted in a bellow that made the children jump. They edged back, motionless and staring as if trying to blend in with the furniture. "Damnit, Hattie, you stay with me. Understand? That's the mill's law Peterson's bringing, not that of working men. The monied and capitalist monopolies make perfume out of skunk scent and people buy. They can easily make a lie out of the truth." He was mocking in a tone as bitter as raw lemon.

John's eyes became glazed as if looking somewhere deep inside. A familiar, dangerous undercurrent changed his voice. "You read what that newsman wrote, people are on my side."

He tramped outside. There was pride to his walk. His eyes were bright. His strong, broad shoulders had lost the sag of defeat.

John met Sheriff Charles Peterson as he crossed the exposed pasture area leading to the farm. John was cordial, talkative, Peterson would later say. And unarmed, as far as he could see. All the proprieties of deep woods hospitality were observed. He was invited inside for coffee, warm bread, butter and the previous season's blackberry jam.

John leaned back in his chair and casually appraised the sheriff. Peterson was a tall, lean man with slicked-down hair parted down the middle and a thick moustache. His cheeks were gaunt, his eyes direct. Charlie liked to do things in friendly fashion. He did not care for the hostility and notoriety that went with his position. In truth, as John had told Hattie, the men went out of his way trying to be liked. "I never could understand why Charlie took up with the law."

"I sure hope you didn't travel all the way down here to try to serve any mill papers," John said to Sheriff Peterson. "That would be a terrible waste of your time and taxpayers' money."

"Now, John, you're getting the burr put on some people's chairs. They don't take kindly..."

"And I should? You want me to lie down in the middle of the street, Charlie? Let them ride their graft wagons over me and my family?"

"No, John." Sheriff Peterson held his hands palm outwards as if trying to calm John. He'd said nothing and already John was out of control. Peterson's mouth became dry. He knew how John had stood in the midst of fifty loggers and taken on two of their best. He'd been there when John had slapped the gun out of Giblin's hand and knocked the sheriff to the floor. John's a tough, bullheaded son of a bitch, his deputy had warned. "No telling how he'll react. You better not carry a gun."

Charlie had agreed. It took a strange man to live in the outback like this.

"I brought along your mail," Charlie said. His voice sounded strange. "Ah, there's a paper in there."

John leaned forward, his eyes level and direct on Sheriff

Peterson's. "What kind of paper?"

It had taken Peterson two days to travel from the county seat in Hayward to this farm. There were too many miles, too much forest, and the few witnesses in between were outlaws unto their own. The sense of isolation sat with Peterson like a yoke on his neck. "Ah, it doesn't amount to a hill of beans, John. But it's my duty to bring it out. You understand that. If not me, they'll send someone else. Judge Parish signed an injunction in favor of the mills. It's a civil thing. It's up to you to decide what to do."

"You'd do the dirty work for the lumber trusts?" John shouted. He jumped to his feet. He was a stocky, towering presence that had absolutely no sense of intimidation because of Peterson's badge. If anything the fact of the law made John more upset. "Do Hines and Connor have you stitched in their hip pockets along with all those other grafters up there? Well, do they?" John shouted.

The attitude struck Sheriff Peterson as dangerous. He couldn't help wondering if John had a pistol concealed inside his dark coat. He spoke quickly as if trying to ward off an attacking bear. "No, no, John. I'm just doing what the judge requires. You do what you want. I'm on your side here."

"That would be for the best," John growled. He jerked his head toward the door, an indication the meeting was concluded and the county sheriff had best get on his way.

Charlie stood, said his goodbyes to the family and, without further word on the injunction, quickly complied.

Sheriff Peterson returned to Hayward and was immediately confronted by officials of the Sawyer County Board, and within hours of that by a number of prominent lumbermen who were livid at Peterson's failure to uphold the law. The next day the Chippewa Lumber and Boom Company returned to court and Judge Parish issued a bench warrant for contempt of the injunction and instructed Sheriff Peterson it was his sworn duty to serve the injunction and uphold the law. After all, the State of Wisconsin granted franchises for dams, in this case to the lumber company. Dietz's ownership of the land upon which the dam sat was irrelevant, the company contended. Judge Parish agreed. Thus two days after he'd returned from the arduous journey, Sheriff Peterson swallowed his misgivings and again made the long, muddy springboard ride back to the Dietz farm.

"If I show up there again, John's going to do something foolish," Peterson informed his deputy, Fred Clark. Fred was older, grey-haired, a soft-spoken, reasonable man who had known John from his days in Rice Lake. Peterson went down to visit with the men in the driving camp below the dam. Old Fred Clark was sent to visit Dietz. Once again the Dietz family was more than hospitable, Fred reported.

But then he informed John the reason for his visit. John lurched to his feet with such force Clark flinched. John's rough voice boomed, "Are you going to pull a gun on me in my own house?"

Clark remained seated, outwardly as calm as he could manage. "Oh, no, John. I'm not armed. If you don't come in peaceably, I imagine they'll send back a posse to smoke you out."

"They won't take me alive," John declared.

"John!" Hattie cried. The girl, Myra, was helping out in the kitchen, Clark reported. Her eyes grew wide, questioning.

Clark reached as if to feel the bulk of the injunction folded inside his jacket. "I don't think you want to do that, Fred," John snapped. The cabin was small, dark, the outside of the cabin logs still held swaths of bark. With the lowered sapling ceiling, John seemed to loom larger than ever. "How can you come out here like this to bother me and my family? I haven't set foot off my own land. I protect what is mine and that is all. You give in to the mills and do their dirty work like some monkey cleaning manure out of sleigh ruts? That's the work of drunkards and boys. Has your integrity dropped that low?"

"John, I'm an officer of the law. I'm sworn to uphold the law."

"The mill's law," John thundered. His face was red, his eyes strangely fixed and glittering with an intensity that took the moisture from Deputy Clark's mouth. John did not give a damn, Fred later said. He could have held a gun on John and it would not have done a bit of good. "He'd have walked straight into the barrel and knocked it away unless I killed him. And I didn't want to do that."

In fact Deputy Clark dared not even reach for the injunction sitting like a rock against his breast. The dark of the cabin reminded Fred of his terrible isolation. That mill attorney Connor could get mad and yell and scream about the duty of the law all he wanted; the man wasn't the one to journey two days through the wilderness and then face John Dietz.

"Well, Sheriff Peterson's down at the driving camp," Clark said in an easy tone. He stood, keeping his movements easy, maintaining a safe distance between himself and John. "You think on what I said. We'll stop back in the morning."

"I know Peterson's working for the lumber trusts. You tell him if he sets foot on my property I'll shoot the son of a bitch on sight."

"If they send the militia after you, John, they will get you."

John squinted as fiercely as a bald-headed eagle atop his nest. "I know they will get me, but I will get a lot of them first."

The words were hard-studded facts. No veiled threat there, Fred understood. John took principle as a simple fact of nature. A man took a position and did what had to be done. "But think of your family, John. Your children."

"What about my children? They're mine. They have a home, food. What more can they want?"

"You're putting them in danger, John."

"No, Fred. That's the doing of you and those bloodthirsty mills. Don't put your blame on me."

He'd pushed as far as he could, Clark thought.

"Don't forget there are six innocent children that live here," Hattie said as Fred walked to the low front door. "Besides, the mills owe us. They've already offered five hundred dollars. That means they know they are wrong."

John stepped outside ahead of Fred. Fred thought of thrusting the injunction in the woman's hands but could not be sure how she would react. John was just steps away. "With all due respect, Mrs. Dietz, as I told John, you cannot knowingly place your own children in harm's way and then pretend you have no responsibility. What happens to your children is entirely dependent upon the actions of yourself and of John. You make the choice, you bear the consequences. As for the mills, the courts have already spoken. If you don't, you should know the next law out won't be sympathetic like Charlie and myself. They'll have guns. And they'll use them."

Fred grinned at the telling as if he'd been triumphant. "That put the Dietz woman to silence," he said.

SOLDIERS AND MINERS FIGHT

**Trouble Between
Union Miners
and Mine Owners
Culminates in Pitched
Battle by Opposing Forces
-
Martial Law Declared
and Union Miners
Deported**

CAMERON DAM OUTLAWS SHOOT

**Two Men are Shot
by the Outlaws
Who are Holding
up the Log Drive -
Dietz Says that He Will Not
Be Taken Alive - Is Still in
Possession**

CHAPTER III

The circle was unbroken, the family kneeling in prayer, heads bowed, hands joined. John Dietz lead the way with his abrupt, rasping voice. "Give us this day our daily bread..."

They said in unison the Lord's Prayer. "And make the trusts see the error of their ways," John continued. "Let them know Your strength and the strength of this country lies in the calloused hands and bent back of the common working man."

John paused for breath. Hattie, as if in continuance, spoke, "Forgive them Lord, for they know not what they say or do."

John scowled, his tirade broken, a hint that Hattie's words were not directed solely at the trusts. They stood.

"Sing, Hattie," John growled. "Whatever the children like."

"Shall We Gather at the River?" Hattie asked.

"The Thornapple?" Leslie asked and was immediately elbowed by Clarence and Myra. Myra giggled, with Leslie they could always have fun.

As usual on Sunday morning, they sang a number of hymns. All of them were contributing members of the family congregation. Hattie could feel their closeness, all of them united in song as if without a care in the world. She looked to the bowed sapling poles of the ceiling and raised her voice in song, a deep-lunged woman born to sing. She was loud, lusty, with clear tones carrying the family as if the union of voices would hold them together for all of time. Surely, she thought, at long last triumph would be theirs.

In the front yard the two dogs barked. Helen and Stanley raced to the window.. "It's Valentine," Stanley called.

"What would you expect, it's time for lunch," Hattie said.

"Now Hattie," John kidded. "Valentine's our friend."

"You could at least tell him to wash," Hattie snapped.

"It's Sunday. Maybe he could shave once. He doesn't come to be friends. Never that. He's always got some reason, some purpose for himself."

But this time Valentine had news, the worst it could possibly be, Hattie thought. They were sending out an armed posse from Hayward, which bothered John not at all. What infuriated John was, in his view, this posse did not represent the law. Sheriff Charles Peterson hadn't deputized anyone. In fact, he'd refused to be part of the doings. In John's opinion these men had been hired directly by the lumber trusts. John was livid. "The goddamn trusts even run the law. There's no chance of justice for the common man."

"That's exactly it, John. Right on the marker," Valentine agreed. He stuffed his mouth with homemade bread dripping with gravy, some of which ran down his unshaven chin.

As soon as they finished eating, John and Valentine departed, rifles in hand. In the scrub grass of the front yard Johnny Ginger, Helen and young Stanley were playing in a piano-sized plank playhouse. Clarence, Leslie and Myra were playing catch with a hardball in the dirt. When they'd lived in Rice Lake and Clarence had been able to go to school, he'd enjoyed the game immensely. Now he had only his brother and his sister, who was using the family's one flat leather glove.

"Can I go along, Pa?" Leslie asked. He was eager.

"No," John growled. But he was pleased at the request. However, if any of the children were injured, Hattie would have a breakdown.

"I could be a lookout," Leslie persisted.

"I said no." The hard undercurrent entered John's voice.

The children edged back. "I thought I told you boys to work on that fencing on the north end. And Myra, that garden needs more to be dug." He seized the children's one baseball from Myra's hands and tossed it down into the long marsh grass. "Now git to it," he said to his cowered brood. He strode away, Valentine scurrying after like a cur trying to catch up with a cruel but beloved master.

At Valentine's suggestion, the two men covered their faces with mud from the marsh. "Not so easy to see thataway," Valentine said.

"Or recognize," John finished Valentine's thought.

"We'll cut across here," John said and set out directly through the thick timber of basswood, birches and maple trees.

"Thick woods here," Valentine whined. Each year a number of men in the North Woods ended up lost for days and sometimes forever in the darkness of the forest.

"I know this forest as good as any Indian," John grunted.

"Yeah," Valentine forced a laugh. "You know what they say about Indians, they never get lost. It's just that sometimes their wigwam moves on 'em."

"Better be quiet now," John said. His anger put a long, ground-eating stride into his walk. Sweat streamed down Valentine's unshaven, mud covered face. Several times the slight German immigrant stumbled trying to keep up. To think that he'd been pushed so far as to be allied with a self-serving weasel like Valentine, John railed. But a man fought with what he had. The Lord could ask no more.

In time they came out to the banks of the narrow logging tote road. "Right on the mark," Valentine said in admiration and relief.

John did not reply. They sat on a nearby log, waiting. Valentine pulled out a half pint of whiskey and offered it to John. "You know I've taken the pledge," John said.

"I'm sorry," Valentine said as if wounded by John's gruffness. "I'm jes' tryin' to help."

John patted the dark sleeve of his neighbor's coat. "I know. You're a good man to stand with me like this. Can't say the same about all the neighbors."

"Some of them work for the mills because that's all there is," Valentine ventured.

"I know the spies," John barked. "Don't think He and me

are unaware. Their day of reckoning will come."

Valentine fell silent. When John was like this he never knew what he could safely say.

They sat for several hours. Presently they heard the creaking of a wagon and the two men ducked back into the woods. At the last minute John seized Valentine's elbow.

"Don't kill anyone unless you have to. These drivers don't know it but the trust sent them out here as bait. They want me to kill someone so they can send out the militia."

Valentine nodded absently. Now that the posse was actually bearing down on them, he was too frightened even to speak.

There were five men on a company wagon pulled by a team of four horses. Ex-sheriff, now deputy William Giblin was in charge along with a deputy Elliot. Both men were from Hayward. Two employees of the boom company, a Pat Magin and foreman John Mulligan, with whom John had had his fight were also present as was hosteler Irwin Giauque. Giblin informed the men he was armed with a bench warrant in a civil action brought by the boom company and also carried a criminal warrant for the arrest of John Dietz.

Giblin recalled his election day humiliation at the hands of Dietz those many years previous. The debt had yet to be repaid. "Dietz is an obstinate man," he declared. His party was in good spirits. "We have to be quick, firm and fast."

"He can shoot," Giauque said. He sat at the back of the wagon on a sack of horse feed. "I saw him at the fair in Rice Lake. He tossed potatoes into the air and blew them to pieces with that automatic Luger pistol of his. He doesn't miss."

At that moment a man with a blackened face and a hat pulled low across his brow stepped out from behind a birch tree. "If you men are looking for John Dietz, he's standing here looking at you."

Giblin grabbed for his rifle. "Git your hands up," Dietz yelled and raised his rifle and began to pump out a flurry of shots. The horses bolted at the sudden explosions, one nag's panic infecting the others. Magin, the driver, was shot through one arm and dropped the reins. The others dropped for cover in the wagon box while Mulligan dove for the reins.

A bullet ticked through Giauque's hat. As the team jerked

forward into a gallop, he was thrown from the back of the wagon and into the dirt at the feet of John Dietz. He stared up in terror as John, standing in the middle of the road, fired three more shots at the racing wagon.

John casually gazed down at the prostrate figure at his feet. He began to slide bullets into the empty breech of the Winchester. "What are you doing out here, Irwin?"

"They just sent me in with LeBoeuf's team to drive it back out. That's all! I swear!" Giauque was rushed and raised his hands as high as he could. "I'm unarmed! Please."

A second man, Valentine Weisenbach, stepped out from behind a tree and fired down the narrow road in the direction the wagon had fled.

"The time to shoot is past, Valentine," John growled.

"Where'd that other one fall? Elliot. Wasn't that him up there with Giblin?"

"Yes sir," Giauque said quickly. "But I don't think he fell. I don't know. I fell myself."

"He's around here." John walked off the road towards where chest-high balsam were growing in the ditch. Giauque scrambled to his feet and started walking down the road. He was quiet, stiff-legged as if he thought he could sneak away in plain view.

"Where do you think you're going?" John yelled.

"I'm going to get LeBoeuf's team. I have to drive it back like I told you."

"You get back here," John ordered. Giauque kept walking. John raised his rifle. "I'll blow your head off."

Giauque stopped. Weisenbach approached. "You working for the trusts?" John asked.

"No. No. I just came along to drive the team back. I don't even have a gun." Giauque's voice quavered and he trembled uncontrollably.

John squinted, calculating. "Get out of here."

Once again Giauque started down the narrow tote road.

Weisenbach laughed and walked after him, his rifle jabbing into the hosteler's back. "You git now, you git," Weisenbach chortled in a high-pitched voice lifted by his excitement.

He kicked Giauque in the rear end. "You git out of here or

I'll fill you so full of shot you will not get out." He kicked him again.

"So I went," Giauque reported. "The wagon had raced off and left me, headed toward the driving camp." He was bitter. "They just left me there. I walked the ten miles back to LeBoeuf's. There were five of us in that wagon and John Dietz stepped out in the open to face us all. Just as calm as you please. He's got hisself a point. And no one's goin' to take it away, least ways not without a gun." The little hosteler's head bobbed with the telling. Five years later he still wore the hat with the hole from a John Dietz bullet. He'd hold the hat out for emphasis. He'd seen John Dietz, met him face to face and lived to tell the tale.

* * *

The four horse team ran for almost a half mile down the dirt tote road before Mulligan managed to seesaw the reins and gain some pull with the bit and bring them back under some reasonable control. Nevertheless he permitted the team to continue at a ground-stomping canter. By the time they pulled into the driving camp the horses were lathered with sweat. Despite the long run the horses were still prancing, eyes rolling. With the exception of the hefty deputy Giblin, the four men were excited, eyes wide, hands gesturing wildly as each interrupted the other to tell the dozen drivers his version of the encounter.

Magin was in great pain from the bullet that had smashed through his forearm and shattered the bone. With the exception of Giblin, the men were all agreed, poor Irwin Giauque probably had been killed.

The log drivers bandaged the pale Magin the best they could. The horses were walked down and cooled, watered and then the two belonging to LeBoeuf hitched to the bullet-splintered wagon for the journey south to Ladysmith and a doctor. Meanwhile, Giblin deputized a half dozen drivers to join him. "It's Dietz who is keeping you from work," he told them. "If you don't help stop him now, you're not going to have a job."

The armed posse slowly walked back towards the ambush site. There was no sign of Giauque. They paused, alone and in silence, surrounded by the vast and tangled forest of northern Wisconsin. The snarls of uprooted and felled trees beside the tote road offered cover for an armed man every step of their route.

"Keep a sharp eye," the fat deputy said. "They had their faces blackened."

"Tell us vat vee need to know," a laconic Frenchman by the name of LaFave muttered. He was a strong, squat man, a hearty singer and drinker. He'd once killed a man in a fair fight and had broken more than one jaw, in return for which his nose had been mangled and permanently skewed off to one side. "I'm a log driver," he told Giblin. "This Dietz' fight ees with the mills, not veeth us."

Giblin nodded. LaFave did not support Dietz, but there was a limit as to how hard he would push to bring Dietz in.

The sun beat down. The road was drying and steaming from a rain the night before. Spring birds, meadowlarks, red-winged blackbirds and robins warbled a dozen songs from the surrounding green foliage. Forty rods ahead a figure stood in the road.

"It's Dietz!" a lumberjack yelled. The rifles came up, but even before a clear sight picture could be formed, the first shot whistled down the road, followed by half a dozen more. The figure disappeared. The men cautiously edged forward. They could see nothing but the trees and the towering greenery. Within minutes the birds resumed their songs. The day was warm. In time the first gnats and mosquitoes of spring began to find their mark.

"Let's move on in and see what we can see in there," Giblin called.

No one moved. "Go ahead, sheriff," LaFave said in his dry, accented voice. "You lead it off. We will be along directly." Several lumberjacks laughed.

Giblin fumed. When he'd been full-time sheriff with his full-time deputies, he could give orders and the men were compelled to obey. These civilian deputies, these loggers did as they damn well pleased.

"You going to let John Dietz beat you?" Giblin chided the tough logger.

"He ces not beating me, Geeblen. I thought you and Elliot

over there vere thee law. Sure doesn't look lak' it to me." LaFave stood, the others with him. They ignored Giblin's anger and started back to camp. On their way in across the clearing they could see the low, squat buildings of the Dietz farm, the small barn, the root cellar, the outhouse, the two-room cabin where the family of eight dwelled. The woman, Hattie, was bent over working in the garden. The three younger children played nearby. The two older boys and oldest girl were not in sight. Nor was John.

"Queer sight there," LaFave growled. "Looks like a nice family to me. But I don't know how a white woman can take to living as isolated as this. Why would a man even bring his family out here to a place like this? The kids have no school. There is nothing here for them. Nothing at all."

* * *

John returned home in late afternoon. He was wet, dirty, his face still streaked with dirt. He poured water from a galvanized pail into a porcelain wash basin and lathered his hands and face.

Hattie appraised her husband, trying to gauge his mood. "The boys thought they heard shooting."

The children, eager to hear the news but unwilling to provoke their father, cautiously crowded into the small log cabin. John dried his face and then leaned back in his rocking chair. He'd removed his boots but still wore wool socks. He wiggled his toes. He had a satisfied, confident look Hattie hadn't seen since John announced he and brother Bill were going into the real estate business. "The trust sent down some of their men. Seems they've decided to use rifles instead of pike poles to try to drive them logs. Which seems like a mighty peculiar use for a Winchester."

"Did you run them off, Pa?" Leslie yelled. He was excited, pressing forward as were Myra and the young ones.

Only Clarence understood the gravity of John's actions, Hattie thought. But of course Clarence couldn't speak, not against his father, not against John Dietz and that temper and those thick, meaty fists.

"We had a talk," John continued with his tale. "I believe they got the point. It doesn't pay to do the dirty work for the trusts."

"Did you shoot anyone?" Leslie asked.

"Leslie!" Hattie admonished as if frightened to hear the reply.

"There was fur that flew," John allowed. "None of it mine. I don't expect they'll bother us again."

"You shot a man?" Hattie railed. "How could you, John? Now they'll never settle. They can't."

John scowled. He'd warned Hattie more than once. He didn't like her snapping at him like that, especially not in front of the children. He was brusque, "They'll settle. They have three hundred thousand dollars worth of timber lying there. They'll want them out of here before the water drops or else the logs will start to rot and be chewed by maggots."

Hattie shrank from the hard tone. She'd stepped onto thin ice.

"How about some supper," John said as if giving an order. "I'm as hungry as a bear. And just about as mean," he said, and seized Stanley and then Helen and began tickling them head to toe. The children squirmed wildly and squealed with delight. Leslie grinned at the game. Clarence rose to go search in the marsh for his only baseball John had tossed away.

"Myra," Hattie said to her daughter, a request to join her in what served as the kitchen. The two women had work.

* * *

Hattie lay in the dark of night. Beside her, John snored. She elbowed him. He grunted, muttered, rolled and ceased to snore. Outside the evening whippoorwill had stopped its nightly call as had the bullfrogs and crickets. The damp, musky smell of motionless fog came through the screen. Silence reigned so complete and total Hattie imagined she could hear her children breathe. Johnny Ginger slept in a small, handmade bed stuffed with swamp grass and set on the floor at the foot of their bed. In the combined living room, kitchen and bedroom the rest of the children slept, Helen and Myra in one bed, Stanley and Leslie in a top bunk, Clarence, the oldest, by himself in the lower bunk. It was tight, cozy, in truth, after twenty-two years of marriage, the smallest house they'd ever owned.

Abruptly John sat up in bed. The bare vestiges of a grey

foggy dawn revealed the frame of the window. John rose and pulled on his clothes. Surely after years of toil they deserved more than what they had, Hattie thought. She spoke with fervor, "Be careful, John."

John grunted, his sign of affection for her support. He took his rifle down off the rack and departed. The front door closed. One of their two dogs, Myra's pup Tippy, barked once and then yelped as if in pain and fell silent.

Hattie, her chest throbbing as if on fire, stared without sleep. Where could it be John was going? She had not even asked.

It was not unusual for ground fog to cover the watery lowlands of the flowage and Thornapple River just down from the house. John strode as easily and confidently as a big mountain man crossing familiar plains. He headed for the dam, Cameron Dam, his dam that was located just up from the driving camp. He paid scant attention to the camp as he strode out onto the center of the dam and inserted the stub end of a solid oak limb into the turning wheel and began to wind up the center sluice gate. Water gushed through in an ever-increasing roar. That'll fix the trust, John thought, as the water drew down. They'll never get their logs out now.

He continued on across the dam and sat in plain view on a stump twenty rods up the hill from the driving camp. He'd slept soundly the night before, woke up with the first rays of dawn just as he'd intended. He knew most of the men in the driving camp, could even call a few of them friend. But they'd turned. Some of the traitors had been with Giblin and Elliot the day before. Even fired on him. As far as he knew they'd put the trusts' henchmen up for the night and were planning on coming for him again today.

"Well here I am," John said aloud as he struck a match and puffed on a pipe. He gestured toward the camp with the pipe as if talking to the men face to face. "You boys won't have far to look."

John sat, waiting. Behind him the roar of water draining from the flowage continued. The camp began to stir. Fresh smoke belched from the chimney, the cooky, or the man they called the bellyrobber, firing up the stove. Several men stumbled outside and urinated just outside the door. Unclean bastards, John thought, too lazy even to go to the outhouse.

Several of them looked in his direction as if puzzled at the roar of water. But no one saw him, even silhouetted as he was in the open on the hill.

An anger began to burn in his chest. The trusts would be nothing without the common working man as their slaves. Just the working man going along was the only strength the trusts really had. Working men made the trusts. And then it was working men the trusts abused the most. Like those fools down in camp risking their lives for less than two dollars a day.

He'd been a driver. He knew what it was like, the dangers, prying logs apart under the massive jaws of a log jam. Setting dynamite and running across the logs. Riding the logs down the river from before dawn until after dark. Wading in water and prying logs out of sloughs and off the shoreline. Waiting until the Wannegan, the trailing supplies and chuck wagon boat brought a hot supper. Then settling down on the shoreline, often without a tent, while animals and bugs gnawed at your body. He'd been with those men. And now they came after him.

Still sitting calmly in the open, John raised his rifle and fired a shot through the driving camp window. The bullet found a mark, shattering the bone in the arm above the elbow of a driver from Park Falls named John Tracy. Tracy dropped to the floor writhing in agony. The other drivers scrambled for cover. Deputy Giblin peeked out the window. A second shot whistled above his head.

"It's Dietz! He's standing right up there in the open. Get your guns," he ordered. None of the drivers moved.

Bill Tromblay, a friend of John's, a man who had said if the dam was on John's land, John should be paid, crawled over to the door. He cracked the door and peered out. A bullet burned his neck and splintered the door jamb beside his head. He sprawled backwards, rolling on the floor. "That bastard! If I come back out here I'm bringing my Winchester and John Dietz is dead."

"Go get him, Geeblin," LaFave chanted. "Go get him, Geeblin. You are the law. He is there waiting for you." The swarthy Frenchman giggled at Giblin's plight. "You have no one to send, eh? And you will not go alone. Hee. Hee."

Giblin was red, fuming. But he did not pick up his rifle and venture to the window to return fire.

The men lay in cover for the better part of an hour. They treated Tracy and left the man lying in the corner, bearing his pain in teeth-clenched silence. After some time LaFave ventured a peek outside. "He is going home," he said of Dietz.

The others looked. Indeed, it was true. John Dietz was walking the open ground up the small rise returning to his farm. The lumberjacks walked outside. Deputy Elliot went up to the dam and the roaring water. When he returned his face was set, solemn. "Well, men, you might as well pack your gear and start walking out. Dietz must have opened the dam. There won't be any drive of those logs this spring. Old John Dietz won this time. But he hasn't made one nickel. And he sure as hell can't make a living on that swamp farm he owns. I can't figure what he's after, turning down the company's offers, and now letting the water out. But he's not going to beat the lumber company. And he's not going to beat the State of Wisconsin. They'll get him, if they have to starve him out to do it. He can't hold out forever."

"Maybe not," LaFave said. "But it appears to me the man is going to try."

A POOR SINFUL MOTORIST'S DAY
Page from the Diary of an Average Driver
A HAIRBREADTH ESCAPE

A Steam Roller Disputes the Way - Shop and Cyclists
These Samples of a Motorist's Difficulties
He Himself a Perpetual Target for Abuse

The first excitement was caused by a small boy - one of the kind whose parents had neglected the teaching of Solomon. When the powerful car was within six yards of this small boy he jumped onto the road in front of it, playing that favorite game of small boys, which consists of running as closely as possible in front of a motorcar without being killed.

DIETZ WOULD GIVE LIFE DEFENDING CAMERON DAM

DUFFY'S PURE MALT WHIS-KEY not only serves to keep the bodily health at the highest notch of excellence, but in typhoid and malaria, especially when the bodily functions are at their lowest ebb and death seems imminent,

CHAPTER IV

Hattie did not even ask why John let the water out of the dam. She was too numb. Perhaps it was her fault. She'd been blinded by the large sums of money and the prospect of a leisurely life. Love not the world, neither the things that are in the world. If any man love the world, the love of the Father is not in him. Perhaps letting the water out was for the best, Hattie thought. Now the sheriff's or mill posses did not come around. They had no cause.

Hattie hitched up her ankle-length calico dress and went to work. In fact and in essence she ran the farm. Under her direction the small garden John and the children had started was quickly doubled in size. The soil was not the best, a sandy loam filled with rocks and low spots of water-retaining or baked-hard clay. "I want five acres of this plowed, John," Hattie said and pointed at the land. "We'll plant rutabagas. It's probably the only thing that will grow. We need something we can market to buy supplies for next winter."

"Hattie, that's six months away." John smiled at his wife's seriousness. "Come fall the boys and I will run trap lines. Just so long as the Lord doesn't decide it's my time and one of those hired agents from the mill doesn't bushwack me."

"I want those five acres," Hattie insisted. She could not be swayed.

John winked at his children. He loved to tease Hattie when she was like this, push her until her exasperation drove her to thin-lipped silence and hard-slamming work as if to demonstrate she'd do everything herself. Then John and the children would do the tasks Hattie had asked. That way it was as if he were giving Hattie something, a gift rather than doing what she said.

"Old Joe Hobbs from over Phillips way said this country was good for sheep," John said. "I figure we'll get a flock. Sell the wool. Sell the mutton. Sheep are easy to keep. I'll need that money out of the sock."

Hattie's stomach sucked back against her spine. She'd hoarded that money, saving pennies, nickels and dimes over the years. She never bought a new dress. She always picked the used, the discards of those monetarily more fortunate than herself. She gave the new clothing to the children and tucked away those pennies, a meager nest egg in case of disaster.

"Don't look at me like I'm a midnight thief," John snapped. He appraised his brood. "Your mother's part pack-rat. Which makes you all mice," he said and grabbed a squealing Helen. "C'mon, let's have some of that rhubarb pie."

The next day John set Clarence and Leslie to plowing the veggie patch. All day long Myra, Stanley and Helen walked behind picking up rocks.

The family bedded with the sun and rose with the sun. Most evenings they did not even bother to turn up the wick in the kerosene lamps. Some evenings, if the deer flies and mosquitoes were not too persistent, the children played hide-and-seek, or blindman's bluff. Clarence, the oldest, the one who whittled toys for the younger children and who helped organize their games, headed the play. On occasion they would ride Old Tom or Leslie would run with a lead rope while Stanley, Helen and sometimes Johnny giggled and bounced on Tom's swayed back.

When they could manage, Myra, Leslie and Clarence went off on their own. They used bamboo cane poles and worms to fish the Thornapple for bass, pan fish and redhorse. A half mile upriver a deep pool had formed at the base of a twenty-foot-high sand bank. There they'd swim, Myra wearing frilly bloomers that covered her from shoulders to knees, the boys wearing knee-length shorts. Often they took soap, for in summer they used the river for their baths.

The passage of weeks with no sign from the law or mills had made them all feel easier. But just the day before, Saturday, John had let Myra ride to the tiny railhead town of Radisson with him and Leslie. They had to chop out several downed trees to get through on the seldom-traveled road. Myra had been terribly excited for she noticed a difference. Everyone stared. Some people pointed. "She's one of them Dietz kids," she heard one lady say. She saw other children, girls her own age. But they all stood off, defiant, and when Myra turned her back she could hear them giggle and talk. She hunched her shoulders, stiffened her back and choked back the lump in her throat.

"What do you think they'll do to Pa?" Myra quietly asked. They ducked neck-deep in the warm water to keep deer flies away. The embarrassment of her visit to town lingered. None of those girls lives as isolated as she, none of them had a father as stubborn as was hers. Nor as tough, she thought in proud confusion.

"If they get a chance they'll put him in jail," Clarence said solemnly. He was serious, reflecting the truth so the others would be prepared. It would then be up to him to run the farm, to stay home. It would be years before he could move out on his own.

"If they come here again he'll just run them off," Leslie retorted. "They'll never take Pa. He said so himself."

That was Leslie. He did not like to have his routine upset. "Pa said they'd never take him alive," Clarence pointed out. His blue eyes were unclouded, direct as if trying to make Leslie see as did he.

"That's not true," Leslie shouted. His face colored with protest. "They're all scared of him, just like you, Clarence. You should have seen him tell that O'Hare from the school board. I want a school for my children, either that or a teacher. So O'Hare said we get our own teacher this year. And then Pa said he wasn't paying for the teacher to eat so O'Hare says we'll give you twenty dollars a month room and board. You should have seen O'Hare shake. Now what do you think of that?"

Clarence shrugged. But his lips were tightly compressed, a part of it his own fear. He'd never seen one hint his father would ever back away. Never. He closed his eyes, faced with the image of a smiling giant blocking the road, the same giant who'd smacked him alongside the head at his slowness to obey, and the next moment knelt patiently and taught him to shoot. Leslie and Myra simply did not understand.

"Besides," Leslie continued, "remember that Joe Buckwheat was here and said Mr. Irvine wanted to talk, settle things peacefully. You wait. Pa's won."

Clarence did not reply.

* * *

William Irvine, Secretary of the Chippewa Lumber and Boom Company, and two assistants sat in the crowded confines of the low-roofed Dietz farmhouse. Irvine had hired Joe Buckwheat as a guide and wagon driver. Dietz had been forewarned. Irvine and his party had arrived unarmed, been greeted cordially enough and invited into the squat log house. It was July 20, the humidity high, the heat a swelter. What thick, blurred glass windows the house possessed had been removed and the openings were covered with rusted screens. Nevertheless, the air did not move.

Irvine mopped his brow. He considered himself a reasonable man, an articulate man who could converse in layman's terms with the assorted breeds and nationalities hired by the mills. But he was beginning to confess, John Dietz put his patience to the test.

He'd already made his offer to drop all civil actions and pay John the same five hundred dollars previously offered. John of course laughed. His price was fifteen thousand. The dam was on his land, built on the flowage where the mill could not possess meander rights. John was leaned back, relaxed, but his voice was pressing like a self-confident attorney unwilling to entertain even a remote suspicion he could be wrong. "The law states the mills are permitted to charge others ten cents per thousand board feet for the use of a mill dam, is that not right?" John demanded.

"Yes," Irvine conceded to John's statement, "but that is only on a dam we have franchised with the state. Like this dam here. You want to charge us for the use of our own dam?"

"A dam built on my property. If the mills can charge others, then of course so can I." John moved forward to the edge of his seat as if coiled in a crouch.

"You do not have a franchise, Mr. Dietz," Irvine said quietly. The words did not penetrate. Was Dietz that set in his ways, or was he just that tough? The visit was a mistake. Irvine looked to his two partners for support, but they were equally exasperated and apprehensive.

"Who does this attorney T.J. Connor work for?" Dietz asked.

"Why the Mississippi River and Logging Company," Irvine said. "That's common knowledge."

John showed his famous smile. "Why, I was informed T.J. Connor works for the Chippewa Lumber and Boom Company? He signed affidavits for their benefit. He's out there hiring gunmen to kill me and my family and he's filing those twenty-thousand-dollar injunctions against my property and you tell me he doesn't work for either company. My, my but he must be a saint or a good Samaritan to take on all those lawyerly tasks. And for no monetary gain. What's the matter?" John goaded the lumbermen with seeming pleasure. "Are you so ashamed of the man you cannot even admit he works for you?"

Irvine was trapped into silence. Dietz knew more about the outside world than a man would believe. Irvine noted Joe Buckwheat showed the trace of a smile. Dietz and his sarcasm was making the mills look bad. Buckwheat would spread the word.

"Why did you send those drivers with rifles out here?" John suddenly demanded into the silence. As quickly as the bitter humor had been raised it was replaced by a tone of threat.

The man wore a pistol under his coat, Irvine was convinced. "I told you those weren't our men. They were deputies from the county."

"Sheriff Peterson did not deputize those men," John roared as if to intimidate. But his anger was not real. He leaned back and smiled. "Was that one of your experiments, driving logs with rifles instead of peaveys? It went like a lot of experiments, didn't it, Mr. Irvine? It did not work."

Irvine wiped the dry spittle from his lips. The water the woman offered in a scratched glass was warm and tasted of iron. He glanced around the low, dark cabin, feeling the closeness, the isolation. The logs still had bark on the outside. The yard was beaten dirt with little grass. The young ones ran dirty and barefoot and they all crowded inside this sweaty little jailhouse to sleep.

Irvine tried to meet John's pale blue eyes direct, to understand the basis of the man's rigid stand. If he didn't know better he would have said there was a madness there.

"Now suppose, John, just suppose I gave you all you asked. Would you sign to us full use of the dam? Would you be satisfied?"

Hattie stopped at the table as if frozen. She did not breathe. Her eyes were wide, questioning if Irvine was serious. She looked to John for his response.

"You want me to speculate on what you will not do?" John said. "Because we live a goodly distance from town we aren't simply ignorant knotholes in a tree. Quite the opposite is true in order to survive in the wilderness. But your kind would not know, Irvine. What I ask in settlement is but a fraction of what those logs are worth or what you mills owe."

Irvine rose and walked the few feet to where Hattie was peeling potatoes. "Mrs. Dietz, I'm here to look for ways to resolve our differences without further bloodshed. Your husband looks only for reasons to oppose me. Surely, madam, you can see the need for compromise, that we can indeed find a common ground for settlement."

Hattie's heart ached. Her head throbbed. But her hesitation was no more than a heartbeat, a minuscule interruption in the twenty-two years living and bedding side-by-side with John. And this wealthy executive dared parade in here in his expensive clothes and ask her to submit like a little waif.

"We have common ground, Mr. Irvine, where that dam sits on our property. We ask you to pay no more than what you can legally ask others to pay for the use of your dams."

"But that dam is ours. The courts have ruled."

"The courts you own," John snapped. "The press knows about me and my stand. They know about the lumber trusts."

"The court says you're in violation. You can't make your own law, John."

With the suddenness of a wildcat, John slammed his fist on a tiny side table, splitting the maple wood with the force of his blow. "And neither can the mills."

Despite himself, Irvine shrank back, humbled to realize the presence of authority made no impact on John Dietz. The man had moved out here to the wilderness, here he stood and would not move. He could be President Theodore Roosevelt himself and it would not hold sway with John Dietz.

From that moment on Irvine looked only for a basis on which to depart. "Mr. Hines has threatened to go to federal court. That would bring out the U.S. marshals and perhaps the militia. You'll be facing the law, not only the State of Wisconsin, but the law of the United States of America."

"Send them out. I'll be here," John said. He contemplated a spot on the floor. Unconsciously the lines of his hard German face softened. "Sure, you can send 'em out. You have that power. What can I do? I've moved as far as I can go." His voice became husky, almost on the verge of breaking. "A man can move only so far and then you have to say enough, Mr. Irvine... Enough."

For some moments those in the tiny cabin were silent. As the men rose to depart, Hattie motioned John off to one side. She whispered urgently in his ear. They must come out of this with something for their trouble. She pleaded with her eyes. How much could John expect?

John scowled at this sudden weakness. Reluctantly he turned to Irvine. "I'll settle for ten thousand. You drop all civil and criminal charges. Get rid of your damn injunctions you've placed against my land."

"That's twenty-five years' wages for a woodsman, John," Irvine protested. Nevertheless he hesitated, contemplating. There were six and one half million feet of logs out there rotting under the soaking of water, the heat of the sun, and the relentless boring of maggots and grubs eating up three hundred thousand dollars worth of prime pine timber.

"That doesn't cover any future drives of course," John suddenly said as if in fear Irvine would accept his compromise offer.

Irvine noticed Hattie close her eyes and turn away. For a second he thought she would weep and for a second his heart went out. But when she looked her eyes were dry, her back firm and straight.

"I tried for reasonableness," Irvine reported. "That was not to be."

Two weeks later newspapers reported that John Dietz, a Mason as was Irvine, refused to argue his case before the Grand Master of the Masons.

* * *

The summer wore on. It was long, hot and much too dry. The rutabaga patch had been planted late and did not fare the best. Heat, humidity, and wood ticks exacted a fearsome toll on the sheep. Coyotes and fox feasted on the Dietz's uncooped chickens. The river dropped to a mere trickle. The mounds of huge logs lay high and dry, exposed to the elements.

It was a summer of work, nothing but work, Hattie thought more than once. And work as they did, they seemed to gain so little.

The mills pushed a railroad spur past Radisson and into the deep woods. The mill town of Winter, less than eleven miles away from the Dietz farm, emerged from the forest. Commerce picked up. The tiny mill town quickly expanded.

Despite the warrants for his arrest, John and one of the boys and sometimes Myra went into town almost once a month. All summer long Hattie went but once. And then she was filled with acute embarrassment, for she saw people look and heard the whispers behind her back. "Never again," she told John. "Next time I'm staying out on the farm."

"Oh, Hattie, they just need something to chew on. Nothing more to it than that."

Hattie glanced at her husband perched high on top of the spring board. She hadn't seen this much fire in him since he was a young man. He looked smug, satisfied, like that slight swagger she'd noted in his walk down the plank sidewalks, arms swinging wide, people moving aside, that Luger pistol jutting defiantly from the holster high on the hip belt used to hold up his pants. Oh, yes, Hattie thought, John Dietz you are a real man. But of course she did not say a word.

On Sundays the Dietz family held their church and, led by Hattie, sang, often for an hour or more. They even "Sundayed," visiting and eating with deep woods neighbors four and five miles down the narrow tote road. "We have to be neighborly," Hattie insisted to John. "I have to get out sometime."

John patted her shoulder as if in understanding. "Of course. I'll tell them to drop by, give them an opportunity to make an excuse."

The visits did not go well. Gottlieb Schmuland, wife Bertha and two kids, hardly talked. Bertha spoke mostly German and seemed nervous. They spoke of the weather, of neighbors, of old Swede Olson down the road who had lost his mind. Each day his wife sent him to the basement to carry coal from one side of the basement to the other, and the next day back to the other side. Eventually the conversation evolved to talk about the mills. Gottlieb listened quietly to John's long lecture against the trusts then commented, "That may be true, Mr. Dietz. Nevertheless, the trusts give us work. Up here in the north they're all we have."

"Then you wouldn't know a thief if you felt his hand in your pocket," John snapped. He lurched to his feet. They would not visit Gottlieb or speak to him again. Hattie patted Bertha's hand when they said goodbye, two pioneer women commiserating with each other. Despite her poor English, Bertha had been nice, even smiling when John got mad.

With the John Abraham family they fared no better. Iris Abraham was a thin, worn woman who, at least it appeared to Hattie, needed no more mouths to feed even on a Sunday. And when the Abrahams visited them, Hattie saw their supplies drop in half. "They must have starved those kids all week," she complained to John.

In September they wagoned into Winter and took the Soo Line to Rice Lake to visit their oldest daughter, Florence May. Stanley and Helen were excited beyond themselves, noses pressed to the window, watching the conductor and all the people, mostly locals on this short spur. They laughed and pointed at every homestead and river and road they passed.

Once they saw a team of coal black horses dancing in their

harness in panic as the train roared past at close to forty miles per hour. Their joy gave Hattie joy. Just watching the two in their excitement made the trip worth the price.

Nevertheless she was deeply worried. Winter would soon be coming on, a bad one Hattie knew; the woolly bear caterpillars had narrow brown bands and the corn husks were hard to pull apart. The children needed boots, Myra a winter coat. She'd canned everything she could, corn, pickles, beans, berry preserves. But the root cellar was only half filled, scarcely enough to last out the winter. Her frontier face was hard, set as if with plaster so no one could read what churned inside.

Try as she may to concentrate on pleasantries, Hattie could think only on the here and now and the prospect of another deep forest winter looming just ahead. It seemed the last one had just passed.

Once in Rice Lake they went to daughter Florence May and John went downtown to visit. He returned in an ebullient mood. He'd met up with Sheriff Charles Peterson from Sawyer County. "Gave him a solid piece of my mind for siding with the trusts. He said he didn't deputize Giblin and those men. Said he was sorry for any trouble he'd caused me. Gave me ten dollars then turned around and gave me three more. Some of those reporters said they're still with us." John showed Hattie the papers. "That shows what I said, a lot of people are counting on me to stick up for their rights."

"That's good, John. Now you don't have to go it alone."

John laughed, grabbed his wife and hugged and kissed her in spite of her resistance. "That's my Hattie, fastest tongue in the north. C'mon, let's take the young'ns to the fair."

A few weeks later they heard the news: Sawyer County had a new sheriff, one who swore he'd do his duty and arrest John Dietz, or die in the attempt, the man said.

The mill capitalists were behind the move, John informed his family. Sheriff Peterson had been tried on a contempt charge before the mill judge, Parish. Peterson had been fined $150.00 and sentenced to thirty days in jail. He'd been replaced by Sheriff Thomas Harrison Grist, a sixty-eight-year-old man who claimed to carry two rifle balls from the civil war.

The mills were moving to put other pressure on him as well,

John was informed by sympathizers. On October 25, 1904, the Sawyer County Board adopted a resolution:

> WHEREAS, the sheriff of this county is unable to apprehend and arrest the said John F. Dietz without assistance because of the natural obstacles to overcome, and, WHEREAS, the failure to apprehend and arrest the said John F. Dietz is a blight and stain upon the fair name of Sawyer County therefore, it is hereby resolved, that the sheriff and district attorney of Sawyer County are hereby authorized and empowered to contract for, and on behalf of said Sawyer County for whatever assistance and necessaries may be necessary to effect and arrest and apprehension of said John F. Dietz in a sum not exceeding $500.00 which shall be paid out of the treasury of Sawyer County in the amount in the manner of other claims.

> S.H.B. Shue, chairman

> Gust Anderson, county clerk

* * *

"So now you've got a five-hundred-dollar reward on my head," John accused the grizzled old sheriff. It was November 19th. The northern deer season was in full swing. A light snow had covered the ground. Sheriff Grist, unarmed but with warrant in hand, had made the long two-day journey down to the Dietz farm. John bent close to the old veteran.

"Well, I'll tell you and you can inform anyone else if they mean to come after John Dietz they can go straight to a place a mite warmer than they're accustomed to. I will gladly assist them or you on their trip."

Hattie came behind John and at Grist. She waved a newspaper they had received in one of their intermittent mail deliveries. "Are these your words, Mr. Grist? 'I will get Dietz or he will get me. I will do my duty if it costs me my life.' Did you make those threats against my husband?"

Hattie was shrill, almost hysterical with this presence of one more representative of the law. "We have so little. And you would do the bidding of the mills and tear this family apart?"

"Now, now, Mrs. Dietz. I'm just trying to do my job."

Immediately Grist was turned back in the opposite direction by John's blunt voice. "Here I stand and there you stand. You wouldn't want the county to lose a sheriff without a formal resignation."

"I ain't packing iron," Grist replied carefully. He stood as if facing a wild, unpredictable bear. He'd been told stories that made John sound like everything from a saint to a wild man. But not an immovable object like this.

"Why not?" John asked in a high, mocking tone. "You're the sheriff. You're entitled to be armed. How are you going to get me if you're not armed?"

"I heard you didn't take kindly to armed visitors." Grist smiled as if trying to make it a joke.

"Why, that's right too," John continued his exaggerated mocking. "Seems you've heard just about everything, including my instructions." John turned and picked up a rifle leaning in the corner. "Here, Sheriff, I'll give you a weapon. You can do with it what you will. But I'm not budging from my home."

The lifting of the rifle so alarmed Grist he swallowed his cud of chewing tobacco. He knew he'd soon be sick, in fact, felt the churning already as he stared at the offered rifle. If he touched it would that be reason for John to pull his pistol? Or even if he held the gun and John refused to move, could he shoot a man in cold blood over a simple injunction by the mills? He stared, frozen in place as firmly as water in a pail on a winter night. Yes, he'd sworn to serve the injunction on John Dietz. He reached for his coat pocket. He silently cursed the trembling of his hand. He was 68 years old, the duly appointed sheriff of Sawyer County, a veteran of the war — he had no reason to fear John Dietz.

Grist later told a reporter:

"I told Dietz I had a warrant for him and took it out and commenced to read it... but he snatched it out of my hand and made some threats that I had been looking for trouble and guessed that I would get it... He got pretty angry... I could have arrested him but I couldn't get him out. He would not walk out and I couldn't carry him."

On his departure Grist paused briefly at the low, wood-plank doorway. "I wish you'd come, John. James Gylland is taking over as sheriff come January. And I heard the mills are going to federal courts to obtain an injunction. That means U.S. marshals and the militia will be out here next. Those men don't fool around."

John leaned casually back in a rocking chair. Grist could see the butt of a Luger pistol tucked in the belt under his coat. "Tell them I'll be here, Grist. A man cannot die before his time. Tell them I'll get a lot of them before they get me. If they want to do the work of the trusts, then that's the cross they'll have to bear."

Grist took his leave. T.J. Connor, the attorney for the mills, returned to court. Shortly thereafter a federal injunction was returned in favor of the mills.

REAL MILITANT TO TAKE STATE FOR SUFFRAGE

Mary Swain Wagner Here to Arouse City by English Methods in Vote Quest

Leader Assures Men no Bricks Will be Thrown and no Heads Cracked

Milwaukee Passive Suffragists Will Now Become Militant

DIETZ STILL MASTER OF THE DAM

Officers Come Out of the Woods, Leaving Dietz at Home

Masonic Influence at Work for the Woodsman

Dietz an Expert With Rifle and Revolver

An exchange says that one of the new fads is men's socks for women. There is a rumor prevalent that some women wear the trousers, but no one imagined that the socks would be appropriated. If the women continue the invasion of the wardrobe of the men there will be very few articles of wearing apparel left that the men can call their own. His hat, shirt, vest, coat, collar, tie and socks are gone.

He has remaining his chewing tobacco and suspenders — not much of a layout for a cold day.

CHAPTER V

The Dietz family spent most of the fall preparing for the winter. They ditched around the cabin, building a levee of insulating dirt against the bottom logs to cut the floor draft. They piled more wood. John and the boys hunted grouse, ducks and deer and trapped muskrat and mink. The days grew short. There were evenings they gathered in the dim light of the kerosene lamps and John slit the skin of muskrats from hind legs to tail and then, with a powerful rip, peeled the skin the length of the body and down over the nose. The bloody carcasses were tossed into the same galvanized tub the family used to take a bath. Hattie, Myra, and Leslie sat with burlap bags on their laps, boat shaped boards over which they stretched the skins and used Hattie's large spoons to scrap fat off the bloody insides of the skins. Meanwhile Clarence stretched scrapped skins, fur side in, and hung the bloody skins in the low rafters to cure.

"Yech. It was a gruesome sight. And the smell," the newcomer to the family reported. She was Ethel Young, the young school teacher who had been assigned to live with and instruct the Dietz children as John had demanded of the local school board. She wasn't worried about living with the outlaw family, Ethel nonchalantly told friends. In fact, she thought it might be stimulating. She did not admit to being distantly related to

Hattie Dietz. Besides, she'd only seen the woman twice.

What Ethel hadn't anticipated was such isolation, such desolation. They were surrounded by jagged stumps and miles and
miles of thick forest. Her combined bedroom and the schoolroom was a drafty little cubicle hitched on one side of the cabin.
The Dietz children's schooling to date had been hit or miss.
Johnny Ginger was very young and barely knew his ABCs.
Helen was a whiz, and Stanley tried only as a form of compe-
tition with Helen. Leslie was inattentive and a prankster. Myra
was a bit of a dreamer, although a strong and hard worker
around the house. But Myra didn't know social protocol and
she didn't know boys. Other than her brothers she'd had very
little contact with males her age.

Once Ethel caught Myra staring at the handsome male mod-
els in the Sears & Roebuck catalogue. "Have you ever kissed
a boy?" Myra asked her.

"Of course," Ethel said. Her face turned red. She was a bit
heavier than she liked. But she was considered pretty. Her
father was a community leader. Besides, she'd graduated from
the eighth grade and had her teacher's certificate. And she
was only twenty years old.

"What was it like?" Myra asked.

"Myra, you don't ask people those questions," Ethel scolded.
"Ask your mother. I'm here to teach you to read and write, not
about life."

"But that's what I want to learn about," Myra protested.
"About people. What are they doing, what are they wearing,
what they say." Her eyes sought Ethel's. "Don't you understand? We've lived out here in the wilderness ever since I was
a little girl. I simply want to talk."

"No," Ethel snapped authoritatively, "you want gossip. I
can't help where you live." She turned away. It would not do
to get too friendly with one of her pupils. Life with the Dietzes
was an experience she would never forget, Ethel said. Hattie
made the children wash daily, however, they only took complete baths two or three times a month. Myra and the boys
toted buckets of water from the spring and filled the galvanized tub sitting on top of the wood stove. After the tub was
hot they set it on the floor.

The family cleared out into the school room or outside and they took turns taking baths, girls first, boys last. By the time they were finished the water was grey, almost black.

"If I hadn't been first I never would have bathed," Ethel said. "That was some family. Those kids were thick as honey."

The oldest boy Clarence was the leader, a puzzle who took his position seriously. Handsome, Ethel thought on first impression. Although he clearly wanted to learn, he thought himself too old to accept instruction from her.

Once, when they were briefly alone in the house, Clarence even made an overture, at least Ethel thought he did.

"Do you have a steady beau, Miss Young?" Clarence asked. His voice rattled with nervousness. His eyes sought hers, then quickly darted away.

Ethel was alarmed. If there was an attraction from this outlaw boy she had to deflect it at once. "Not at the moment," she said in a bright tone. His blue eyes were watching. There was a narrowness of vision there, she later insisted, like with his father, John. "I want something more from life than living in the woods or on a farm, Clarence. Look at your mother. She never gets a break. The only thing she ever does for fun is 'Sunday' once in a while. And then she cooks or does dishes. Or when she sings. But that's all."

"I wasn't asking you that," Clarence snapped. He turned crimson with embarrassment. "You think everyone who lives in the woods stays there? I wasn't asking you anything." He spun on his heel.

Thereafter, despite Hattie's insistence, Clarence rarely attended Miss Young's class. She may be a teacher, he thought, but she understood no more than the rest.

By December winter was upon them full force. Within a number of miles there were several logging camps that had hired crews and taken to the woods. After a supper of boiled rutabagas, fried venison hash and Hattie's green beans and prunes, the family played games. Stanley and Helen played checkers. Despite Helen's superiority in school, Stanley was the whiz at checkers, able to beat everyone in the family, even the teacher Miss Young, and on occasion his father.

This particular evening John was feeling expansive. He lit a pipe and leaned back in his rocker, feet upon a trunk. The pot-bellied stove glowed warm. The kerosene lamp flickered as a raw wind buffeted the log cabin and ice crystals rattled off the windows. This was a moment for which a man lived, John thought — home, a warm fire and the close togetherness of his family.

Clarence mentioned the subject first; the Kaiser Lumber Company had a camp and crew cutting less than four miles away. He'd been hunting snowshoe rabbits and had talked to a couple of cruisers. Kaiser was still hiring, the men had said, but of this Clarence remained silent. His hands trembled and his one leg jiggled up and down like a race horse anticipating the sound of the gun. Several times the words gathered in his throat, but he could not force them out. "Kaiser company is cutting not far away," Clarence finally managed to say.

"I spent my time in the woods," John said in reply. "Started as a road monkey keeping the ice ruts free of manure. Swamper, brushing out the roads. Sawer. In eighty-eight, Joe Klecko and I won the two man crosscut sawing contest in Rice Lake. Ax throwing. Teamster, skidder, you name it, I've done it." A veil seemed to cover John's eyes. His big hands clenched and unclenched like a man fighting off spasms of pain.

"Worked some spring drives. Used to stand on those logs right down through the rapids. Slough over on the Flambeau, guy drowned there. Waist deep in that freezing water, pike pole for balance, squatted low just back of center." He smiled with the memory, with the adventure, for there had been part of it he had enjoyed. "Not many men could ride those sluice gates and those rapids all the way through."

The children and the school teacher were enthralled. Hattie continued to stitch on a calico dress for Myra who sat in her usual place paging through the wish book.

"A lot of men got hurt; crushed by a tree; runaway wagon down an iced hill. Seen one overloaded wagon caught up to the team and killed two horses and two men. Drownings. Yeah, I worked the pineries. Back when we had real trees. Men with language so foul it took the bark off the trees."

A scowl came over John's face. The remembered adventure of seconds before had never existed. "The lumber trusts use men. Men risk life and limb for twenty dollars a month as a road monkey. Thirty-five as a teamster. Meanwhile the bosses rake in their thousands over the bent backs of slave labor. Look at their huge mansions down there on the Chippewa. There is not a parcel of land in this state they cannot take hold of. Now they want ours. No, you work first light until last, sometimes twenty-four hours if you're on a river drive. They don't care if you're hurt. Can't work, you don't get paid. A good draft horse is worth more to the mill than a man. Doesn't cost a nickel to replace a man."

Why, in the face of John's most bitter mood, Clarence spoke just then, he could not explain, not even to himself, he later said. But the fire was there, a seldom demonstrated passion which would stand no rein. He knew how John had turned on Valentine Weisenbach. A warrant had been issued for Valentine's arrest. Valentine in fact had been arrested and was now out on bail awaiting trial for his part in the ambush of Giblin. Despite the charges, John asserted Valentine had been favored and was working for the mills. The bastard was a spy, John said of his former ally.

"Kaiser camp four over here still needs men," Clarence ventured. It seemed as though the words put him naked on a stage. His voice became strained. "We were short on our land tax money this year. We could use some money home here."

Despite himself, he looked to Hattie for support. Her eyes were wide and she shook her head in warning. No, no, no! A heavy silence pervaded the cabin. Wind buffeted the log walls. Imperceptibly the other children shrank away.

"Maybe Clarence and I should get more wood," Leslie said.

"Shut up," John snapped. His boots clicked on the plank floor. "You saying I don't provide?"

"No. It's just that Uncle Bill said if we don't pay all the tax, the mills will pay and they'll take over the land. They already changed the records at the court house."

Clarence was giddy, almost dizzy with his fear. Surely his father could understand. "I'm getting older, Pa. I have to do something."

"Do something? What do you call this farm? You want to leave, work for the trusts? The ones who pushed us here?

Fine, Clarence. Leave. Stab me in the back. Just don't let me see your face."

"John, please," Hattie cried.

"No," John roared in a voice that shook the walls.

"Valentine makes me a mockery, trying to cut himself a deal. And now my own flesh."

"I'm not against you, Pa. I just want my own life."

"Oh, you deserve more than the rest of us? Maybe you want it all, a mansion, your own company, men you can order around like slaves. Is that what it is, you don't have enough?"

Clarence, his face as ruddy as dried blood, rose, crouched as if preparing for the blow. "I have enough," he screamed. "You seem to forget, the rest of us have lives, too."

John swung. Despite Clarence's readiness the punch took him full and knocked him over a trunk and into the wet boots set in a line under the bunk beds. "Go then. Covet my enemies. Work for the trusts. Just don't come back."

Hattie moved between them then, yelling as loud as did John. "Enough of this. Have we not supported you all the way?" she chided John. She glared, warning Clarence to hold his tongue. Myra knelt at Clarence's side. The younger children were pressed to the walls as was Ethel Young. Somehow Hattie managed to head John off for the chill of their bedroom. He was still shaking with rage.

"Oh, Clarence," Hattie said as she helped her son to his feet. She took his head in her hands. Her eyes were filled with tears. "Why did you do that? Why? You have to bide your time, give your father a chance."

"Chance for what?" Clarence retorted in a fierce whisper that would not carry to the back bedroom. "To take our lives with his? Look at you, Ma. You always said you wanted a nice house some day. Is this where you want to be? Pa's so turned against the trusts now he'll never give you nice things. Never."

"Hush now." Hattie was angry as if Clarence's words struck home. "Don't you talk to me like that. You still have your place. You should think twice before you give it up."

She whirled and joined John in the tiny bedroom.

* * *

Shortly before Christmas the weather broke and on a warm, sunny twenty-five degree day John declared they would sleigh into the town of Winter. Clarence curtly refused John's request to join him. "Don't then," John snapped. He took Leslie, Myra, and the teacher in the two-seat cutter.

The two sorrels had not been hitched up for some weeks and were spirited. There were no fallen trees blocking the tote road that had been packed firm by buckboards and bobsleds dragged to the logging camps. They covered the eleven miles in little less than two hours.

It was on the frozen dirt street of Winter that Ethel met the attorney lumberman T.J. Connor. He was polite, gracious towards her feminine status, yet forceful and intimidating. He wanted to know all she would tell him about the outlaw Dietz family. Did the entire family support John and his stand?

"Oh, yes," Ethel said brightly. "They can all shoot. Even little Helen and Stanley, and they're barely big enough to lift a gun. Little Johnny plays with toy guns all the time. Mr. Dietz even asked me if I wanted to fire a few shots. Said I never knew when knowing how to shoot might come in handy."

"Dietz is an anarchist, a killer. Do you support that?"

Connor's face loomed over Ethel like an approaching train, smoke belching from the puffing of his cigar. He wanted — no, he insisted — on her assistance, Ethel said. He pressed fifty dollars into her hand, knowing she made less than three hundred dollars teaching a year. He wanted drawings of the farm, a count of weapons, the location of firing ports.

Perhaps she could secretly deplete their stockpiles of ammunition. That way, if it came to a siege the family would soon run out of ammunition and no one would be hurt.

"Mr. Dietz would kill me," Ethel said. But with her fear there was excitement, involvement in more than what the world had shown her to date. The family had already made the house into a fort, she told Connor, by piling dirt up around the bottom logs.

Connor thanked her and promised more money and positively no efforts against Dietz while she was still on the farm. "Then we'll send in the U.S. marshals," Connor said. "I've already got the injunction in process. Dietz is an anarchist.

He'd destroy this country and our free capitalistic system that has made us so great. He deserves to be hung."

"Yes sir," Ethel said. A young woman did not disagree with a man like T.J. Connor.

The Dietzes were in town! It seemed everyone knew five minutes before they arrived. So badly Myra had wanted to come to visit at the general store and see the latest bonnets and talk with girls her own age. But now, with the whispers and stares she already wanted to leave.

"Shot any lawmen lately?" Two boys laughed at her and Leslie.

"It ain't the season," Leslie said goodnaturedly to the bigger boys. He smiled and deliberately reached into the pocket of his dark wool coat. Abruptly, as if goaded by some inner and unnatural fear they did not understand, the two boys backed away. There'd been so many stories.

"He's got a gun in his coat pocket," one whispered. They turned, straining to keep their walk from breaking into a run.

"Wonder what's with them?" Leslie said as he pulled a pair of deerskin mittens from his pocket.

"That was mean, Leslie," Myra scolded. She hugged her brother's arm, for once feeling as big as did he. "I just can't understand why everyone holds back and stares. What do they think we are?"

"Outlaws," Leslie said with wide-eyed exaggeration. Unlike Myra he was not bothered in the least.

After the leisurely lunch they picked up their mail, including a mail-order package from Wards, and stopped by the general store.

"Ask about credit for just over the winter," Hattie had asked John.

"I owe no man," John had responded sharply. "A man takes on debt and sells the trust his soul. It's exactly what they want."

John ignored Hattie's distress and appropriated what he thought was her last five dollars and with that purchased what he could of flour, yeast, dried beans, cornmeal, side pork, and a tin of lard. They loaded the sleigh; John clucked to the horses and they headed for home, their big day complete.

"There he is," Leslie yelled. He pointed out a large, dapper man wearing a knee-length beaver-skin coat. "The attorney, Connor! Look at him, dressed like he's a king."

Leslie's bitterness was deep, genuine. "I bet that coat cost more than all of Ma's clothes put together."

"Your mother does not want," John growled. He refused to even give Connor a look.

"Weren't you talking to that Connor earlier?" Myra asked Ethel, who was sitting beside her in the back seat.

"Me?" Ethel's voice squeaked. She flushed. "Land's sake, I ah ... I guess he did say hi." She gave Myra a look, a plea really not to ask more.

Myra stared at her father's broad back. He sat straight and erect, eyes straight ahead as if he had not heard. Myra shrugged and fell silent. Ethel closed her eyes and breathed a sigh of relief. Myra would not tell, she thought. The girl was young, naive — she really wasn't an outlaw like the rest.

* * *

"Pa," Helen said, "Stanley and I saw Miss Young looking through your papers. "

"And then she took some bullets," Stanley eagerly cut in, "just like last time."

"I figured," John said. "Ever since Myra saw her talking to Connor." It was a pleasant winter day. The entire family, including Myra and Hattie, had gathered on the flowage behind the dam to saw ice blocks to store in sawdust in the root cellar. Hattie wanted enough to last throughout the summer. The younger children, Helen, Stanley and Johnny, ostensibly had been sent up the hill behind the house to sled on the slide Clarence had built. In fact John had instructed them to sneak back to the house and spy through the window.

The entire family strode en masse back to the cabin. Ethel was sitting serenely in a rocking chair reading one of her many pulp novels.

"Always reading," John said. "Those books a bit more interesting than personal papers?"

Ethel's mouth gaped like a bass gulping for air. The family crowded past into her combination schoolroom and bedroom. They seemed so united as a group, their combined presence soaking up the space and forcing Ethel back against the wall.

Young Stanley went directly to her dresser and pulled open the top drawer. He hesitated then pointed at the white silk of Ethel's bloomers. "Under there."

John flipped aside the bloomers. Approximately two dozen bullets lay scattered in the drawer. Ethel shrank against one wall. The eyes of the family, as if united as one unit, swung in her direction. Her heart hammered in her throat. She felt an urgent need to urinate.

John rattled several bullets in the palm of his callused hand. His blue eyes glinted like cold steel. "Our stores have been going down quite a bit." His lips curled in a smile that belied the look in his eyes. "You been figuring on teaching the young'ns to shoot, Miss Young?"

Ethel tried to speak, to protest her innocence. But her lungs and throat hurt too much. She could only manage a croak.

"How much did the mills pay you? How much?" John bellowed. Ethel so jumped she almost peed her bloomers. The others froze, stilled by the raw force of John's shouts.

"Pack your things. Get outta here."

"How will I.. " Ethel stammered.

"Walk," John said. "It's only four miles to the lumber camp. Maybe the trust needs a new bellyrobber to cook, or else they'll give you a ride. But you git, and you git now."

"I can give her a ride, Pa," Clarence said.

"No," John roared. "She walks."

He would not kill her, Ethel realized. She gained courage. Her contempt surfaced. A man who would bring his family to live like this. A family that would go along.

"I'll walk. I can't stand this shack anyhow. You won't last long. This spring they're sending in the U.S. marshals."

"That will be fine." John was amused at the young teacher's defiance. "You can stay if you wish. You can pass the ammunition."

"It's in the river," Ethel said. "They'll kill you. Who knows how many they'll send. "

"They can come and try," John said. "They will not be the first."

"You want them to come, don't you?" Ethel said. She was almost in awe as if she'd just arrived at a realization.

"Of course he does," Clarence said. "That way Pa looks big."

John slowly turned on his son.

"No," Hattie yelled. "John, don't you dare. Not again."

The words passed John by. His eyes were bright, glittering on his son. The teacher, Hattie, the children, all ceased to exist. He'd experienced life, John thought, faced everything the Lord could throw and still stood tall. He didn't have much, but he still survived, facing the mills, and now his own flesh and blood. His toes dug in against the soles of his boots, anchoring his being as firmly as the roots of an oak. An oak never budged. It lived out its time and then it died.

He smiled as he spoke to Clarence, like one man taunting another to his death. "So now you want to be a man. Well don't think I'm the way, for you or the mills."

"Oh no you don't," Hattie said. She fearlessly stepped in front of John. "Would you tear this family apart just for the sake of your own pride?"

"For what's right, Hattie," John snapped. "I'm doing this for you, the children, for Clarence there, but he's too blind to see, too filled with himself." John eased his tone.

Hattie propelled Clarence into the living room. She hissed a warning, an order. "You're smarter than that, Clarence. Why do you push? You know your father would never quit in a fight. Never. You'd have to kill him first. What do you think you could gain?"

"Freedom, Mother," Clarence said softly. "And not just for me."

Hattie turned away. Clarence did not understand all that she and John had faced. But he did understand one thing, Hattie thought, even as had that Irvine from the mills. What happened now was between her and John and the children. Only John thought it had to do with the mills.

ELEVEN DROWNED NEAR HOLCOMBE

Overloaded Batteau in Which 15 Log Drivers Were Attempting to Reach a Jam, Capsized in the Chippewa River and 11 of them Drowned.

DIETZ APPEARS TO HAVE THE BEST OF IT

Officers Who Sought Him Leave Cameron Dam and Return Home

TAKE OFF FAT WHERE IT SHOWS

Most women suffer much humiliation because of great quantities of fat so located, that, no matter how they dress, everybody sees that they are abnormal. This is the day of the figure, and fat women are simply not tolerated either in business or social affairs. Women may not know it, but men when they see a fat woman on the street or in public places make all manner of sympathetic remarks about her. They do not mean to be unkind or to seem unmanly, but it is natural for a man to dislike fat on a woman.

The famous Marmoia prescription goes into your system just like food. The tablets stop the stomach and digestive apparatus from producing fat and reduce the fat upon the body at the rate of from 12 to 15 ounces a day.

CHAPTER VI

The spring of 1905 brought a parade of sheriffs, deputies, agents and U.S. marshals to the Dietz farm. The majority of posse members were from out of the area, recruited in taverns in Milwaukee and Chicago, young men and down-and-outers looking for adventure or out to make a dollar and a bottle of fermented corn. They journeyed north by railroad and then by canoe or on foot dozens of miles more into the tall timber of the north.

The very size of the wilderness intimidated. In addition to which, they faced John Dietz. They read newspaper stories and heard tales; Dietz could toss pennies into the sky and pluck them out of the air with a pistol; he'd handed one sheriff a rifle and dared him to shoot; he'd taken on two of the toughest men the loggers had ever seen and whipped them both; he'd stepped out and taken on a posse as bold as you could please; he moved like an Indian in the forest and could magically materialize two feet from your side. The posse members were far from home, without comforts, surrounded by Dietz sympathizers. The view from the depths of a forest filled with insects, bears, wolves, Indians, and outlaws had undergone considerable transformation from what they'd imagined in the bawdy safety of a saloon. The eager seeking of adventure had somehow ebbed.

The first effort against John in 1905 was not an effort at all. Word reached Hayward that John and members of his family were openly visiting John's daughter, brother, and father in John's old home town of Rice Lake. Goaded by intense public pressure, then Sawyer County Sheriff James Gylland pocketed the numerous warrants and injunctions against John Dietz and boarded the train for Rice Lake. He looked throughout the small town, Gylland reported. John Dietz could not be located.

But John was there and making no effort to hide, Rice Lake residents said with a wink and a knowing smile. Those sheriffs from Sawyer County were truly was a disgrace. Meanwhile, T.J. Connor formerly had title to the Cameron Dam conveyed from the Chippewa Lumber & Boom Company to the parent company, The Mississippi River Logging Company, an interstate company which could thereby, and in fact on February 28 did apply to U.S. Circuit Court for a federal injunction to restrain one John Dietz from interfering with their log drive. The injunction was duly signed and the first posse from the south boarded a train for the deep woods north.

The outsiders did not go unnoticed. The first group of six disembarked in Phillips and walked through the forest, across the Flambeau River and through the wet slush of melting snow some 25 miles to the Dietz homestead. On April 3, 1905, some nine grueling days after they set out on their journey, three of the men arrived at the driving camp a hundred yards from the dam. All three men were deputies acting under instructions from Charles Lewiston, U.S. marshal for the Western District who, along with a chancellor's subpoena, a demurrer and injunction order, had a summons and complaint to be served on one John Dietz for a hearing in federal court scheduled for May 1, 1905.

The first deputy marshal, Henry J. Conlin, hailed John and had John row him across the flowage behind the dam. He offered John a dollar for the ride.

"I don't charge for this kind of service," John growled. His eyes were sharp, alert on Conlin's hands and eyes. Conlin stayed but briefly, failed to mention his purpose, then abruptly, as if his nerve had left him, stood and left, walking for Winter.

"Strange fellow there," John said to his family. "The way he shook he must have had a block of ice in his pants."

He showed his famous grin, as if he enjoyed this business immensely.

"He was from the mills wasn't he, Pa?" Leslie chortled.

John shrugged. "The man didn't make his purpose known. Took a stroll way out here in the forest just to row across the flowage near as I can tell."

"Don't think he was alone," Hattie snapped. She wore her sun bonnet, preparatory to going out and work in the garden.

John's smugness grated. Could he not see the consequence? "They said there were a dozen men that got off the train. We've never gotten a dime for all our trouble. Now the rest of those men could be lying out there in ambush. I don't know why you're acting so smart. If something happens this family could be ruined."

"Now, Hattie dear," John cautioned. He was in a favorable mood and did not want that swayed. "No posse's moving me and you know that."

"No, John," Hattie agreed. Despite efforts to convince herself to go along with John, she was bitter. "No posse's moving you; of that I'm sure."

John winked at his children. "Your mother must have been gnawed on by bed bugs last night. She gets on something and bores in like a tick. You better get outside and give her a hand, children. Otherwise I'm scared she'll work herself to death."

Hattie showed the trace of a smile that John could so disarm her. She picked up her bags of seeds and went outside. Almost immediately her attention turned to the flowage and across to the distant woods. There were men watching her. She was convinced. The feeling of impending doom returned.

Later that day, the two Dietz watchdogs loudly announced the approach of Deputy Herman Jonas of Madison. John, unarmed, stepped out on the porch to greet the visitor.

"It isn't every day a feller can earn a dollar before breakfast," John said in reference to Conlin's visit. Jonas feigned ignorance. He was a landlooker, a cruiser looking over timber for the Jonas Mercantile Company, Jonas explained. He'd hurt his knee falling over a log and wanted to buy some eggs. Their few chicks weren't laying very good, Hattie explained and then proceeded to give him their last raw egg in a glass of fresh, warm cow's milk. Jonas drank the mixture down while John asked questions, mainly about Jonas's work.

"Strange fellow there," John said after Jonas departed. He was leaned back in his rocking chair, feet propped up. His blue eyes twinkled like sunlight on a lake. Who could have dreamed the mills would send out such men as these? "Man claims to be a cruiser and doesn't even know how many acres in a quarter section or that there's sixteen and a half feet in a rod. Wonder who all these fellows are? Getting to be a regular way station here. Maybe your mother should open up a restaurant."

Later that same afternoon, Jonas returned, this time accompanied by a Deputy Callaghan. They were again greeted by the watchdogs. This time the Dietz family had other visitors, two men who'd brought in the mail, which John leaned back and read as the two deputies made hesitant conversation with the visitors, Surdson and LaLonde.

A man couldn't help but be aware of his distance from the rest of civilization, Jonas later said. More than one man had ventured into the deep wilderness never to be heard from again. He suspected Dietz was onto them, but the woodsman never gave a sign, invited them into his home and fed them tea and bread. Everyone was peaceful, easy, but Jonas could not relax. Once he met John's steel blue eyes. They were hard, piercing, laughing with the knowledge of a fox bouncing high in the marsh grass toying with a mouse.

"Ma, could you help me a second?" Myra called. She seemed to want to be near the visitors and have some contact with the outside world.

Jonas exchanged glances with Callaghan. Callaghan swallowed and then approached Hattie. Jonas pulled out his own injunction.

Hattie observed the two men rise and watched the young one hold a legal-looking piece of paper towards her face. It was up to her, of course. After all, the land title lay in her name.

"Mrs. Dietz?" the man who'd just eaten of her corn bread

asked nervously, as if he did not know.

She saw his approach with fangs gleaming and mouth drooling as if he were a wolf putting her and her family under attack. Hattie cried, "Don't take them, John! They are detectives!" She slapped at the papers Callaghan pushed at her and seconds later found herself grappling with the lawman.

John exploded to his feet. The rocking chair flipped end over end behind him. A Luger pistol magically materialized in his hand. "You son of a bitch! You bastards come here and eat my food and lie and call yourselves men?"

All of Jonas's force-fed resolve seemed to flow away like water over a falls. He held out his hands as if to ward off a train. "I'm an officer of the law."

The words were not heard. John hit Deputy U.S. marshal Jonas a crushing blow in the face. Both lips split inside and blood spurted from his mouth. As Jonas whirled away in his confusion he was struck again, this time by the butt of a pistol, he later claimed. He sprawled face first on the plank floor.

Without hesitation John turned on Callaghan. The man's defenses were ineffectual and completely ignored. Relentlessly John bore forward and knocked Callaghan to the floor.

Leslie and Clarence burst into the cabin and stared at the two downed lawmen. One guest, Surdson, who'd backed against the wall to try to avoid the fight, whispered to Leslie, "I'd give twenty-five dollars if I wasn't here."

Leslie grinned. "Don't worry. Pa's got things under control."

Within seconds the two deputies managed to crawl to their feet. In abject and bloody surrender, they held their hands palm outwards over their head and backed side by side from the cabin. The family trailed them outside, but then John turned back. "Watch them, Hattie. I'm getting my rifle."

"Pa's awful mad. You men better get," Leslie said with a wide grin.

The two deputies whirled and ran across the open field with their hands still high in the air. John came out and raised a Winchester rifle to his shoulder. Hattie yelled, "No! Don't shoot, John. Don't shoot. We're just as well off as we were before."

"Are you going to intercede for these parties?" John asked with exaggerated gruffness as if putting on a show for his guests. Again he raised the rifle. Again Hattie begged him no. Reluctantly John lowered the weapon to his side.

Despite his beating, Jonas remained in the vicinity of the Dietz farm. He telegraphed U.S. marshal Charles Lewiston. The mills received the dismal reports and demanded more action. Spring logging drives would soon be in full force. A crew for the Thornapple drive was already under contract.

Several days after the Jonas visit, a posse of eleven men headed by Superintendent J.J. Hopper, an agent of the McQuire and White detective agency out of Chicago, met Jonas in the deep woods of northern Wisconsin.

"Seems as we have more visitors hereabouts," John said to Clarence and Leslie. The two boys were struggling with a huge boulder in the newly plowed rutabaga field. "City boys judging by their clothes and the way they stare at the woods like it was going to bite. If they circled the wrong way around a tree they would be lost. They must have mistaken me for a wild bear because they all turned around and ducked into the brush."

"Twelve of them ran?" Leslie laughed.

"They don't understand there is no purpose to being frightened, Leslie. I've told you and your brother; when it's a man's time, it's time. If not you could walk across the open fields of Gettysburg under shot and shell and not be touched. If it is your time you could hide in a hole like a shivering rabbit and a shell would find its way. Might as well stand up and be a man, take what comes as it comes, be it a bear, be it a man." John pointedly appraised his oldest son.

Clarence made no response.

"Get down the road there, Clarence, and keep an eye out," John said gruffly. "See if those fellows have a mind to continue down this way. See what they do. Show 'em how Dietz men stand before those trust agents from the big city. Show them what real workingmen are worth."

For some period of time Clarence did not move or acknowledge the order. He slowly, deliberately wiped his muddy hands on his heavy linen pants. He glanced across the barren and stump-filled ground of their scrub, backwoods farm. It was half swamp, wet and sloppy in spring, dry and cracked in mid-summer. Home. He glanced to the soft green of emerging spring leaves and buds. Meadowlarks sang. Two thin, winter-grey deer browsed at the edge of the forest forty rods away. And now Pa wanted him to go out and spy on these men.

"I'll go," Leslie blurted into the gap of Clarence's defiance.

"Shut up," John barked. Leslie recoiled as if he'd been struck. John's light blue eyes never left those of his eldest son. "A man can get old just standing around. If you have something to say, it better get said soon. I don't believe you understand what it is I'm taking on here. There is no room for dissent."

In his mind Clarence tried to speak, to explain what John was costing them. But the man stood there like a ten-foot-high mountain man. Clarence's throat became dry, seemingly clogged by a huge lump. A line had been drawn in the sand and if he did not cross, he'd be forever confined to this side.

"My hair is turning grey standing here," John said.

Clarence's eyes dropped from John's. He turned and started walking towards the forest. Tears of humiliation clouded his vision. He broke into a run. Red Mulligan was one of the toughest men anyone knew and he couldn't stand up to John. Those marshals shivered in their boots. How could he face John?

For a moment Clarence vowed revenge, but was taken with an image of John's amused eyes and heard his mocking laugh. Coward, that's what John thought. Clarence ran faster, dancing as quickly as he could over the jumble of huge logs floating on the flowage. He was determined. He had to find that posse, keep track, report back to his Pa.

The Chicago detectives hired to kill John lurked in the nearby woods for weeks. They seemed reluctant to press an attack. One night the dogs burst into wild barking. John seized his rifle and stepped outside. "John Dietz is right here waiting on you boys," he bellowed. "Come on up."

The night wind blew. Bullfrogs in the marsh croaked a steady din. An owl hooted. Young coyote pups yipped from out in the forest. This time the dogs settled down. John returned to bed.

The next day John walked up to a man standing just inside the tree line and staring at the farm. John snatched the man's rifle from his hands and smacked the man alongside the head with the barrel of his own weapon. "You spying on us for the trusts?"

"No, no," the young man stammered. He struggled to regain his balance. The lines of his face were stretched taut as if facing death itself. He could barely manage to speak. "I'm just passing through. Honest."

"Bullshit. Where're you from?"

"Winter," the man blurted.

"I know every man there is in Winter and you're not one."

"No sir,' the lad agreed. "I meant Rice Lake."

"That's my home town."

"It is?" The boy's eyes rolled in wild movements around the wild and tangled forest. "I gotta go." He shook his head as if negating what he said. But his legs were moving, slowly backing away. He backed into a tree, patted it as if in apology then turned and suddenly ran.

"He was a strange one," John told his attentive family. "Just forgot all about his rifle and took off running. I hope he knew where he was headed because it wasn't in the direction of any trail."

Leslie clapped his hands. "Gee, Pa, I wish I could have seen his face."

"Well, here's his rifle," John said solemnly. "I'll set it over in the corner in case he returns and wants it back."

* * *

In late May even more men came to the North Woods, this time a posse of twenty-five men. Charles Lewiston, chief U.S. marshal for the Western District, oversaw the operations which were directed by Special Deputy William H. Appleby. The posse consisted of men brought up from Milwaukee's Fourth Ward, and others recruited in Fifield and Park Falls. In order to avoid publicity and the expected harassment from the local Dietz sympathizers, the posse canoed down the Flambeau river and walked the last number of miles into the area of the Dietz farm.

Neighbors gave John the word that another large group of

agents hired by the mills were lurking nearby.

"Grab your rifle," John ordered Clarence.

"Yes, Pa," Clarence said. He ran for his rifle and quickly returned, walking side by side with his father as they patrolled the farm. It was almost as if John thought him equal, Clarence thought proudly. But in the next moment he felt misgivings that he could so easily be taken in.

Once they spotted two men, Special Deputy Appleby and another. John raised his rifle as did Clarence. John yelled, "You goddamn spying sons of bitches get out of here."

The two men promptly disappeared.

Two days later Deputy U.S. Marshal Appleby and another man called to John across the flowage that they wanted to talk. "The answer's no. Get the hell off my land," John yelled.

U.S. Marshal Lewiston enlisted the help of a neighbor, Charles O'Hare, to invite John to talk to Lewiston. O'Hare talked to John for half a day, passing on Lewiston's message that he simply had a civil warrant and that by talking to a judge things could be fixed up in a satisfactory way. O'Hare's efforts were fruitless. John refused to talk. Hattie became upset when she was informed the warrants named her as well as Clarence.

"He won't come out or let you come in," O'Hare informed Lewiston. "The only way you'll ever get John Dietz is lay siege to his home. And then you have Mrs. Dietz and the six children present." O'Hare shook his head as if in admonition at the idea of killing children over a civil warrant issued by the mills. They'd never hear the end.

So Lewiston laid off, watching the trails and the tote road, biding his time. They set up camp in a Kaiser company driving shanty four miles away, and a tent campsite closer to the farm. Time, weather, insects, lack of comforts, lack of liquor, the elements, all began to exact a toll. On the train ride north one of the elite posse members had suffered from alcohol withdrawal pains and had been left behind in Phillips where he subsequently passed away. The remaining men became disgruntled, lax. Their ambushes in which they sat day after day were easily detected. In fact Leslie looked at spotting them as a game.

But less than a week after the new posse arrived disaster

struck the Dietz farm. Their sheep began to die.

"Poisoned," John railed. Tick fever, Hattie thought.

Then their new milk cow became sick. Forty-five dollars they'd paid for that animal, drawing Hattie's painfully earned savings down to almost zero. At John's instructions Myra and Clarence had even carried pails of milk down to the loggers in the driving camp, a peace offering from John.

"Tell 'em my argument isn't with them," he instructed Clarence. "My argument's with the mills."

"Yes, Pa," Clarence replied as obediently as a dog. He cursed his surrender, but knew he had no means with which to stand up to John.

The next day Myra became deathly ill, racked with fever and convulsions and stabbing pains that burned in the bones of her arms and left her dehydrated and numb with paralysis.

"By God, they did poison the water!" John boomed.

"Twenty-eight dead sheep. One dead cow. And now," he gestured helplessly to where Myra lay on his and Hattie's bed. Hattie had given Myra an emetic in an effort to induce vomiting and expunge the poison. Myra peered up through a rheumy film covering her eyes. Her voice was small, plaintive. "Pa, you won't let me die?"

A great sadness brought a lump to John's throat; the agents of the mills had done this, poisoned a young girl. He scowled with wild rage, big, powerful hands knotting into fists. "I swear," he muttered. He sat on the lumpy straw mattress and took Myra's hand between his callused palms. Her skin burned. "Almyra, you are a queen. I met your mother when she was the same age as you." The hint of moisture came to his eyes. The force of his voice slackened, restricted by a lump in his throat. "I cannot believe there is a reason for His taking you at this time. Lie back. Sleep. Your mother and I will be at your side. Trust that all will turn out well." He touched the back of his hand to her cheek then left her lying in his and Hattie's bed.

As John stepped into the outer room Hattie looked at him, questioning with her eyes. John shook his head in the negative, it did not look good. "No!" Hattie cried. First Henry died, and then Leanna. And now Almyra? Her pure voice was the pearl of the family chorus. How much did the Lord expect a woman to bear?

"We must send for a doctor," Hattie pleaded what had already been discussed.

"I'll go," Clarence said eagerly.

"No," John said, a single forceful command. "No doctor can change what's already meant to be. It's too late. We must stand firm and let fate take its course."

"You could kill her," Clarence protested.

John slowly pivoted. "I thought you'd found your place, Clarence. You best stay there; it's where you were meant to be."

Clarence turned red with embarrassment that he could so often stand up to John and then be forced to back away. He simply looked the fool.

"Almyra needs a doctor," Hattie said with some force. "Damn you John, why must we always believe as you believe?"

"You can believe whatever you want," John said mildly. "Clarence as well. I'm no dictator. But believing one way doesn't change the other. I know what I see with my own two eyes and that's what is. There's no way you two can change that unless you have some strange powers not yet revealed."

"What you want is what's going to be," Hattie said coldly. "Even it it's your daughter's life. Some day, John..."

"Some day what?" John snapped.

"Some..." Hattie trailed off as if in despair. She took a pan of cool water and a dish cloth and went in to look after Myra. Whatever will be, will be, John said. And all Hattie could do was watch and work and pray.

Somehow Myra recovered, although for weeks she moped around in a weakened condition, barely able to life her arms, spending hours on end lying in bed. There were times, as lawmen after lawmen came around, Hattie thought she was going to burst. Frequently her hands trembled uncontrollably, her knees became weak, her stomach as upset as if she had morning sickness. She could stand at the cabin door and look across the glen and see deer at the distant spring. She'd be filled with peace and contentment and in the next moment drowned by inconsolable loneliness. She had no friends, no other woman with whom she could identify or confide in. Still the mills and the law made their attempts on the Dietz family.

The mills' attorney, T.J. Connor, submitted a bill to the county for $147.50 for ten rifles, reportedly supplied to the Milwaukee posse members. On July 3, 1905, Sheriff Gylland traveled to the Dietz farm to serve a subpoena for Dietz to appear at Valentine Weisenbach's trial scheduled for early 1906. The trial was to be for Valentine's part in John's ambush of Giblin and his deputies.

John was not home, the family informed the sheriff, although they and visitors knew John happened to be up near the barn and without benefit of a weapon.

In October of 1905 Deputy Sheriff Ackley and another man from Chippewa County approached the Dietz farm. The dogs barked their warning. John stepped out the front door with rifle in hand and ran the two men off.

During the November deer season, John's brother, William, came down from Rice Lake to join in the annual hunt. John, who regularly killed more deer than anyone, always moved carefully in the forest, never taking the same trail twice. William, however, moved openly and often repeated his tracks. One day eleven men with rifles surround him and yelled for him to put up his hands. For an instant William thought they would shoot him. He was bitter. "Strangers, probably from downstate. They thought I was John."

In December, with winter hard upon the family, two men came by light bobsled and took dinner with the family. At first the two were extremely talkative. Their voices were high-pitched and the two continually glanced back and forth at each other and made what John described as the most peculiar faces. As soon as dinner was over the two men coughed their thanks and took their leave without explaining the nature of their visit to the isolated farm deep in the forest.

After those men, with the exception of area loggers, they seldom had visitors. The winter was upon them full. The family pulled within itself. In an effort to assail Hattie's increased physical ailments, John had a Wurlitzer organ sledded to the farm. Now their Sunday and evening concerts often lasted for hours.

The music became Hattie's refuge, a reprieve from the distressing workings of her body. At one time she thought she had consumption, another time a cancer eating out her stomach. In one moment of privacy she begged John, "We have to resolve this, John. We can't go on never knowing when we'll be attacked. The children have their lives."

"You want me to go to the mill courts?" John asked. "Take the few pennies from your sock and toss them down the two-holer against the gold mines owned by the mills? Would that be justice? I think not my dear." He patted her shoulders and bussed her cheek as if both to comfort and dismiss her. These were simply Hattie's normal complaints and the ailments that one time or another beset all women.

In truth, John thought, the family was getting on just fine. Besides, he thought with one of his wry grins, the mills had yet to touch those six million board feet of prime saw logs.

* * *

On April 13th the first official callers of 1906 arrived at the farm. They were Deputy U.S. Marshal William Pugh and Henry J. Conlin who had visited the Dietz farm with Jonas the previous spring. Conlin informed reporters how this visit went:

"We went up to the house and met one of the boys. He asked us what we wanted and we said that we wanted to see Mr. Dietz; said he guessed that Mr. Dietz didn't want to see us. So we passed by him and Mr. Dietz commanded us to stop where we was; at that time we were about fifteen feet I should judge, from the door. So Mr. Pugh pulled out his papers and showed the names of the judge and also the clerk of the federal court, and Mr. Dietz said if we come any further he would blow our goddamn heads off. Mr. Pugh left the papers on a pile of lumber twelve or fifteen feet from the door."

John later claimed he thought the package, done up in oil-cloth, might be some sort of infernal machine so he took a pitchfork and tossed it into the river.

"Pa ran two more guys off," Leslie laughed to his brother and sister. "You shoulda seen 'em run. Like they had a pack of wolves on their tail."

"Those mills sure know better than to mess with Pa," Myra quietly agreed. She was proud of her father, of the way he stood and other men quaked. Yet she hated their isolation, the lack of friends. She even confessed her loneliness to Clarence and Leslie and wondered aloud how many more years this could go on. There were other times, when they went to town and people pointed and stared, that Myra could feel a stiffening in her spine, a lifting of her head. She was a Dietz. They weren't just farmers, not anymore.

"As soon as those men lay eyes on Pa, they started to shake," Myra said.

"He's something all right," Clarence grudgingly acknowledged.

"Something?" Leslie chortled at the understatement. "He's braver than you'll ever be."

Clarence turned as bright red as if he'd been chastised by John himself. "Maybe he is," he admitted. "But one of these days they'll send out a lot of men with guns, guys who won't turn and run the minute Pa looks them in the eye."

"Let them try," Leslie retorted. "I'll be there side by side with Pa. What about you?"

For just long enough for the hesitation to be noticed, Clarence did not speak. "I'll be there," he said with some vehemence. "What other choice do I have?"

HANG AND BURN
THREE NEGROES

Mob at Springfield, Mo.
Revenges Attack Made
on White Girl

Rope Breaks Precipitating
Victim into Burning Embers
of Pyre Where Two Others
Had Preceeded Him - But Mob
of 5,000 is Relentless

BLOODY FIGHT
TAKES PLACE
AT THORNAPPLE DAM

Sheriff of Sawyer County
and Deputies with Six
Militiamen Attempt the
Capture of Dietz and are
Repulsed with Loss
of One Man

In the Encounter Dietz's
Son and One of Militiamen
are Shot, Probably Fatally
Not known How Serious
are the Wounds

HUNTING SEASON FATALITIES
Seventy-four persons dead and
seventy injured, some of them so
seriously that death may result, is
the record of fatalities for the hunting season thruout the country.
Northern Michigan and Wisconsin
went ahead of the record for last
year in death, twenty-eight being
reported this year, and twenty-six
for the previous one. Many of the
deaths were those of boys who
were hunting, and mistaken for
deer accounts for a large number
of others.

CHAPTER VII

They were some of the most powerful men of Sawyer County. They physically blocked the path of Sheriff James Gylland, their duly elected representative of the law. Just when, they had demanded, was Gylland going to do something about John Dietz?

Gylland was a round-faced man with baby-fat cheeks, what appeared to be a pasted-on moustache and large blue eyes. He'd spent too many years seeking this job, knowing the right people, projecting the proper image. Now every time he turned around someone mentioned John Dietz, as if totally ignorant of his journey to the deep wilderness the April past. Such was the measure of his irritation that, to these men to whom he'd once so eagerly smiled and fawned, he now snapped, "I'm in the process of putting a posse together right now. You men can join."

The community leaders tolerated no insubordination from any man, especially not one favored. Attorney T. J. Connor spoke on the company's behalf. "You are the one that ran for sheriff, Gylland. We gave you our support. We can take that support away. You made promises. Arresting Dietz was one of the first. If you can't get men up here, go back to Milwaukee. Sufficient funds are available. But this time do something like a man, like a true representative of the law. Just as soon as you get to the Dietz farm move in and attack. Get after the anarchist. If he puts his family in harm's way, that is his decision, not yours. No holds barred."

"Yes sir," Gylland said in a voice devoid of the defiance of seconds before. For a second he tried to look Connor in the eye, but got no further than the thin, scornful line of the lumberman's lips. "That still does not solve the problem of how do I round up a posse."

Connor held up a thick roll of money. "Money," he said. "You can always get men with that."

In mid-July, 1906 Sheriff James Gylland of Sawyer County arrived in Milwaukee, three hundred miles from the seat of the conflict. He set up headquarters in the Fourth Ward in a saloon owned by John Hoeft. John's son, Arthur, was a policeman who had visited the Dietz farm with the hired detectives the previous spring and reportedly once by himself. Arthur Hoeft was appointed chief deputy. With the promise of an easy mission and seven dollars a day, a number of young men who worked in nearby tanneries and frequented the saloon were hired to travel north to assist in the arrest of some old backwoods farmer by the name of John Dietz.

For more than two years northern newspapers had speculated on the governor ordering the militia in after John Dietz. But a great many people supported Dietz and his stand against the lumber trusts. Governor Davidson strongly believed in law and order. But he also read the political winds. Davidson stated he could not call out the militia until all the resources of Sawyer County had been exhausted.

Sheriff Gylland had an idea, brilliant, he thought; the men would rent and dress in the khaki uniforms of militiamen. Dietz might be intimidated and hesitate to shoot. The uniforms would provide a cover from the prying eyes of Dietz sympathizers and outwardly give his hired posse a legitimate appearance — which of course it had in fact, Gylland was heard to argue.

On Sunday night, July 22nd, the posse members boarded the train for Hayward. The men settled in for the long ride. In time a deck of cards materialized. A secretive flask made the rounds. As they traveled into the north people began to take notice. A passenger recognized Sheriff Gylland from Sawyer County. Others joined the militiamen in their card game.

"You men after John Dietz?" one man asked.

The posse members were confused that the secret was out. Gylland was visiting in another car. Young Hoeft took the lead. "What business is that of yours?"

The card player shrugged. He was a slim, leathered man with a large nose and protruding ears. His picked his cards, looked once and never looked again. "You men know Dietz?"

Most of the men said no. They'd heard a few stories, rumors. Some had never heard his name. Young Hoeft had been there but had never met Dietz, had never even been allowed to draw his gun.

The old card player continued in a slow voice that rattled as if his throat were clogged with dust. "The way I hear, Dietz has taken on posse's twice the size of your'n. Last fall six hired guns from Chicago went in after Dietz. Every one of them was a crack shot." He paused, looking at each young man until the man looked away. "They went out there. And they never came back."

The card player sipped at his flask of whiskey and passed it across the aisle. It was early morning. The car was dimly lit. Most of the passengers were asleep. The groan and clank and rattle of the train over systematic rail joints continued as a relentless throbbing and swaying from side to side. "Better have a snort, enjoy life while you can. Dietz never goes after men; he just takes those that come to him. He doesn't take kindly to trespassers or strangers. Shoots first then goes to see who he got."

"Go grab a cow catcher," Hoeft growled. "I've been there. I know what it's like. You're just telling stories."

"Dietz has been out there two years since he first fired on the mills. They haven't budged him yet. Think on that. Don't think you men are the first. Dietz ain't alone. He has two sons just as big and mean as they come. They love to kill. His wife shoots, oldest daughter shoots. That oldest one, she's a looker as well. Heard tell she meets men from some of the lumber camps.

Always packs a gun."

He bent close and gave a conspiratorial wink. "Always, no matter what she's doing." He laid down his cards and raked in the small pot of coins.

"It's a bit of a shame," the card player continued. He leaned back, no longer a part of the game. "Young men in your prime siding with the trusts against a common man who does nothing more than stay on his own land."

"Those stories are horse manure and you know it," young Hoeft said. He was defiant, his voice raised despite others trying to sleep. The card player's sad brown eyes sought those of Hoeft. He shrugged as if in apology; what could he tell those who were too young and brash to listen? He pulled his hat low over his eyes and seemed to go to sleep.

One of the young posse members turned down the lantern. They leaned back, trying to sleep, each man alone with his thoughts.

* * *

The afternoon threatened rain. The hand-cut hay had laid for two complete days and had cured and dried. But rain just now would ruin it all. At John's urging, the entire family had set to work loading hay on the wagon and then raising it up to the loft of the barn.

The boys had just finished driving a new wagon of hay from the field. Clarence stood on the hay wagon with a pitch fork and piled loose hay on the wide hay fork that was suspended by rope from a track in the gable at the top of the barn. Hattie stood out away from the wagon, handling the guide rope to keep the hay fork away from the side of the barn. Myra, wearing her usual ankle length dress as was Hattie, stood with Old Tom who was hooked up to the hoisting rope that ran through the pulleys at the base and roof of the barn. Leslie and John stood in the loft of the barn where they spread and trampled down the hay. Helen, Stanley, and Johnny played nearby.

John leaned out the open loft door. He was sweating freely. "Let's move it along down there loading that fork, Clarence. This humidity up here is getting worse and that thunderstorm isn't given to patience while we dally."

"Yeah, yeah," Clarence grumbled in a voice only Myra and

his mother could hear. "Leslie and I did most of the field loading and now he rushes us." He dug deep into the mounded hay
with the pitchfork, all but breaking the homemade oak handle.

"Just a few more forks," Hattie cautioned. She gazed at the
darkening sky. If they lost this crop they'd have to cut down
the herd for the winter, she thought. It was a poor dirt farm,
she had finally admitted. How they'd survived this many years
she was hard pressed to understand.

Hattie gazed down over the farm. One night that spring, when
the water had been at its highest, one wing of the dam had
washed away, or been blown, John alleged. The flowage in
front of the house had dried up and now consisted of tall marsh
grass and numerous old stumps. No one had come around since
the dam had been washed out. There was no need, Hattie
thought. They could not move those logs now. They had left
only the farm, their lives and her sorely aching back.

"There you go," Clarence said to Myra. Myra spoke softly
to Old Tom and led the driving horse forward, pulling on the
rope through the pulleys on the gable. The rusted pulleys
creaked.

Hattie leaned back on the separate guide rope to keep the
hay fork away from the barn. Her strong, broad back strained.
Beads of perspiration sprinkled her temples. She glanced to
the sky; if the storm brought hail her tomatoes would be ruined. She had a boiled dinner simmering on the stove. It should
be checked and another stick of wood added to the fire. Several of their beef cows milled nearby and for a moment she felt
a sense of pride, the exact opposite of seconds before. It had
been more difficult than anyone could imagine, but they'd made
a home here, a farm, such as it was.

One of their cows, black with a white spotted face, had
ambled down toward the marsh and stood with its ears perked
forward and head cocked as if watching something in the grass.
Must be a porcupine or something, Hattie thought. She called
to Helen, "Run down to the marsh and see what old White
Face is sniffing the air at."

Helen took off at her usual headlong tear. She'd run about
seventy-five yards when she suddenly whirled and ran back
towards the barn. "Daddy, Daddy, there are men down there

with guns." She jumped up and down, pointing and yelling excitedly at the top of her lungs.

Sheriff Gylland had deployed the six men dressed as militia into the marsh in front of the cabin. He'd instructed them to sneak through the tall grass in an effort to get between the family and the heavily fortified log cabin. He, Gylland, moved behind, keeping an overview and remaining in position to fire the signal shot to commence firing. He also claimed he would protect the men from an ambush from the rear.

But then the little girl came and took off running and yelling at the top of her lungs.

What the hell was he to do now, Gylland fumed. A deep anger seized him. If he failed this time he was finished as sheriff. This farmer Dietz was ruining his life. A man — Dietz, Gylland presumed — came running from the barn and jumped up on a stump right out in the open and started bellowing. "I see you sons o' bitches. Get off my land, you hear. If you value your lives, move."

As Gylland watched he noticed movement in the tall grass as two men started scurrying backwards. Such was his rage he all but rose to confront the two deserters. But the mud between him and them was deep. And he realized that if he rose Dietz would spot him as well.

The moment passed. Gylland stayed low, undecided. One thing, those deserters would not receive their seven dollars pay for this day. Then Gylland saw the outlaw woman and the oldest girl run from the house with their arms filled with rifles. They gave one each to the boys and the last one to the man on the stump. The three male outlaws started down towards the marsh.

"There goes two of them, Pa," Leslie yelled. Sure enough, a good thirty rods away they glimpsed the figures of two men dressed in brown khakis scurrying through the brush.

"I think they're militiamen," Clarence said in a high voice. "They did just what they said and sent out the army."

He crouched down near a rail fence beside the garden. "Now we're done for," he accused his father.

Leslie hunched forward as well. The army? He was uncertain if he should join Clarence or follow his father.

"They were sent here by the mills," John snapped. "We fight to the finish." He moved across the rutabaga field paralleling the two fleeing men. The rage built from deep inside. For over a year now he'd minded his own business, staying on his farm and struggled to raise his family and survive. Now, in the middle of the summer heat with a thunderstorm threatening his crop, the mills sent men deep into the wilderness trying to kill him. With civilized justice sold out to those who paid the most, the frontier was the proper place to be.

Twice John raised his rifle, front bead and back vee lined up on the body of a man. Each time he stayed his pull on the cold steel trigger. Those were militiamen here, working men, representatives of the State. Should he kill them he would bring down the wrath of Cain.

"Git you sons o' bitches," John bellowed in a voice that carried like the braying of a mule. Militiamen or not, they were sent here by the mills. A profound sadness gripped him, as if he already lay dead. He had no choice — if they fired, he fired.

As to what would happen to Hattie and the family, at the moment he could not consider. This simply was the way things were meant to be, John thought. No sense shedding tears.

"Pa," Leslie called. John turned back. Myra was herding a reluctant Stanley, Helen and Johnny into the cabin. Clarence and Leslie were still standing near the garden fence. John returned to his boys.

"We saw two more crawl off," Leslie said.

"I think there's more in there," Clarence quietly declared.

"Well go run 'em off," John snapped in irritation. "We've got hay to put up and that storm isn't going to wait."

"Sure, Pa, I'll go run them off," Clarence said. He rose and walked down the open ground of the incline leading to the marsh. In contrast to the sunlight still falling on the farm, the black towering thunderhead of the approaching storm loomed over them like the powerful plunge of a one hundred and twenty foot high white pine. The air hung motionless and Clarence's linen clothes clung like wet toilet paper. He held the lever action Winchester .30.30 cross arms as if ready to fire. But what if he saw a man, a militiaman? What was he suppose to do?

A shot cracked from down on the opposite side of the marsh.

Clarence crouched. Could that have been at him? His mouth was dry and sticking. The tangle of chest-high grass and stumps appeared as impenetrable as a wall. Thunder rumbled in the distance. A sense of dread took him, of fear. What was he to do? He could not turn away. Pa stood behind him on the hill watching his every move.

The pale straw of the marsh grass moved. Clarence turned to see the wide-brimmed hat of a militiaman and the black bore of a rifle. He could not move. Flame spurted. Clarence thumped on his back as if he'd been felled with an ax. A great confusion gripped him. Had he been shot? He was on the ground before he realized he'd been struck in the head. He put his hand to his face and it came away a mass of red blood. Pa would see, he thought and tried to climb to his feet. His vision whirled. His ears rang. His legs wobbled in uncertain coordination. He thought he detected the thunder of shooting, but then thought it all a part of his mind.

"Pa," he said in a firm but quiet voice. "I've been shot.' He said it matter-of-factly, trying to be nonchalant in order not to show John his fear.

A dark figure loomed. "Clarence," the voice cried.

"Ma," Clarence called plaintively. He seemed to smile then pitched face first into the dirt.

John saw the spurt of flame and Clarence drop to the ground. The sound of the shot followed an instant later. The telltale white smoke of someone using black power drifted from the marsh. John ran a few steps down the hill to be clear of where Clarence lay, raised his rifle and levered out seven shots just as fast as he could. He was answered by a fusillade of shots from far across the river where the other militiamen had taken their retreat.

Leslie, firing in his own time, suddenly dropped to the ground behind the garden fence.

"You hit?" John asked as he ran back to secure more ammunition.

"No!" Leslie yelled excitedly. He was embarrassed to show his fear. "A bullet went right past my head."

"Too late to duck once they're past," John dryly observed. He stared down to where Hattie was struggling to help Clarence to his feet. "Don't let them see you grovel. Looks like your brother's still alive," he said grimly.

"Bastards," he breathed. "Almyra," he yelled orders towards the house. "We need ammo."

Myra ran from the cabin, rifle in one hand, several boxes of ammunition in the other. Sporadic shooting continued from far across the river. Bullets swarmed through the warm, moist air like passing bees. Nevertheless John stood tall and in the open. Tentatively Leslie broke from his crouch to join his father.

"Pa," Myra pleaded as if for guidance. She handed John the ammunition. Her face, grown thin from depression over the past months, was contorted with fear and uncertainty. Nevertheless she was poised as if ready for instant obedience for any order from her father.

"Your brother's been shot," John said bitterly. "Help your mother get him back to the house." He was still sweating from his work in the barn and ran down to confront the invaders. He was in a rage, yet markedly in control. "Lester and I will put those men on the run." John moved across the open ground to get a better view of the opposing wood line more than forty rods away.

Hattie had watched Clarence advancing on the marsh. Sent there by John, she thought angrily. Yet she had not called Clarence back to where he could not come while John watched his every move. There had been one lone shot, as if some kind of signal, and seconds later another and Clarence dropped like a rock to the earth. Such had been the jolt, Hattie thought her heart had stopped. Before she even thought, she was running down the hill, her heavy ankle-length work dress pulling at her legs. "Clarence! Clarence!" She wailed for her fallen son.

She saw clearly and yet everything rushed as if in a blur. An enraged John moved forward, firing his rifle as fast as he could. "Get them, John," Hattie called encouragement. "They shot Clarence. Kill them back." Had she a gun, she would have fired it herself.

Clarence struggled to his feet, staggered a few steps and then fell on his face. Hattie lumbered to his side and seized him under his shoulders and forcefully pulled him to his feet. One

side of his head and the entire front of his face streamed rivu-
lets of bright red blood. Hattie knew then he was dead.

"Lord, please," Hattie begged. How much could He expect
one woman to bear? Her strength knew no bounds. She all but
physically lifted Clarence by herself. Clarence staggered with
his mother. "Where's my gun, Ma? I have to shoot. Pa will
want me to shoot. I never fired a shot."

The crazed babbling brought a huge lump to Hattie's throat.
Was this what John had wrought?

Myra rushed up to her brother and mother. "Oh, Clarence,"
she cried in anguish at the gushing red blood. Without hesitation or thought of personal safety, Myra took Clarence's other
arm and draped it over her shoulders. "You can make it,
Clarence. Please." She still carried the rifle in her other hand.
The shooting continued, isolated blasts of thunder from agents
of the mills sent out to the squalid, isolated Dietz farm to clear
the outlaws out. Myra felt close to tears.

By the time the two women and Clarence reached the house,
Stanley and Helen were peeking outside, looking to see what
was going on. "Damn you kids, get inside," Myra screamed.
"Lie down!"

As they dragged Clarence inside the low cabin door they
heard several bullets striking wood. One bullet came through
the logs and smacked into a dresser just beside Johnny Jr.'s
head. The young boy with long, curly locks began to bawl.

"Lie down!" Myra screamed again in a voice that approached
hysteria. Could it really be Clarence would die? Stanley and
Helen, wide-eyed and uncertain that their sister could be like
this and seeing the blood streaming from their brother's head,
grabbed their wailing brother and lay down with him on the
floor, forcefully holding the young boy from running in and
clinging at the security of his mother's side.

"Jesus, God, let me die. My head is going to break," Clarence
mumbled. His legs sagged, but the two strong women held
him up, dragging him into the bedroom and laying him down
on John and Hattie's bed. Myra seized a towel and Hattie held
her boy's head while he bled onto her lap. She gently mopped
at the blood. Head wounds could appear so bad, she knew,
recalling the time Stanley had gone down the hill on a sled, hit

a tree and split his head. But that had been a tree. This was a bullet. Clarence bled from his nose, his mouth, his ears, and of course from the gaping wound. One hand had been nicked as well, from a bullet or his fall she could not tell. Hattie choked back thoughts of collapse. She had to be strong. She always had to be strong.

The bullet had tracked a deep furrow above Clarence's right eye. They could see the skull had split. As Hattie carefully dabbed at the blood she was certain she could see part of Clarence's brain exposed inside. She looked at Myra and shook her head in despair.

"Am I gonna die, Ma?" Clarence asked.

"No," Hattie said quickly. But her voice broke, giving away what she believed to be a lie. Johnny Jr. continued to scream for comfort in the living quarters. Rifle fire cracked outside.

"I saw a uniform. I think that's the militia," Clarence said in a thick voice. He moaned with his terrible agony.

"If not they'll be coming. Don't let Pa take you and the kids with him, Ma. It's not right."

"You're not dying," Myra yelled as if by force of her shout she could will it not so. "So don't start talking stupid over what you know we cannot do. Pa and Leslie are running them off. They're running through the woods. Listen. The shooting is letting up."

The tears formed but Myra grimly held them back. Clarence couldn't die. Who would she confide in? No, not Clarence, the best of them all.

"We going to get Clarence a doctor?" Myra asked.

"Hush now," Hattie said sharply. "Get me some warm water. And keep an eye out that front window. There could be more men sneaking around from the north."

"Shall I shoot them?"

Hattie hesitated. Myra's distressed tone sounded so much like asking if she should commit murder. The rawness of it jolted her, just like the opening of Clarence's skull.

Clarence was right, she could no longer subject the children to this danger. If she had a duty to John, she had one to the children as well.

"Shall I shoot them?" Myra yelled.

"Easy, Almyra," Hattie cautioned. "John hasn't killed any-one yet. We don't want to give the mills a real cause."

"No. No cause," Myra said. She turned and faced Helen, Stanley and little Johnny who were all peering into the bed-room as if trying to join the protective presence of their mother and sister. A shot thumped against the cabin wall. Myra yelled, "Get out and lie down like I told you. You want to get shot like Clarence?"

The three youngsters scrambled back under the bunks. An-other flurry of shots thundered from outside.

* * *

Sheriff Gylland was raging to himself. He'd completely lost contact and thereby control of his men. Only young Rogich had heeded his signal shot and taken out one of the boys. The only other man still in the marsh was Hoeft and after Dietz had charged forward to protect his women and his boy, Gylland thought even Hoeft had fled, firing from an ineffectual dis-tance far across the river.

Ruination loomed more heavily than the approaching storm. Gylland moved his bulk in one direction and became mired in the mud. Sweat soaked his clothes, adding to his weight. He labored for air in the hot, humid air, struggling like a wallow-ing buffalo before finally crawling free. Just then a bullet smacked a grey tree trunk inches from his head. Sharp slivers of wood splattered Gylland's face, drawing blood. A whine escaped his lips. He clawed on muddied hands and knees for cover behind the stump.

When he reached the safety of the stump, Gylland lay back, chest heaving, staring up where approaching black clouds cut a squall line across brilliant blue sky. His rifle was caked with mud, useless. Somewhere someone moaned and cried out for help. For a long, long time the sheriff just lay there and tried to breathe. He hadn't even lost a man, Gylland thought, as if just that fact was a failure.

Not one man had remained long enough to take a blow. They'd all turned and run. Which would make it appear they hadn't really tried. Deputies' cowardice was the cause of the failure, but he would be to blame, Gylland thought, a laugh-ingstock. He'd never live it down.

John emerged from behind the corner of the house and again joined Leslie near the garden fence. "I checked to the north and no one's there," John said. Leslie fumbled and dropped a shell as he tried to jam more into the breech of the Winchester.

"Take your time," John advised sourly. "Appears to me you're already loaded. Even you can't squeeze eight bullets into a six-bullet breech."

"There's one," Leslie cried and pointed. More than forty rods away on the opposite side of the marsh, a man emerged, tried to stand and run along the woods.

"That's the one that ambushed Clarence," John said.

"Looks like he's carrying quite a load." John sounded almost sympathetic. Then he shrugged. "Might as well give him some more, Lester."

Obediently Leslie raised his rifle. He'd been firing at puffs of smoke and movement, but never lined directly up on a man. The man was well over two hundred yards and clearly struggling towards the forest line. Leslie held as steady as he could and lined his sights, aware of his father standing at his side. He squeezed the shot. The man dropped and disappeared as if poleaxed from above.

"Good shot, Leslie. You just killed yourself the rattlesnake that ambushed your brother."

John clapped Leslie on the shoulder. He spoke with pride. "You conducted yourself well out here today, son. Like a Dietz. You should be proud."

Leslie's head bobbed with embarrassment. It was so seldom John gave any of them praise.

John turned his attention from the woods to the sky. "We don't have much time. Let's check Clarence and get Myra and see if we can save some of that hay. I hate to let the mills think they ruined our crop."

"Should we check on that man I shot?" Leslie asked. At the time he'd been pleased his shot hit home. Now he could not expunge the image of a man lying in the deep green of the forest and slowly bleeding to death — from his shot.

"Naw. Most likely he's dead. If not he's a load that posse will have to tend, if they stop running long enough to pay one of their own a mind."

John, still squinting fiercely towards the forest, walked down past the outhouse towards the river. He spotted another man, James Hedrington, a foreman for the Chippewa Lumber and Boom Company, sitting on a bank far across the river as if watching the spectacle of the fight. It did not appear Hedrington was armed.

"Damn spying bastard," John yelled and fired a shot that splattered into the tree next to where Hedrington sat. Within an instant the scrambling foreman disappeared into the thick greenery of the forest.

John walked the marsh line then returned back to where Leslie stood. His stride was elongated, almost a swagger as he strode the open ground. He thumped his rifle stock as if in satisfaction. "I think that's all of them. There weren't many and they weren't very brave for being militiamen. Now that we've killed one, I guess next time they'll send out a battalion to get me instead of a squad."

John turned on Leslie, trying to get him to understand the obvious. "The mills can do that. They have the power to do whatever they want. You've been witness. They take this nation's liberty and hold it in their wallets. They can come out here and kill a man and his family inside his own home."

John grimly spat to one side. The muscles of his jaw worked as if on a chew of tobacco. "To think this nation has come down to this. The mills can send out more militia. But we'll take a few before we fall. Isn't that right?"

"Yes, Pa," Leslie responded. He could feel a trembling in his loins and could see it in his hands. He tried to smile and gripped the rifle tighter in hopes his father would not witness his deep uncertainty and fear.

John took a few steps forward, a farmer in baggy pants and loose fitting shirt standing clear in the open surveying his domain. All his life he'd struggled against the monied interests, breaking his back and remaining dirt poor while the mill executives did nothing and lived in mansions halfway to the sky. He'd been on their property and each time they knocked him to the ground. But not here, he thought, not on his own land. He'd fought them to a standstill. They'd gone so far as to call out the army against one man. That they had that much power, he only prayed the people could see, understand the injustice, rise up and take to arms.

He would lead the way.

ARCTIC EXPLORER NEAR NORTH POLE

Robert E. Peary and His Party Reach Beyond 87 Degrees.

Compelled to Subsist on Dog Meat and Musk Oxen When Caches are Swept Away by Ice Thrown up by Gale

---

DIETZ FEUD IS BROUGHT TO A CLIMAX

Outlaw sends out His Last Defiance He Awaits Finish Believed he Will be Caught in Two Weeks Says he will Shoot Down Every Man who Approaches Governor Davidson to Decide on Militia Hoeft's Hat - Dietz so Close, Powder Traces on Hat.

CHAPTER VIII

John Rogich lay behind a log where the third and last bullet to rip his flesh had knocked him down. He was in the wood line south of the farm, but still across the river from the driving camp. He'd crawled through the marsh grass and mud and stumps for more than 150 yards. Visiting reporters would later see the deep imprint of his knees and hands and the dark splotches of dried blood.

When he reached the tree line he'd stood, hobbling the best he could. The heel of his left foot had been blown away and another slug had hacked a huge chunk of flesh out of the side of his neck. He'd thought he was well out of range when the last bullet smacked like a sledgehammer into his thigh.

He lay and blinked at the thick green foliage crowding him on every side. The greenery reached for his face and body, soft, offering comfort and concealing him as if in a coffin.

Thunder rumbled.

His life's blood oozed away. And yet John Rogich did not panic. He was not that kind. "Help," he called in as loud and calm a voice as he could manage. "I've been shot. Come and give me help."

No one replied.

"I'm a goner," Rogich said aloud. The bastards had lied. He was a short, stocky man of 22. His father had worked in a slaughterhouse. He worked in a tannery. He'd struggled. He frequented saloons such as Hoeft's. He was not a man to pick a fight, but if someone pushed or taunted he did not hesitate to raise his fists. When Dietz yelled, he'd held his ground. Stories on the train had made him a skeptic. People made things up, made a guy sound like more than he could ever be. Of course Dietz hadn't looked frightened. Jumped up on a stump right out in the open and started bellowing.

Spies, agents of the mills, he'd called them. Rogich had experienced a sense of guilt — Dietz was a working man just like him.

But then Gylland, way the hell back behind them where he had no business being, fired a signal shot. And one of the Dietz outlaws walked down the open field to where Rogich lay. He hadn't traveled three hundred miles to turn and run, Rogich thought. He knew about the five hundred dollar reward. And the men in Hoeft's saloon would know how John Rogich stood his ground. Besides, Gylland had signaled to shoot. Rogich's father had trained him well; when authority spoke, he obeyed. Rogich recalled the act of raising his rifle and aiming at the outlaw's head. Just a kid, he'd thought as the rifle bucked under the impact of the shot.

After that all hell broke loose. Dietz had bellowed like a monster possessed. The demon force of the man's rage still gave Rogich a chill. Bullets had rained down on him on every side.

And now he lay and waited to die. Deer flies and mosquitoes homed in on the fresh blood of his wounds. He called again, "Help. I've been shot."

Two figures loomed, Sheriff Gylland and young Hoeft, who'd crossed the river. They'd taken their time, remaining concealed inside the tree line and out of direct sight of the farm. Gylland was covered with mud and sopping wet with sweat and river water. He gazed at Rogich's wounds then looked at Hoeft and shook his head in the negative.

"I ain't dead yet," Rogich said angrily.

The two men broke off a short tree limb and had Rogich sit on that with his arms around their shoulders for balance. The three set off side by side, struggling through the trees. By the time they reached the driving camp, Rogich was almost delirious with pain and exhaustion. The other posse members were at the camp as well as the foreman, James Hedrington, who'd fed them and pointed the way to the Dietz farm when the attack had begun.

"Dietz and his boy will be down here soon," Hedrington warned. His head bobbed up and down peering furtively out the window. "He put that shot right past my head. Couldn't have been more than half an inch away. "

"We'll never get out of here alive," one of the posse members moaned.

"Not the way you ran," Gylland snapped.

"I didn't see you up there," the man retorted. "I fired. Emptied my rifle twice. I couldn't see from that marsh. It was too low. I moved back to get a clear shot. I wasn't alone either."

"We didn't see you shoot," another member charged Gylland. They were a wild-looking lot, wet, filthy with mud and faces contorted with bitterness and shame.

"Enough of that," Hoeft, the chief deputy, called.

They bound Rogich's wounds with strips from a dirty towel and made a stretcher out of the frame from a bunk.

"Dietz is coming. Let's get going," Hedrington moaned.

He peered out the window toward the Dietz farm. He could see tiny figures in the front yard, some of the children keeping watch. "Did you see those women shoot? Both of them firing like hell. Must have been two hundred shots in that exchange."

The ragtag posse quickly exited the back of the camp, not even bothering to redress Rogich in his pants.

"I can run ahead and send back a doctor and a team," Hedrington volunteered.

"Yes," Gylland said. "That would be the thing to do. I'll contact the governor. He'll send out a company of militia now. You men stay on the trail and keep moving as fast as you can."

"You leaving us, Gylland?" one of the posse members taunted. "Running off?"

"I'm getting help," Gylland snarled. He scurried off after Hedrington, leaving five men and Rogich moving down the narrow woods trail. They were headed toward Ladysmith, twenty miles to the south, rather than pass in sight of the Dietz farm and take the trail to Winter which was half as far away.

Very soon exhaustion began to exact its toll of the posse. There had been the train ride, the long night camping out, the twelve-mile walk out to the driving camp, the pumping adrenaline and the trauma of the gunfight. And Rogich was not light. Soon, every hundred yards, the men dropped Rogich to the ground and lay in repose themselves. But each time they stopped deer flies and mosquitoes swarmed in on Rogich's exposed flesh and bloodied wounds.

"C'mon, c'mn, you cowards," Rogich moaned. They had not stood strong in the marsh as he had, he reminded them more than once. "Where are my pants? These flies are killing me. C'mon, let's go."

Four men carried the litter, their rifles in their off-litter hand. The fifth man walked ahead, keeping an eye out for Dietz or any of the other numerous outlaws and Dietz sympathizers that frequented these woods. More than once they thought they'd lost the thin trace of the seldom-traveled trail.

Suddenly the leading man crouched, his hand held high warning the others to stop. Off to their right they could hear distinct crashing and movement through the brush.

"Dietz," one man whispered.

"Rogich shot his kid. He's going to kill us," another man said. Panic throttled his voice. They dropped Rogich under the brush beside the trail.

"Be still and silent. We'll be back," Hoeft whispered.

And then the men were gone.

How long he lay Rogich could not say. He heard movement in the brush, the posse members in one direction, Dietz in the other. He kept silent, even against the attacking swarms of deer flies and mosquitoes. If Dietz found him, he was dead.

Time passed. He could no longer tolerate the feasting insects. He thrashed wildly. Finally he yelled, "Where are you guys? Over here."

The deep green of the lush summer forest silently greeted his cry. Insects buzzed. Thunder rumbled. The first drops of rain splattered overhead leaves. It was then Rogich realized the other posse members were not coming back.

They'd whispered the word Dietz and ran like a pack of cowards — and left him here to die.

He closed his eyes. He could not stand and walk. He rolled on his good side where no bullets had struck and slowly began to crawl. Rain poured down in sheets. Lightning flashed. Thunder crashed. But at least for a while the insects were gone.

Soon he began to shiver with cold. He crawled on. In time darkness enveloped the forest. Rogich realized he'd lost the trail. He had no idea where he was located or which direction to head. Once he whimpered.

But then he found resolve. "Those bastards will pay." He spoke of his fellow posse members. The anger gave him strength. He crawled on into the night.

* * *

Myra, John and Leslie came in from the storm dripping wet. They'd loaded and tramped what hay they could. Another wagon and a half lay soaking in the field. Two cows were freshening and Myra had completed the milking. They'd carried water from the spring, fed and settled the animals and now returned to the humid confines of the squat log cabin. They were still ebullient, for they'd faced a siege and beaten off a contingent of militia. They were racked by concern Clarence might die. They were apprehensive; they'd killed a man. The militia would return. Next time there would be a much larger force, this time with cannon.

John, his heavy cotton clothes clinging to his stout frame, immediately crossed the room to look in on Clarence.

"How's my boy? Walked down there to that marsh just as fearless as you please. Showed those mill agents some courage. We got that bushwhacker, Clarence. Leslie hit him the last time and he dropped like he'd been hit with an ax."

Clarence feebly waved. A dark splotch of blood and pus covered the strips of white sheet wrapped completely around the top of his head and one eye.

"He can't see out of the one eye anyhow," Hattie whispered to Myra and Leslie. They stood behind John in the living room. "His vision is blurry in the other. He's still bleeding from his ears and says he had a sharp ringing." Her lips were a compressed line. The weight of terrible trials sat on her shoulders like a yoke. What a woman had to bear... She spoke with grim firmness, "He's taken fever now. I put wet towels on his chest, but then he claims he's cold."

"We must get a doctor," Myra said to Hattie in a quiet voice so her father could not hear.

"I'm doing everything I can," Hattie snapped as if Myra had accused her of outright neglect.

John peeled off his wet shirt to reveal the pure white and wrinkled skin of his upper body that contrasted sharply with the ruddy, weathered skin of his face, neck and arms.

He lay the sodden shirt on a wooden chair. Two kerosene lamps provided a dim, red glow. The gloom made the cabin seem smaller than it was. Hattie and the children eyed John as if silently gauging his mood. John swallowed with pride.

"We were a family out there today. Hattie spotting that cow, helping Clarence back to the house. Helen seeing those men. Stanley grabbing Old Tom. Myra grabbing guns, ammunition, taking care of Clarence and the kids. Clarence going down to the marsh. Leslie holding his ground, firing back at them just as fast as they fired at us." He shook his head as if in admiration. Tears welled in his eyes. "Your mother counted a dozen bullet holes in our house. One of them went right past Johnny Ginger's head and even he stood his ground."

"Johnny cried, Pa," Helen piped up.

"I wasn't even scared," young Stanley added. "They shot right beside my head too."

John rumpled Stanley's hair. "We all did fine, just fine. The mills never saw a family stand like that out there today." For a moment they were silent, proud, all of them bound as one. It truly had been a family stand.

Eventually Hattie spoke, "I have a boiled dinner ready."

She kneaded her hands on her apron, wiped them on her sides then kneaded them again. "There's no need to be quite so taken with yourself, John. Clarence is badly hurt. We lost some hay. And it's certain those men will soon be back."

Hattie was firm as if through force of conviction she could alter what already had passed.

"Do you think they'll be back tonight?" Leslie asked.

"Nope. The cowards ran. They'll be back in a week or so," John stated matter of factly. His voice carried an undercurrent, a pumping of adrenaline from his accomplishment. "They'll probably have a company then."

"Then what will we do?" Hattie demanded as if laying the blame entirely with her husband.

"Stand and fight," John growled. "This is our home." He scowled, irritated his good mood should be so disrupted. "If you want words, woman, I'm ready to oblige."

Clarence staggered to the doorway and leaned in the frame. Myra immediately jumped to his side to lend her support. Clarence's voice was thick, almost as if he was drunk. "We don't count, Ma. None of us, Helen, Stanley, Johnny."

"That's not so," Myra softly protested.

John had sat on a wooden trunk and pulled off his wet boots and wet pants. He stood in boxer shorts. He peered at his oldest boy. His blue eyes glinted, angered that in the face of triumph he had to face betrayal that ruined it all.

"Patrick Henry said it first, Clarence, give me liberty or give me death. For how much would you sell your soul to be a slave to the mills? No one is holding you or anyone else. Members of this family are free. You can leave anytime you like — right now would be fine."

"No, John," Hattie yelled. "For God's sake, the boy's been shot." She was furious.

"Then what the hell does the boy want from me?" John yelled. "If I stand up for my rights, I'm in the wrong. If I turn and run, I'm a coward. He's just like the mills, he wants it both ways."

Hattie searched desperately between her son and her husband; there seemed to be no way she could support one without alienating the other. Unconsciously she kneaded her apron. What test could the Lord possibly have in mind? She'd never been so proud as when John jumped up on top of that stump to attack those men. And she'd never felt such anguish as watching Clarence fall to the ground. One moment she felt the powerful defiance of a bull, the next the weakness of a lamb. She knew one thing, if this family held, if it stayed together, it would all depend upon her.

"What are you asking, John?" Hattie challenged. "Clarence did your bidding and now you want to kick him out?"

"I said he can leave or stay. I don't give a goddamn." John's shout drove the younger children back against the wall in crouched, wide-eyed silence. "But if he stays he minds his goddamn tongue. That goes all the way around."

For some seconds a heavy silence filled the cabin. Hattie turned to the low wood fire under the cast iron cooking kettle. John struck a wooden match on the cooking stove and furiously puffed on a cigar. "Those rifles are wet, Leslie. You better get them cleaned and loaded so we're set in case callers come around."

"Don't do it," Clarence mumbled. He firmly resisted his sister's efforts to drag him into the bedroom.

"I shot that man," Leslie said slowly, as if explaining to a child. "We saw him fall. Later the others went over there and picked him up. Those militiamen. They'll be back, Clarence." He looked to his father and then back to his brother, pleading with his eyes for understanding. "We have to be ready," he mumbled as if in justification. He picked up a Winchester, pointed the muzzle at the rough plank floor, and ejected the shells. He kept his head lowered, steadfastly refusing to meet his brother's eyes.

"Mmmmm," Clarence moaned. His knees almost buckled. Hattie rushed to help Myra put him back in bed.

"Should we get a doctor?" Myra managed to ask. "I'll go."

"Do you think a doctor can alter what the Lord has already decreed?" John asked.

Myra hesitated, her arguments held within. When she spoke, her reply was weak, filled with defeat, "No, Pa."

After Clarence was settled and seemed to doze, Myra returned to the outer room. John and Leslie had eaten. Leslie sat on the floor with three rifles stripped down at his feet. He seemed industrious, preoccupied as if preparing for the opening of deer season in the fall.

"Nothing is going to happen that wasn't meant to happen, Almyra," John quietly lectured. He tried to be soothing. "We've led a lawful, righteous life. We have nothing to fear."

"Yes, Pa," Myra agreed. But she was unable to meet her father's eyes. He could be so strong, so fearless, not at all like other men. Just do not oppose what John believed.

Then she drifted to a dresser and lay her hand on the cover

of a Wards catalogue and thought of the countless items within, material goods from the world far outside their farm. An entire society of people. A melancholy mood gripped her. She drifted to the organ. Music would soothe her. But Clarence lay writhing in pain.

"Play something," John softly urged.

"What about Clarence?"

"It might do him some good to hear an angel sing," John said solemnly.

Myra swallowed nervously. Her father did love her. Just as his rage that afternoon against those men proved his love for Clarence. Everything else was a lie.

Myra sat down. She fingered the ivory keys, something clean, pure, far from the violence of exploding guns. Something that fit her mood; Stephan Foster, *Swanee River, Far, Far From Home*. She struck up the first chord.

The family sat silent, taken by the song, the mood. Leslie silently oiled the guns. Hattie sat in the bedroom with a damp cloth and sponged at Clarence's fevered cheeks. Johnny clung to her side, just as he had done all day ever since the bullet smashed just beside his head. Helen and Stanley sat side by side on a bunk, leaned back hiding in the gloom, Helen clutching a rag doll, Stanley gripping a toy gun. John sat in his rocker. His eyes were soft, his jaw relaxed. But as the sad melody took hold he became transformed, eyes narrowed and squinting fiercely, muscles of his jaw working as if chewing on a cud.

"*...the old folks dwell*," Myra sang.

The force of the rocker erupted, slamming the chair arm and rising to his feet. "Let the goddamn trusts send out the militia," he roared. "They think they can shoot, well, we're pretty damn good shots ourselves." He squinted around the room, commanding their attention. "Don't you people understand? There's going to be a revolution. Ours is but the first fight. The trusts have snatched our freedom just as wantonly as a king. Trapped us here. The common man has one choice left, stand tall and fight." His rage washed over them with the crushing force of a spring flood.

"Easy, John," Hattie cautioned. She was firm, not a woman to back away. She knew John's mood, that now was not a time

Photo courtesy of Chippewa Valley Museum
The Dietz family several days after Clarence was shot in the head. From left, Stanley, Helen, Johnny, Leslie, Clarence, Myra, Hattie, John.

to push. But she was all that stood between John and the children. "We're with you," Hattie said. "You saw that today."

"I saw nothing but opposition. Even Leslie there ducked behind the garden fence before he fired a shot." He seized one of Leslie's freshly oiled guns. The boy ducked away as if about to be struck. "You better duck," John chided. He glared around the room. "What are you staring at? Play, Almyra. It sounds good."

Myra struck up a chord. John slammed outside and into the black of the deep forest night. A brilliant sheen of stars filled the sky down to the horizon. Bullfrogs croaked, crickets chirped. The dogs stirred, recognized John's scent and immediately lay down, alert, ears perked forward in case John called them to his side. John hefted his rifle and stepped away from the tiny cabin, striding upright and bold as if daring any man to stand and be his foe.

John laughed, a bitter, mocking sound filling the night. The

Lord gave it to a man; poor all his life, stomped on by the mills, attacked by the law, even opposed by his own family for whom he'd willingly sacrifice his life. The weight of the growing opposition bore down upon his shoulders. John looked to the sky and the millions of stars covering right down to the horizon. He shrugged, "Well, if that's what there is to be, that's what I'll have to face."

He rubbed at his jaw as if in contemplation. The Man best not expect him to break.

Inside the cabin, Myra continued to play. The pure tones of her voice drifted through the night and were swallowed by the vast expanses of the surrounding forest.

The music brought tears to John's eyes and a lump to his throat. All he wanted was for him and his family to live in peace. But the mills would not let him be.

In time John returned to the cabin. He was calm, joking. "Not a soul out there. They even abandoned the driving camp. Must have been in a hurry for some reason — they left the door wide open when they left, food still lying on the table."

Leslie grinned nervously. John patted Leslie's shoulder. "You did a man's work out there today, Lester. Stood your ground. Gave back better than what you got."

"Thanks," Leslie mumbled. He beamed with pride. "If you want, I can sit outside and keep watch?" He was eager.

"No. Let the dogs earn their keep," John said. He looked in on Clarence then the family settled down for the night.

John and Leslie kept guns at their sides. Myra was instructed to defend the north side if men happened to approach during the night.

"Be listening for the dogs," John said as he crawled into Clarence's bunk. "They can sniff a polecat five miles off."

Hattie hooked the screen door and blew out the kerosene lamp. She quietly drifted in and sat in a rocking chair beside her son. Clarence, tormented by a sharp ringing in his ears and throbbing pain in his head, moaned most of the night. Whenever he looked his mother was there. Toward dawn, he became silent. Just sleeping, Hattie thought and again prayed.

In the morning Clarence was still alive. The family held hands and knelt in prayer and thanked the Lord.

* * *

Somehow John Rogich also survived the night. His ordeal pushed him to the outer limits of human tolerance. The man-made rents in his flesh became clogged with congealed blood and clods of dirt. The pouring rain and wet foliage had left him shivering. And then in the steamy depths of a black July night, swarms of insects returned. Brambles raked at his hands, face and sides. A fallen log took a supreme and agonizing effort simply to surmount. Tangles of fallen trees completely blocked his path, forcing a retracing of a painful crawl that led he knew not where. Inch by inch the indiscriminating forces of nature began to exact their toll.

On more occasions than Rogich could recall, he sought the smooth, pine needle carpet under a tree and curled into a fetal ball, giving himself to the narcotic drug of exhaustion and willing himself to die. But insects swarmed in, angry bites pricking his consciousness. He recalled his fellow posse members, panic in their voices, dropping him unceremoniously in the brush and running away like a flock of frightened sheep. The cowards! The traitors! If he ever got back alive ... He picked up and crawled on.

Sometime during the night he came upon a stream. It was a narrow body of water lined with tag alders and fallen tangles of trees. At first he thought to just cross the stream, perhaps find a deep hole and allow himself to drown. But the water was much too shallow for that. And the cool brine soothed the dirt-filled and infected agony of his wounds. And insects could not gnaw at his naked flesh.

Rogich turned and began to crawl with the stream. Morning dawned bright, sunny and clear. Red-winged blackbirds warbled nearby. Muskrats ducked back into their lodges. Two deer gazed with frightened and puzzled curiosity at the sodden form groping along the stream like a beaver with only a head sticking above water.

More than once that day Rogich's head dropped into the water. And more than once he lay for long stretches with his head resting on a log while his body lay submerged.

Eventually his pain and exhausted mind would fix on distant thoughts of revenge, of all the world he had yet to see and experience. In time strength and resolve would build and he would pick up and crawl a few yards more. But with each effort he covered less ground before he quit.

His senses lost their acuity. His vision blurred. He could not hear beyond his own labored breathing. Although once he swore he heard a train, and men talking. He yelled and yelled at the top of his lungs. No one replied.

In time birds again resumed their song. John Rogich crawled on. A log lying across the stream loomed as high as a mountain. Rogich strained. He could not make the climb. He dropped into the water with his head resting on a branch and lay still.

Toward noon, a settler named Charles Johnson spotted what appeared to be a human head in the stream down from his cabin. "What the devil!" He picked up a rifle and cautiously worked down to the stream. "By God," he thought, it was a man. He stepped into the calf-deep water. The man moaned and turned. John Rogich was still alive.

EIGHTY ARE KILLED IN RAILROAD WRECK

Defective Rail Throws Cars Into Stream and Occupants are Trapped, Few Succeed in Making Their Escape Through Windows

---

DIETZ AND HIS RIFLE WILL KEEP THE LAW AT BAY

Stubborn Fight Gives Him Public Sympathy

CHAPTER IX

S warms of strangers beat a path towards the Dietz farm. They were not gun-carrying sheriffs or militia, but camera-toting and pencil-carrying reporters from local papers and big city dailies such as Milwaukee, Minneapolis, and St. Paul. Throughout the upper Midwest John Dietz's brave and lonely stand against the mills became front page news.

One such reporter was Alfred E. Roese, editor of the *Osceola Sun*. Only recently had Roese been taken by the Dietz cause, and in fact had visited the family a few days prior to Gylland's attack and had initiated a series of stories on the Dietz stand against the lumber trusts. He'd been incensed by the cowardly subterfuge, disguises and bushwhacking methods of hired guns sent out by the mills. As soon as he could break free, Roese again made the long trek by train and then wagon out to the Dietz farm.

As usual he was greeted by the wild barking of the dogs. Two of the younger children, Helen and Stanley, ran for the cabin. Hattie and Myra turned from where they were hanging wash on the clothes line. Roese's heart went out for the isolation and persecution of this struggling family.

Certainly they had no excess of money. The Dietz woman was stout, hard working. Roese had judged her quickly, clean house, clean children, strong, red callused hands. The last time she had been polite, hospitable. He'd been surprised when she later deigned to speak her mind. He'd thought more of her than that.

John stepped to the door and watched closely while Roese forded the Thornapple on the submerged logs laid in the mud. The man was unarmed, Roese was pleased to observe. That was John Dietz, as fearless and tough as they came. A champion.

Roese was greeted warmly. John had readily taken to the stream of reporters. After all, they were here to tell the world about his fight.

As Roese entered the house, Clarence rose from where he'd been lying on his bunk. A white, pus-soaked bandage still covered the lad's head. Vision in one eye was clear and blurred vision had returned to the eye just below the rent in his skull. Hattie indicated that Clarence still suffered from ringing in his ears and severe headaches. But he did not complain. A hero just like his father, Roese told the young man.

Other reporters and neighbors had passed on some of the news, however, Roese had brought dozens of clippings from stories throughout the Midwest. "The mills have been made to look like fools, John. The people are with you." Roese was enthusiastic. "You cannot lose."

"What about this story they are sending the real militia?" Hattie asked with deep concern. The lines of her face had deepened. Her eyes had a haunted, furtive look. "They mean to tear us apart."

She showed Roese an article from the Milwaukee Journal:

MAY SEND TROOPS

Madison, Wis.: As a result of the conferences Tuesday between Governor Davidson and Sheriff Peter Gylland of Sawyer County, it is likely that several companies of the Wisconsin militia will be called out to capture John F. Dietz, who has for years defied the authorities who are now seeking to serve a warrant charging him with assault with intent to kill.

* * *

"But you have nothing to fear," Roese all but shouted with elation. He was a tall man with a thick moustache and round spectacles. His manner was intense like a man consumed with a cause.

"I've told the woman that ten thousand times," John grumbled. "If there's one cloud in the sky, Hattie sees rain."

Roese rummaged wildly through his stacks of papers and clippings. "Look at these later articles. Ninety percent of the people are with you."

PUBLIC SENTIMENT STRONG

So strong has become the sentiment in favor of Dietz in this section of the state that petitions of protection against the recent action of the sheriff and his posse and demanding that no further attacks be made upon his home have been sent to Governor Davidson. These petitions have been signed by the most prominent citizens of Sawyer County and vicinity, who assert that they are prepared to back their position with money and political influence.

At Spooner, Rice Lake and other towns of the neighborhoods of Cameron Dam, citizens of prominence talk seriously of organizing home guard companies and marching them into the woods to help Dietz in the event of further attempts to arrest him.

Dietz for Sheriff?

"Why we're going to run John Dietz for sheriff of the county in opposition to Gylland in the next election," declared a merchant at Winter. "There are not ten men in this county who will vote for Gylland again. He is down and out forever up there and he might as well get out of the country so far as holding public office is concerned."

Improbably as it may seem, the entire district has hailed this idea with great enthusiasm and it is very likely that either John Dietz or his brother William will be the next sheriff of Sawyer County.

"Bill doesn't even live in Sawyer County," John sagely observed.

"But don't you see, you have the people's support," Roese

argued.

"I see," John growled. He was gruff, at long last basking in the glow of what he viewed as long overdue public approbation.

Roese held out another clipping. "The governor has been forced to back away from you. Put the issue back up to Sawyer County." Only then, Roese thought, did the mood and tension within the family began to ease.

Could this be true? They had won? They picked through the other clippings with more interest, seeing themselves in a different light, showing off photographs of one another that had made the front pages of large metropolitan and local papers. On one day in the *Milwaukee Journal* there were front page headlines and pictures of John, Clarence and Myra, captioned "John Dietz, Wounded Son and Plucky Daughter." The caption under Myra further read, "Almyra Dietz is Expert in Use of the rifle, but not withstanding the statements of imaginative deputies, she declares that she did not fire a single shot during the fight. One deputy stated that she fired 40 or 50 shots."

Other days showed group pictures of the entire family, and individual shots of Hattie and Johnny Jr., Helen, and Stanley and even a photograph, later made into a post card, of the white-faced cow with the caption "Cow That Acted as a Scout."

"I wonder why they didn't print any of those pictures of you," Myra said to Leslie.

"I didn't want any pictures anyhow," Leslie said. "They had Clarence sitting there with his umbrella and bandaged head. That other paper said he was the hero of the fight and he never fired a shot. Just like they claimed you fired forty or fifty shots."

"Those reporters make these things up, not us," Clarence said to his brother. He was sympathetic. "You know that one reporter from the *Journal* had eyes for Myra. They talked more about her than any of us."

Leslie shrugged. "Ah, it doesn't matter." He turned away from the pile of clippings and began to grease his boots with goose grease.

"Pa told them the way it was," Myra said. "Look at this story here." She handed Leslie a clipping. "He gave you all the credit."

"Yeah," Leslie mumbled, "now they'll put a warrant out on

me." Nevertheless he took the clipping to read:

HIS WOMEN DID NOT SHOOT

In the recent battle fought on Dietz land the women of the family did not fire a shot. Lester and myself were the only ones who handled guns that day, said Dietz to a Journal representative. "Neither Almyra nor my wife mixed up in the affair, and it is fortunate for the men who came in here that they did not.

"I will not permit my women to fight, however, unless they send a more ferocious gang than the last crowd that came in here."

Cowardice is Charged

John Rogich, the wounded man, is still at the hotel in Spooner, where he is receiving medical attention. He is improving and desires to be removed to Milwaukee, so that he may come face to face with his erstwhile comrades who deserted him in the woods.

"They left me in there to die and ran away to save their own skins," he stated with a bitter smile.

The nature of the sound in the woods at which the bearers of the stretcher upon which Rogich had been placed became frightened has now been brought to light.

A party of assessors passing through the timber shortly after the battle approached within a short distance of the retreating deputies who upon hearing the crackling of the underbrush believed that Dietz had gone out to ambush them, and scattered like the wind, leaving the wounded man to take care of himself.

While they were returning to Milwaukee, these deputies passed through two or three rough experiences at the small stations along the route. When their identity became known, Dietz sympathizers flocked to the train and threatened to mob the party.

"Sheriff Gylland apparently spent the night lost in the forest," Roese interrupted the avid reading of the articles. "The company foreman Hedrington reached Ladysmith about two o'clock in the morning and sent a wagon and doctor back along the trail. But the doctor never saw a soul. Gylland must have been so exhausted and filled with shame at his cowardice that he staggered into the woods and spent the night. The other deputies just disappeared."

"I gave those Milwaukee reporters one of my poems about Gylland," John said. He'd assumed a seat in his customary rocking chair, feet propped up as he leaned back and relaxed. He read the articles as they passed from hand to hand, laughing and commenting on the many inaccuracies. One story concluded:

> ...As the newspapermen took to the woods amid the waving of hands, their ears were greeted by a hymn sung by the entire outlaw family, as they marched back up the hill to again take up the bitter fight against the world.

"Are these boys from the *Journal* part of the lumber trust bureau, Alfred?" John grumbled. "The trusts do own their own newspapers."

"Oh, absolutely," Roese agreed. He rummaged through the clippings. "It just appears these men like to embellish things a little. You can count them on your side. Look, they did publish your poem."

> ...See the mighty host advancing, Gylland leading on,
> Mighty men and heroes falling, courage almost gone —
> Hold the fort, for I am coming, with my pepper gun:
> Watch the smoke, and watch the shooting—
> Watch the sheriff run.

John laughed, enjoying the sounds of his own words. "They came here bringing death, but they sure know how to make a man feel alive."

"Here's another article that describes what all you people think you are," Leslie said. He dropped the paper on the floor between them and quietly drifted to the front door and went outside.

Myra picked up the article. It did not mention Leslie once.

"Let me see that, Myra," John said. He held out a gnarled and muscled hand.

Myra hesitated. She'd spoken to the reporter in confidence; someone with whom she could converse. She hadn't thought any of her words would actually find print.

Nervously she handed her father the paper. She backed across the room to help her mother at the wooden table and cook stove. Pa was in a good mood, she thought. He was taken with all the coverage, the pictures, the petitions of support, the way even Governor Davidson had backed down and refused to call out the militia. Perhaps, she prayed, Pa would not get mad.

"Dietz trusts no man," John read the headline aloud in a dramatic voice. He glared around the cabin and fixed Stanley with a wicked eye. "Is that true?" he roared.

Stanley squealed with laughter. "No, Pa."

"Unless they're agents for the trusts," John said.

Hattie suddenly whirled from where she was chopping up and canning beans. "We do have work." She glared at the scattering of clippings. She'd seen John's preening, reading the articles through time and again as if each article anointed him as king. In truth, as she well knew, they simply put him deeper in his trench. And she and the children were taken along.

"We also have company," John replied. He fixed Hattie with a steady gaze, a warning. "And you're being most inhospitable, dear."

Hattie glanced at Roese; the man thought writing about John was helping him. She sighed and turned back to her beans. All the world was moving beyond her control.

Roese shifted uncomfortably. He hadn't imagined Hattie could speak like that. Not that it bothered John, he'd immersed himself in the long article:

DIETZ TRUSTS NO MAN

In two years John Dietz, his wife and six children have never left the 160-acre clearing which, to protect, he has jeopardized his own life and courted the destruction of his family. And in this same length of time but few have ventured into the outlaw's stronghold. The Indian, the lumbermen, and a few scattered settlers of the neighborhood make detours in the woods when the trails they are following lead in the direction of the Dietz homestead. Because of this and because all avenues of communication with the outside world have been virtually closed to him, John Dietz trusts no man.

Two representatives of the Journal followed the faint trail through the woods from Winter, 12 miles to Dietz's cabin, spending a day upon the forbidden premises as guests of the famous outlaw. They found there the simple farmer, the husband and father. The notorious outlaw, the desperado, the blood-lustful woodsman was not present.

Dietz is of German extraction, a man in the prime of life, about five feet ten inches in height, wiry and active. His complexion is ruddy and his hair and mustache are sandy in color. He is a skilled woodsman, a shrewd politician, a reader of standard literature and a dead shot with rifle and re-volver. He is a Mason of many years standing, having at one time occupied a prominent position in the Rice Lake lodge, in which town he has held the office of justice of the peace.

NOT A FIGHTING MAN

To one who approaches him as a friend, Dietz is not the terrible fighting man pictured by the residents of the dis-trict. His face, frank and open, is seared with lines of irre-pressible good spirits. His blue eyes sparkle with humor.

The mouth is expressive and almost tender. This is the John Dietz who welcomed the representatives of the Jour-nal.

The enemies of Dietz, however, describe him as an en-tirely different personage. When he is aroused the human eyes narrow to a pair of slits, cold and repellent. The lines of humor give way to deeper ones of determination and ha-tred. The mouth strengthens and compresses until it is like a scar left by the slash of a saber. This is the other John Dietz — the terror to sheriffs and posses, the fugitive.

While Dietz usually seems perfectly rational at time, he might also be called a monomaniac upon the one subject which has occupied his waking and sleeping hours for two years.

Although he is industrious and causes his little farm to yield bounteously every season, he finds time at night to study and to write bitter poems and songs in which sheriffs,

district attorneys and corporations are heaped with con-
tumely. This scribbling is Dietz's sole relaxation.

HE HAS NO RIVALS

"I am the poet laureate of Thornapple River," he remarked
with a grin. "I haven't any rivals or competitors or critics to
contend with, and admirers of my work are restricted to seven
persons. I don't believe my poetry will ever become popular. I tried it on an outsider once," he finished with a chuckle,
"and it came near getting me shot.

"You may think I am getting too humorous," he said apolo-
getically. "But it is so seldom I have a chance to exchange
courtesies other than little steel bullets with outsiders, that
when I do find a friend I immediately make him my enemy
by talking him half to death."

With his family of seven, Dietz has made himself a wonderful home in the forest. He has cleared 160 acres of land,
all of which is under cultivation, feeds a herd of several cows,
a few sheep and poultry. His famous cabin is built on a crown
of a hill, commanding a sweep of cleared country for 200
yards on all sides. A little spring of sweet water bubbles at
the foot of this hill, attracting thirsty deer from the forest.
He is able to kill these animals from the back door of his
cabin.

HE LOVES HIS FARM

To drive a wagon through the woods to Cameron Dam is
an impossibility, the little clearing being surrounded on all
sides by almost impenetrable forest. The lumber road at one
time led from Winter straight to Dietz's clearing, but this
trail has long since become choked with logs and windfalls.

Yet with all its drawbacks Dietz says that he loves his
farm and could remain contented there if he was free from
molestation.

Miss Almyra Dietz, "the girl who can shoot like a man,"
is above all things, a woman. She is the one member of the
outlawed family who is not quite content with her lot. Her
pride and love for her father, however, will not permit her to
complain.

"I'm with him through it all," she said simply, "if death
awaits at the end I can ask nothing better than to go with

father and my brothers.

"People think I am an amazon," she complained. "Why I've never fired a shot in anger. The day may come when it may be necessary for me to use my rifle in defense of my home, though. When I'm forced to that I think I can provide good measure. I've been known to bark squirrels at 100 yards."

In the meantime Miss Dietz follows the pursuits of a farmer's daughter. Her recreation is simple. She possesses an excellent contralto voice and she plays unusually well on an organ which her father brought over the trail on his sled, a number of years ago. In the long evenings, assessors and others who have been overtaken by the night and forced to pitch camp near the Dietz clearing, have been startled upon hearing the plaintive notes of a little forgotten love song, floating across the clearing into the woods. It is the voice of Almyra Dietz, the girl who never had a lover, and who does not herself know she is calling to the man who only exists in her dreams — who may never come to her.

... The mother of the outlaw family, Mrs. Hattie Dietz, is happy with her children. At one time a school mistress, Mrs. Dietz has expended infinite pains upon the education of her boys and girls. Upon a table in the living room of the cabin is a stack of dog-eared text books. Even Clarence, the oldest boy, and Johnny "Ginger" Jr. the youngest, are not exempt from discipline, being forced to devote a certain period each day to their studies.

"I can not bring myself to believe that the end of it all will be a tragedy," Mrs. Dietz said. "Every thing is so beautiful and so green in the woods, and the very songs of the birds renew my hope that it is bound to come out all right in the end. A mother can not predict defeat for her children, no matter what the prospects. It is too much to expect. I'm giving them what education I can with the hope that some day they may become good and useful citizens."

HERO TO THE CHILDREN

Not because he has been shot and is a man in daring and fighting prowess, if not in years, but because he is a master in woodcraft — a leader in boyish sports — Clarence, the oldest son, is a wonderful hero to his brothers and sisters. Because he has no companions of his own age, he has adjusted his amusements to fit the appreciation of his younger relatives, permitting them to participate in his games.

In the winter it is Clarence who builds the slide from the cabin down to the river brink, who makes the sleds and the snow forts, and who can cut his own name in the ice with skates. Again it is Clarence who can pitch curves with the baseball. He can run like a deer, knock squirrels from tall trees with his rifle, and perform strange feats in the water. The younger children are proud of Clarence.

As a family the Dietzes are happy. They have their home, the forest, the river and their simple pleasures. The life they have been forced to lead has made them strong and robust, and a mutual, constant danger has drawn the ties closer and closer until their understanding of one another is perfect. Dietz has expressed his position, at the same time accounting for the great fight he has made, when he said: "I care for nothing in the world but my family and my home. I shall never give up either."

John let the article fall to the floor. He looked across the tiny, crowded room to where his daughter set porcelain plates around the dining table. His voice took on a hard, angered edge as if railing against the subterfuge and power of the trusts. "What is it you are not content with, Myra? You do not have a warm house, a roof over your head and food in your belly? You never had a lover? What do you think you were saying to those reporters?"

"He asked if I ever had a boyfriend out here and I said no," Myra desperately explained.

"John, John, it's just a reporter's romantic interpretation," Roese said.

John snapped as if at one of his enemies, "I'll thank you not to step in between a man and his family."

Roese quickly apologized. "Yes, of course, John. You're absolutely correct. A man's family is his own affair. It's just that this is a day for celebration. You've all but won. The governor has backed down. Gylland could never raise another posse."

"But the mills can hire agents," John said. "They've done it before, they'll do it again. I've heard talk they plan to starve us out."

"Not if I have anything to say about it," Roese proclaimed as if to a huge crowd. "This is a fight for liberty, John. As you said so yourself. The first step in a revolution. You're no longer alone."

"Supper's ready," Hattie said firmly as if to divert the talk.

Myra glanced at Roese and nodded her thanks for diverting her father's attention. She must hide that article, she thought, or John would read it again.

Roese accepted an invitation and stayed the night. He refused Hattie's offer to take her and John's bed and reluctantly accepted Leslie and Stanley's bunk while Stanley crawled in with Clarence. Leslie took the floor against the wall behind the stove. It was a warm night, Roese observed, a family not crowded upon one another as much as residing together in cozy brotherhood and easy harmony. Roese was proud to share their humble abode.

In the morning Roese ate a hearty breakfast and walked the farm, surveying bullet holes in the house and following the course of the fights, learning how John had slipped up beside an intruder during the moonlight; how on another occasion he handed his rifle to a deputy to inspect.

"Yes, there have been more men sneaking around these woods than we could possibly count," Leslie said. He was jocular, proud of John's exploits. "Clarence and I have run some off. Pa has walked up to a dozen men sneaking around the woods. He says you can tell an agent of the mills easy enough; Pa stands and talks polite-like and they start quivering and stammering and cannot even look you in the eye."

"You children are most fortunate to have a man like John for your father. Men such as him are rare. You ought to be most proud."

"Oh, but we are," Clarence said with exaggerated emphasis. He looked Roese straight in the eye, being the kind of man Roese said he appreciated. "There is no other way we could be."

"Good, that's what I like to hear." Roese accepted the words as pride.

The children looked at one another and grinned. Only Leslie seemed irritated Clarence could mock him so. And yet the children grew to like Roese. He was sympathetic, an outsider who took an intense interest in their fight with the mills.

"Do you think the mills will settle now?" Hattie asked Roese. "Will we not gain something for all that we have faced?"

"Oh no, the mills cannot settle now. They would look bad if they did that. This is just the beginning. John is one in a million, someone working men can rally around. People are with you, Mrs. Dietz. There is no way you can lose."

"You said the mills would not settle," Hattie was perplexed. "So we lose."

"Not your cause," Roese replied as if it was obvious. He reached for a second piece of homemade bread and hand-churned butter. He sought to change the subject, "I swear this is the best butter I ever tasted. If you could jar enough I could sell it and make you a fortune."

Hattie blushed. The man put her off, and yet she was pleased. Roese was filled with compliments, for her, the children, John, even the alertness of their dogs. If Roese had the pups from John Dietz's dogs, he claimed, he could make a fortune.

Yes, Roese promised to champion John and his stand. He would help them in every way. He'd ask for public contributions to fight the mills and to assist the Dietz family. He'd print John's story in its entirety, in John's own words. He'd help John contact editors and drum up support. He'd help them obtain sufficient supplies to survive. If Hattie, Myra and Helen sewed mittens and moccasins from deer skins, he could see the goods were sold at a fair price. He knew trustworthy members of the Bangor Hunt Club, Dietz sympathizers all, who would pay John, Clarence and Leslie to act as drivers and guides for the fall deer season.

"You are no longer alone," Roese assured them time and again as he made ready to take his leave. "This is a war and we've just begun to fight."

Only as the weeks passed did Hattie truly understand the full impact of Roese's words. They'd won nothing and John became more driven and taken with himself than ever.

On October 25, 1906, Alfred E. Roese devoted an entire issue of the *Osceola Sun* to the John Dietz story. JOHN F. DIETZ
BEFORE ALL MEN, the banner headline read.

> True Recounting of Entire Struggle
> From Lips and Pen of the "Human Target."
> Complete Story of the Bitter Fight Waged
> Against the Man of Thornapple Dam

In addition to his normal circulation of 1,700 papers, Roese
printed an additional 4,000 copies which he sold for 25 cents.
He also sold pictures of the family and farm for 25 and 50
cents. All proceeds in excess of production costs were to go to
the Dietz family and their fight against the monied forces.

Besides the description of the long fight in John's own words,
Roese and other writers railed against the power of the trusts:

THE CONTROLLING POWER

Isn't it true that money is the controlling power, and that
the possessor of unlimited quantities of gold is exempt to a
certain degree from the laws that bind the man in less fortunate circumstances? Cannot the billion-dollar corporation
do with impunity acts that the common individual would
not dare do? ... No one is safe from these vultures. No man
knows at what time the little he possesses may be coveted
by these avaricious birds of prey and when that time comes,
under the present system he has no alternative but to give it
to them. True, he may take it to the courts whereof wrongs
are supposed to be adjusted. Here, again, the man with the
millions at his disposal has all the advantages. Skillful lawyers will carry the case thru court after court, every obstacle
will be placed in the path to defeat the true ends of justice,
and in the end the power of gold will prevail...

THE HERO OF THORNAPPLE DAM

Once in a great while, the monied forces mark a man as
their victim, and, when they come to carry out their well-
laid plans, find that they have singled out the wrong man.
They find a man who is willing to stand up for what he
considers right, even at the risk of losing his own life and

sacrificing the lives of his wife and children and all else that
he holds dear; a man who cannot be swerved from the stand
he has taken when he knows that stand is for the cause of
justice; a man who cannot be frightened or coerced into giving up his just dues. Such a man is John F. Dietz, the persecuted hero of the Thornapple Dam.

John F. Dietz is a man in every sense of the word. He is a
type of the sturdy pioneer who reclaimed his land from the
wilderness and made it the abode of a thrifty people. All his
life accustomed to the dangers and hardships which beset
the pioneer in the wilderness, he fears no man. To know the
man is to respect and honor him and even the most bitter of
his enemies will do him the justice to admit that he is honest
in his convictions.

Hattie stared at John, once again reading that Osceola paper
along with all the other clippings Roese sent in his weekly
letters. The children had glued many clippings into a scrapbook that now rested on John's lap.

Hattie slammed a kettle on top of the wood stove. She
dropped the water pail with a bang back on the floor. John did
not stir. Hattie bent forward, one hand on the table, the other
holding her back. The ailments were catching up, rheumatism
eating away her spine, gout causing constant agony and sap-
ping her strength. She wiped her brow. "This work is killing
me." John did not move. "Haven't you finished reading that
paper yet?" Hattie snapped.

John cocked one eyebrow and peered over the paper. "I've
seen stories on Rockefeller, Morgan, Vanderbilt. I've never seen
an entire issue of a paper devoted to them. Look at this," he
commanded Hattie and thrust the paper in her face:

> ...The "press bureau" of the lumber company would have
> the general public believe that he is an outlaw little better
> than a savage, and one who would stop at nothing to attain
> his ends, be those ends right or wrong. If there is a more
> peaceable, quiet, law-abiding and liberty-loving citizen of
> Wisconsin than John F. Dietz, the editor of the Sun has not

yet made his acquaintance ...

He is a firm believer in the cause of good government and
is ready to fight to the last drop of his blood for what he
considers right. He is one man whom money cannot corrupt
or threats intimidate. If the true character of John F. Dietz
was generally known, if his worth was truly appreciated,
his name would be emblazoned in Wisconsin's hall of fame
as one of the greatest men this state has ever produced.

John grinned playfully as Hattie read the familiar words.
"That Alfred has a way with words doesn't he?"

"We can't eat paper, John."

Like the passing of a cloud over the sun, John's mood was
transformed. "No, but we eat, damnit. We've got guiding in a
couple weeks. Trapping. You'll have your deer hides to make
mittens and moccasins. Alfred and Hamilton said they'll send
supplies," he said of a sympathetic building contractor from
downstate.

John bunched the paper in his fists and strode over to where
Hattie was rolling pie crust on the counter. He glared fiercely.
For a moment Hattie was perplexed that she actually felt in-
timidated.

Suddenly John smiled. "You've been a dear. Maybe I have
slacked off on the farm work. Guess I figured the boys can
handle that. There are greater things at stake here, Hattie. I've
got the mills." Almost immediately his voice took an edge. "I
don't need you and the children to fight as well."

"But we're with you, John," Hattie snapped recklessly as
Clarence, Myra and Leslie trooped into the cabin. "Look at
Clarence's head. Didn't Myra almost die?" She faced him as
boldly as if her fear had been an illusion. "Is that not proof of
support?" John remained silent. Hattie shouted, forcing the
admission. "Is that not proof, John?"

"Proof enough," John conceded. He doffed his hat and strode
towards the front door. "Your mother says I have work," he
said to the children. The mirth was in his eyes. "Says all this
press business is going to my head. Maybe I ought to take that
Milwaukee theatrical offer."

John referred to articles written in several papers that John had been offered $300.00 a week for forty weeks to appear on stage in Milwaukee. "Do you think I could be a hit? An old German North Woods man strutting on a stage?"

"If you carried your Lugers the audience would pay you mind," Leslie said.

"True," John said and affectionately tousled Leslie's hair. And then he was gone, working hard for two hours in the fields until a reporter from Eau Claire showed up.

After John went outside, the children moved in close to the potbellied stove to warm up. Stanley, Helen and Johnny Jr. soon followed at a run.

"You look in pain, Ma," Myra observed as Hattie continued her work.

"Oh, it's nothing," Hattie protested. "You know how this cold and damp sometimes makes the rheumatism flare."

"People think Pa's the great one in this family," Clarence said to his mother. He wore small, round, thick spectacles Roese had brought in an effort to aid the poor vision in his eye. Now he looked like a professor, Leslie had laughed. Clarence snitched a piece of cut apple off the table. When Hattie turned to stop him, Leslie swiped a piece from the other side. "But they don't know you," Clarence said as he deftly avoided his mother's slap. "You're the glue that holds this family together. Always have been."

Hattie grimaced, a sort of a smile of appreciation. The deep furrow in Clarence's skull still jarred painful reminders of that terrifying and bloody afternoon. "We have to be careful," she said to her brood. "What with all this press and everything, your father's not himself just yet. He's a little more rigid than usual. He has duties, obligations. Whatever you do, don't think of getting in his way."

The children were momentarily silent, much too aware their mother's words were true.

"Ma's in a lot of pain," Myra observed after Hattie left the cabin for the root cellar.

"She's always in pain," Leslie said as if to imply the pain lay in her head.

"But aren't we all," Clarence snapped. "Ma's doing her best

to keep us together. Who can tell what's going to happen next? They might send the militia. How, with all of this, are we ever going to lead normal lives? Think on that." He seized a copy of the *Milwaukee Journal* and turned to his favorite passage out of dozens of stories. He read in a loud, melodramatic voice:

> What manner of man is John F. Dietz? What is the life of his lonely family on the banks of the Thornapple River? Is the famous Cameron Dam outlaw of the same type as Tracy, Jesse James, — notorious fighting men and "killers?"
>
> "These are among the questions that have recently come to the people of Wisconsin — questions that cannot be answered even by the former friends of this sturdy settler. The terrible successes of the game fighter who has pitted himself, single-handedly, against corporation and government, has made him a man not of the 20th Century. To neighbors who used to know him before he became a fugitive of justice, John Dietz has become as a character in a thrilling book of romance. His exploits have made him a man apart, and although the sympathies of Sawyer County are with him, the residents fear him and shun him and speak of him with awe, forgetting the time when he had a place in the midst of them."

Clarence dropped the newspaper clipping back on the table. "That's us as well, of course." He became flippant. "Pa loves this stuff. But then the people are with us. Why should we be concerned? The governor will not send out the militia — so the papers say. We're wanted now too, of course. But, as long as we remain on the farm and near Pa, they'll never get us. Never."

Myra exchanged glances with Leslie. Ever since Clarence had been shot he'd seemed to change as if the bullet had actually touched his brain. "Then we never will move back to town?" Myra asked.

"Of course not," Clarence shouted with glee. "Now you're beginning to see. We'll live out here forever, all of us, growing old. You might as well get used to it. You and Leslie didn't want me to go against Pa before. Well, now I won't. He's caught up in this now. If all the power of the mills and the government can't move him, I guess I'd be crazy to try." Clarence was almost cheerful at the prospect.

But his voice was higher than normal and his one good eye gleamed wickedly like a mad pirate who'd taken of too much rum. "I told you," he said as if to mock.

In the afternoon more reporters, from Chippewa Falls and Eau Claire, visited. "I've heard reports the mills are trying to form another posse," one reporter said. "Do you think they'll try again?"

"Oh yes," John replied, as if eager for the conflict. The mills have the gold to try. The company has persecuted me for three years, sending in young fools to be killed, killing my cattle and sheep, stealing my dogs and daring me to come off my land onto theirs."

The reporter scribbled furiously, taking John's words down verbatim.

"I suppose that some day they will get me, but John Dietz, whom they call the desperado and outlaw, is going out of here feet first leaving his empty gun behind him, and the place they will take him will be to the cemetery. Sure, they can kill me like John Brown — and then I suppose there will be another revolution."

The reporter suppressed a smile. He turned to the surrounding family. "Do you all support your father?"

Clarence snorted as if the reporter was stupid for even asking a question such as that. "Of course," he replied, as if it were obvious. "You see us all standing here don't you? What do you think that means?"

RENAMING THE SIOUX

Some 25,000 Indians are Receiving Christian Names Educated Indian Tribesmen Selected by the "Great Father" to Re-Christian Braves Bob-tailed Coyote Become Robert T. Wolf

---

DIETZ RAID A FARCE Much Amusement Afforded Entire State by the Bluff of Calling a Posse

FEW WILL OBEY THE SUMMONS

And There is Practically No Danger of the Defender of the Dam Being Molested

---

JOYS OF MATERNITY

The darkest days of husband and wife are when they come to look forward to childless and lonely old age.

Many a wife has found herself incapable of motherhood owing to a displacement of the womb or lack of strength in the generative organs. Frequent backaches and distressing pains, accompanied by offensive discharges and generally by irregular and scanty menstruation indicate a displacement or nerve degeneration of the womb and surrounding organs. The question that troubles women is how can a woman who has some female trouble bear healthy children?

Actual sterility in women is very rare. If any woman thinks she is sterile, let her try Lydia E. Pinkham's Vegetable Compound.

CHAPTER X

Nineteen-hundred-seven was the year of the underground to the beleaguered family at the Cameron Dam; or as John sometimes signed his weekly letters to A. E. Roese, the dam family. A. E. Roese spearheaded the campaign with his frequent visits to the family, editorials, articles and his complete issue treatment of the Dietz affair in October, 1906. But many other newspaper editors, working men and ordinary citizens in the Midwest, became Dietz sympathizers in word, deed and in small contributions mailed directly to the family.

Numerous letters to the editors were in favor of John and his stand against the powerful trusts. In his turn and at Roese's urging, John picked up his pencil and joined friendly press against the mills and what John referred to as the mill press bureau:

> Can it truthfully be said, that in Wisconsin, justice can not be had when the money powers forbid it? It has been stated in the public press that the purpose of my persecutors was to murder my whole family if they could not get me without... It has been their open boast that they would starve us out and that such is the intention is shown by the fact the local market at Winter has been closed against us, so we cannot sell any of the produce of our farm ...

The county treasurer of Sawyer County has issued a tax certificate, on the sale of 1905, on the forty the dam is on to the Mississippi River Logging Company, notwithstanding I had paid the tax for the year 1904.

So we began to realize that Count Leo Tolstoy told the truth, when he said "the American people were greater slaves than the Russian peasants, but they did not know it. They were slaves to a system." The present cold wave, the circumstances that surround us, and the appeal for justice without relief, reminds us that possibly that we are not living in Wisconsin but instead have been banished to Siberia.

In conclusion, I will say, that no man is a stricter adherent to law and order than I am and I demand justice let it fall where it may, for it is high time this disgraceful conspiracy was brought to a close and if this appeal does not bring the required relief, then it can be truthfully heralded from the housetops, that in Wisconsin, justice can not be had for the asking, but is sold at auction to the highest bidder.

Yours very truly, John F. Dietz

In another letter, John wrote in part:

I have been termed an 'outlaw!' Well, if I am, that occupation would appear to be more honorable than law and order. I have never paraded in disguise or under an assumed name; I have never tried to gain any advantage on false pretenses, or 'bellied' around thru the grass, as the agents of the so-called department of justice have done; I have never been afraid to meet any man or body of men face to face, and I have never been ashamed to tell the truth about what I have done, as they have; and I have never struck a blow without warning as Rogich did — even a rattlesnake wouldn't do that.

John glared around the tiny cabin at his family. His fist was clenched, jaw thrust forward, blood throbbing hotly through a vein in his temple. He concluded in a booming voice as if an evangelist addressing a packed tent, "I am, yours for liberty or death, John F. Dietz."

For some seconds, the family, bathed in red by the dim flame of a kerosene lamp, sat silent as if in fear or awe.

Myra spoke first in her small, pure voice, "That's really good, Pa. That should bring the people running."

"You really told them that time," Leslie added with enthusiasm as if he was impressed at ravings he did not fully understand.

John fixed on Clarence as if waiting for his approbation.

"Oh, that's the best one yet, Pa," Clarence agreed in an excited, high-pitched voice. "Of all the dozens of letters, and poems and songs you've written, I think this one tells them best of all.

John scowled at the exaggerated enthusiasm. "Ye who worship false prophets, and ye who offers false praise tend to end up in hell and damnation, Clarence; in the hereafter on one hand and in the present on the other."

Clarence turned red with embarrassment. No matter which tack he assumed, John knew how to knock him down. He stared at the worn, grey-brown planks of their floor. Would there ever be a time, his time? Unconsciously his fingers probed the deep cleft splitting his skull.

His bitterness ran deep and yet he found himself muttering an abject reply. "That was good, Pa. That's all I meant." His head hung like that of a whipped dog.

John grunted as if doubting the words. Nevertheless, he was pleased. "I have to write Alfred again, remind him next time he visits to be certain to bring along a flag. Strike our colors. Show these bushwacking mill agents exactly where John Dietz stands. If the Lord says they get me, you wrap my body in that flag, Clarence. Show people where John Dietz stands."

"Let's sing some songs," Hattie declared. These days diversion was her only way of stopping John. "Myra, you play the organ. Everyone now. We'll sing some split chorus. If that's all right with you, John?"

John grinned wryly at Hattie's sarcasm. The letter was complete, his passion spent. "Play Myra. Clarence, Leslie, Stanley, get over here. We'll find out who can drown out who, boys or the girls."

And so they sang, the dam family on the Thornapple.

* * *

The war that fall and winter was conducted without benefit of the gun. John, with the sponsoring help of A. E. Roese and other editors, joined the fight with his pen. In fact, part of one lengthy John Dietz poem alluded to his present course:

> 'Tis said the pen is mightier than the sword,
> So I'll apply it to this oppressive horde,
> And with the aid of some printer's ink
> May be able to stop their obnoxious stink.

Meanwhile, the family carried on, carefully treading the best they could around John's obsessions and his war with the mills. Myra dryly chronicled events in her diary. In October the boys dug the last of the potatoes. The Bangor Hunt Club journeyed north and camped nearby. The members took dinner with the family. John and the boys guided the hunt.

John, the hunter who moved through the forest with the caution of one who is also the hunted, wrote Roese that he shot six deer. The boys did not even get a smell.

John captured a live eagle, that fierce symbol of liberty and freedom. He shipped the eagle to Roese who shipped the same to the governor. Regretfully, Governor Davidson could not accept such a gift. The eagle expired during its travels. Roese had the eagle stuffed and sent to even more sympathetic Minnesotans.

A new teacher, Eugene Graham of Phillips, arrived. The man was the nervous type, another agent for the mills, John asserted. Except for his time teaching, Graham spent his time alone, even taking his meals alone in his room.

Leslie trapped a mink. John trapped a bear and also shot a silver fox. Hattie and Myra made moccasins and mittens out of deer skins and Roese sold their wares. For Christmas, Roese sent in a large package of used clothes, foodstuffs and ammunition. John was convinced the local postmaster had been bought out by the mills and that all his mail was tampered with. Protests were lodged with the postal department. Thereafter Roese sent all letters with his special seal. With each letter he also mailed a blank envelope without the seal, always

Deer season at the Dietz farm, probably 1907. From left, editor A.E. Roese, Matt Egstad, Harry Roese, W.E. Moses (a log jobber who convinced John to let him move the logs in return for John receiving back wages) and an unidentified member of the Bangor Hunt Club.

cautioning John to watch the seal to see that the dummy letter also arrived. In his turn John was to use Roese's seal on his letters out.

Roese, along with John's brother William, worked for several months to clarify John's payment of real estate taxes on the dam forty. Clearly the county tax records had been erased and the entries of the tax payments altered. The county had even accepted payment on the dam forty from the mills. Payments sent by John were not applied to the forty on which the washed-out dam had been built. No county official could explain why.

"They'll stop at nothing," John shouted to his family. "They lie, they cheat, they alter the county record. There is no one they cannot buy."

"Yes, John," Hattie agreed. These days he was like a runaway bull. No one could get him to stop.

On January 5th, 1907, with the temperature twelve above zero, John killed a steer on the fresh white snow and the entire family participated in processing the meat and hide. On February 4th, the temperature dropped to 44 below zero. The next day the thermometer froze. The boys and Myra carried wood continuously and Hattie fed the stove throughout the night.

On February 9th, John and Hattie invited several neighbors and celebrated their silver wedding anniversary. Hattie was made to sit and relax while Myra and Helen cooked a sumptuous meal. The O'Hares and Van Alstynes, neighbors to whom the Dietz family had sold potatoes, milk and beef, were part of the gathering. One member of the mill press bureau reported more than 200 guests had partied long into the night. In truth, there were fewer than a dozen outsiders who sleighed through cold and winter snow to crowd the tiny cabin on the isolated farm. They stayed but a few hours and then the Dietz family was once again alone.

The days of the winter of 1907 blended one into the other; carrying firewood, hunting for snowshoe rabbits, feeding the livestock morning and evening, cutting ice, attending school with the uneasy Graham, ice skating on the flowage pond, sledding off the roof of the root cellar, making snow forts, and pulling the sled behind Old Tom. And to the outside world, with the exception of a few ardent Dietz sympathizers like Roese, the story began to die.

On February 14, 1907, headlines in the *Osceola Sun* read:

HELP IN A GOOD CAUSE
Readers of the Sun are Asked to Contribute
to Relief of John F. Dietz
SUPPLIES OF ALL KINDS ARE NEEDED
... John F. Dietz is worthy of your aid if ever a man was
worthy. No man in the United States is more patriotic or has
higher ideals of life than he; no man is a better citizen, a
kinder father, a more loving husband, a truer friend than he.

The supplies were delivered during a March thaw. On April 5, Graham left, claiming his mother was worried he might become involved in the battle and be gunned down by the militia. In late April, the cows wandered off. John heard men hollering and driving the cows down the tote road. He gave chase and the would-be rustlers all frantically took to the woods.

Uncle Will visited. The tax problem was settled once and then it cropped up again. "More mill subterfuge," John said simply. They had the gold. They would never relent.

Uncle Will had purchased the Weisenbach homestead. The little German had been sentenced to twelve years in prison for aiding John in shooting at the first mill posse almost three years earlier.

"It's a ruse!" John shouted at his brother. "Don't you understand the way the mills work yet? They gave him that sentence to try to frighten me. Valentine isn't in prison. He's working hand and fist with the mills now. He's brought more than one group around here trying to bushwhack me."

"I was at the trial, John," Will said. He was as firm as John, yet careful. If he even hinted at being in opposition, John screamed betrayal. "They sent Valentine to Waupun. He's there."

"The hell he is!" John shouted.

"You'd argue with the damn sun," William snapped. He shook his head helplessly to Hattie. John was John, there was nothing William could do to alter nature.

"Myra, why don't you try that phonograph out?" William said. "Just give it a few cranks and you'll hear some real recorded songs. Something pleasant to listen to around here."

"One pleasant sound would be the creak of your wagon wheels disappearing around the bend," John said.

William ignored the remark.

While Myra and the boys worked at setting up the phonograph Uncle Will had delivered, William stood beside Hattie at the kitchen table and poured himself a cup of coffee and buttered a piece of corn bread. He spoke in a low voice that was partially drowned by the tinny sounds of the song *Red Bird* from the hand-cranked record player. "There's talk of a log jobber named Moses hauling those logs by steam hauler over to the Flambeau river. I'm sure he'll be offering a good settlement. I don't know how, but we have to get John to accept. Either that or you're going to end up with nothing."

"The Lord will provide." Hattie looked at Will's hard, dark eyes then quickly looked away. Will was with her, she understood, and yet she pushed him and put herself hard at John's side.

For a heartbeat anger flashed in the form of muscles clenching in William's face. But then he gained control. "Well, I've tried. It is your life." He moved off towards the children.

Hattie lowered her head in shame. How could she explain? There had been twenty-five years between her and John. Hard times. She knew no other way.

"You two whispering secrets behind my back?" John suddenly demanded. He was leaned back in his rocker with his feet propped on a trunk. "I won't stand for it in my own house."

Hattie lashed out with all the fury of a winter blizzard. "Don't you dare yell at me, John Dietz. I've stood at your side through thick and thin and I don't need your suspicions now."

"Then why the hell the whispering behind my back?"

"Will's your brother," Hattie yelled in a voice that stopped the children cold. They'd seldom heard their mother as impassioned as this. "He's on your side, same as I am. But all you see are lies. Will thinks the mills are going to offer a settlement, a good one. And he doesn't think you'll accept."

"Well, at least he's right about one thing," John sneered. "Is that what you're doing now, Will? Working for the mills? Bringing their offers? Taking gold from robber barons and stabbing your own brother in the back? Is that your game?" Spittle flew with the force of John's shouts. "Is that why you came out here all dressed up and nice and polite? You're a spy delivering messages for the mill."

William quietly reached for his coat. "I'd best be going now."

"Yeah, you go," John railed. "Report back I did not budge an inch. Dip your hands in those satchels of gold."

"I'll get your team, Uncle Will," Clarence said.

"I'll help," Leslie added. Both boys were eager to escape the house.

"Goodbye, Hattie. Thanks for the meal. As usual it was superb. Children. Myra." He hugged the young girl briefly, donned his hat and, without looking at his brother, took his leave.

"You boys watch yourselves now," William said as he climbed onto the springboard. "The law has warrants in all your names, even your mother and Myra. I don't think they can prove anything, but if they caught you alone they'd certainly try. You stay close here. Be kind to your sister. She's in the prime of her life and life is passing her by. She feels that. You can see it in her eyes. And don't go anywhere without your pa. No one's going to try anything if they're looking eye-to-eye with John."

"Is there really going to be a settlement, Uncle Will?" Clarence asked.

"There'll be an offer. After that I don't know." William sighed. "It's up to John. There's nothing more I can do." He clucked to his horse and the animal took off at a slow controlled trot.

In May of 1907, after many months isolated on the farm, John told Clarence to fetch his semi-automatic Luger pistol. The two of them were going to town.

"Yes, Pa," Clarence said obediently. There was no hint of opposition. He promised Johnny, Helen and Stanley candy, and Myra ribbons and yarn, a jackknife for Leslie. They hooked Old Tom to the wagon and set out on their way.

Just that week Roese had written in his paper and then informed John by letter that the now Sawyer County Sheriff Clark was attempting to form a new posse to go after John.

"He'll never get the men," John said to Clarence on the ride into town. "Van Alstyne said no one would volunteer. So then the Sawyer County slaves did the corporate bidding and voted to increase the reward on my head to one thousand dollars." John chuckled as if in pleasure at the board rumblings. "You watch, today there won't be a single soul that will take them up on that reward."

The walls of the spring-greening forest seemed to fade. Clarence understood, John was going to town precisely because of the increased reward and news of the posse. John would spite them all. Clarence felt the bulge of the pistol in his coat pocket. He'd simply been dragged along as part of the bait.

Simply entering the muddy streets of Winter, the Dietz men created a stir. People pointed and stared. Heads appeared at windows. Their every move was watched. They dined in the friendly confines of the Phelan Hotel with its blue-checkered table clothes. Clarence sat silently while John conversed with men across the room, offering up opinions about the weather, the growing season ahead, baiting people to show their colors and speak up about the mills. No one did.

In June of 1907 a man named Moses started to call at the Dietz farm. "I'll tell you straight and I'll tell you honest," William Moses said to John. "I'm an independent log jobber from Northfield, Minnesota. I sign contracts with Weyerhaeuser. They own those logs now. We want to make settlement, move those logs by steam hauler cross country to the Flambeau River." Moses was a wiry, tough man with a thick moustache and curly hair, both of which were heavily frosted with grey. He was also a patient man, which was fortunate, for on his first visit John roared off on a too familiar diatribe against the mills.

"Great chow, Mrs. Dietz," Moses said as he stood to take his leave. His only argument with John had been that he had no argument with John. He was bidding independently to move the logs to the mills. The logs that had settled on John's land were John's, he said. "Must be a hundred thousand board feet. Yours to do with what you want. Build a mansion for Mrs. Dietz. I want to work with you, John. Reach a settlement you can live with. Let your family resume normal lives. I can get those indictments and warrants quashed."

Moses, a look-the-man-in-the-eye and get-the-job-done contractor, immediately realized his mistake. John had the grin of a Cheshire cat after eating a fish. "The mills can do all that? Command the law to come after me and then command them to stop? Why it must be nice that the mills have so much power they can instruct the principals of justice to respond exactly as it pleases the mills. Just set out your satchels of gold. Buy yourself a judge. Is that how you got Judge Parish to issue those twenty-thousand dollar injunctions placed against my wife's homestead?"

Without backing away, Moses attempted to explain. The mills would not pursue their civil claims. Naturally, criminal warrants would have to be answered — if ever served.

John only hooted with more derision.

As soon as he gracefully could, Moses ended the argument and took his leave. But he'd return, he promised. "Give you some time to think over what you need," he said to John, and immediately thereafter gave a knowing look to Hattie.

The first meeting had not been a success, Moses concluded. But he had met John Dietz, got a measure of the man. He'd seen the children, the woman Hattie; there was leverage there, at least so he believed. He'd also work on that editor, that Roese who presented himself as John's fraternal brother in the "Cause." This would take time. He had time. He had to push a road cross-country to the Flambeau River. He had a promised contract for close to fifty thousand dollars to move those logs. Moses knew men. Dealt with all kinds. Even stubborn men like John Dietz. Sooner or later he'd move those logs. At least so Moses believed.

During the sweltering dog days of August, 1907, with horse flies and deer flies swarming in the forest, and green algae scum forming on backwaters, Moses visited the Dietz family once again. Moses sat in a straight-backed wooden chair while John sat in his rocker. "Well, John, it seems as if you've won."

John stared, waiting for the punch line. Moses smiled, realizing Dietz was not stupid. "The company is giving in. They've conceded your wages for the two years at Price Dam. They'll pay you cash, a thousand dollars and a hundred thousand board feet of those big logs. House-building logs. Mrs. Dietz could have that house she spoke of. You drop all your contentions against the mills and they'll drop all their contentions against you."

For perhaps ten seconds John considered the matter. Hattie, working ten feet away at the kitchen table, had her head cocked. The leathered lines of John's face scowled and then suddenly broke into a grin. "Haw, drop my contentions after I've been shot at, my son shot in the head, my daughter poisoned, my livestock poisoned, my cattle run off, my family almost starved. The mills don't want much from me, do they? First they try to kill a man and then they want him to apologize because they missed their shot."

"John, the mills don't want anything from you. I'm trying to work a contract to move those logs. The company, myself, we want to pay you your back wages. Move those logs before they rot all the way through. That's all. If you need more to cover your wages, we could go higher, say seventeen hundred dollars for your wages, plus all that timber."

Both men heard Hattie suck in her breath.

John jerked to his feet. He shouted, "People know you mills. They know me. You'd ask me to sell my birthright and betray their trust. Do you think I'm as small as all that?"

"No, John," Moses said quietly. "All I'm doing is offering to pay wages for what you've earned. Nothing more."

Moses stood. "Many thanks for the hospitality, Mrs. Dietz." He donned his grey fedora. He met Hattie's gaze, a firm, forthright look as if the two of them had somehow reached an understanding without talking to each other. Now all they had to do was induce John to go along.

For a long time after Moses departed, John and Hattie were silent. Hattie worked furiously, slamming pots and pans as she worked over the hot stove at the table, making blackberry jam and sauce. John leaned back in his rocker and watched her slave. Gradually a smile crept underneath his thick moustache. He rubbed a callused hand where the hair was thinning on top of his head. "You got words, Hattie, they might as well get said. Otherwise I think you're going to burst."

"We should take that settlement," Hattie said. She was firm. She straightened and he'd her back, wincing against the gnawing pain of rheumatism. There had been too many years of too much work. "We should get something out of this. All these years trapped out here, the children unable to go on with their lives."

"The children get on," John groused. "They don't want."

He walked to Hattie's side and stared at her plump red hands with the fingernails chewed down to the nub. "I'm the people's champion. Alfred said that. You want me to sell them out?"

Hattie hesitated, knowing she must say the exact right words. "You're not betraying the people, John. The money is for your wages. The children deserve at least that much. You have to think of your family."

"The family is all I ever think of. Why do you think I sacrifice?" John yelled. "Why do you think I'm doing this?"

"For yourself and you know it," Hattie shouted right back. "Have we not stood by you all these years? Risked our lives the same as you? Clarence, Myra, Leslie, they are old enough to start lives of their own. But they cannot."

"I'm not stopping them," John snapped. "Any time they want to leave, they can leave."

"I've worked my fingers to the bone, John. I've slaved. I'm tired of being poor. Take the money. Take the logs. For your wages. At least get something out of the mills." Hattie breathed deeply, gasping for air. "Something, please."

John angrily donned his hat and went outside. He stood beside the cabin. He tugged at the sapling flagpole to check its firmness then gazed up the crooked pole at the stars and stripes moving listlessly under a hint of breeze. The flag was becoming tattered, weathered. He'd have to write Roese and tell him to send another. John cleared his throat and spat to one side. Up near the barn Leslie and Clarence were repairing the hay wagon. Helen, Stanley and Johnny were playing tag among the piles of giant logs where the flowage used to lie. The spring posse Sheriff Clark had been attempting to gather had never made a show. Few reporters stopped by. Newspaper accounts of his fight were just as sparse. He'd stood for their cause and then the people had turned their backs. Just like Weisenbach, and then his brother Will.

But not me, John thought. He'd never sign a damn thing.

* * *

"There's your money, John," Moses said. "Seventeen hundred and seventeen dollars for your wages. And then we'll set flags to mark the logs lying on your land." Moses stood at the kitchen table, the money piled in stacks before him.

Hattie, John and the six children had gathered behind him as had his brother William who had, by chance, arrived at the same time as the logger.

Moses stood back. He'd brought the money in small bills to make it seem like more. After all, the Dietz family had never had much. He could see their eyes on the money, the wonderment that they could actually receive so much, three to four years of wages for a laboring man.

"I've told you before, I'm not going to sign any agreements," John said. He was defiant. And ready to move in either direction, Moses realized.

He spoke quietly as if soothing a wild animal. "You don't have to sign anything, John. That's money for your wages,

Some of the logs held up by John Dietz at Cameron Dam. From left, Leslie, Clarence, Harry Roese, Alfred E. Roese and family friend Matt Egstad.

that's all. I'll leave it there. I know you won't bother my men when they come to move those logs. If you or your two boys there want, I've got work on my crew. It'll be right here close by. They can live at home."

Both Leslie and Clarence perked up at the offer. A job right here next to home where they could earn their own money. Hope gleamed in their eyes and their poised postures.

"You want my boys to get out in the woods where they can be ambushed by the mills? Not likely," John snorted. He did not notice the sagging expression on the faces of his two oldest sons.

More talk could lead to disaster, Moses realized. He looked at Hattie but she would not look him in the face. He admired the woman for that. She may have argued with John in private, but in public she stood as firm as a rock. Moses reached for his hat. "I must get moving. I'll leave the money there, John. I know you're a man of your word."

John scowled, clearly uncertain. On impulse Moses he'd out his hand. "Congratulations, John. You've held out and won."

John's blue eyes had narrowed. He searched Moses's face

for a hint of deceit. "Those wages are for my family," he said. "I give them everything I can." Slowly, as if with a stiffened elbow, his hand came up and gripped that of Moses, briefly, firmly, in John's mind and Moses's completely sealing the deal.

Moses made his departure. Before the family could fully comprehend their new wealth, John turned on Will. "You son of a bitch," he snarled. "You stand there all that time and watch me grovel. You came with him to move me. You're in league with them sure as hell."

"John, you're seeing crooked again," William retorted. He was a stocky, moustached man, hard, but easygoing unless pushed. Stories circulated in Rice Lake how then Sheriff William Dietz had once single-handedly quelled a mob of two hundred drunken lumberjacks.

"Don't lie to me," John yelled. He was purple with his rage. "You two arrive at the same time. I saw you talking together walking down here from the barn."

"John, Will's helped us all he could," Hattie said. "He's gone to court, paid our taxes, wrote letters."

John whirled like a bear to the attack. "I saw you pleading as well, turning your back on me. Putting me on the spot in front of outsiders."

"I'd best be going," Will said quietly. One more exchange and he knew he and John would be trading blows. He gathered his things, nodded his goodbyes to all but John and slowly walked to the door.

"Go, collect your gold. And don't you come back... ever!" John said as if to hammer home the last nail in the coffin.

For maybe three or four seconds William hesitated. The six children and Hattie held back, silent, watchful. He looked at his brother, hoping for one last plea for reasonableness. But John had moved into that narrowly defined world no explanation could penetrate.

"Goodbye," William said simply.

"And don't come back," John responded.

And then Will was gone, for good. One more link with the outside, Hattie thought. Although they did have the money just as she wanted, at the moment it gave her little joy.

That evening John wrote his public, informing them the way things really were:

"On June 10, 1907 one W.E. Moses made his appearance on Thornapple, claiming to be a direct agent for F. Weyerhaeuser. Every time Moses comes here he has some excuse that he is doing his best. He invited our whole family up to his camp for dinner on one Sunday. If we had gone I am satisfied that when we returned we would have found our home in ashes. The fact is Moses hasn't tried to do any of the hundred and one things he has promised, but is simply trying to cut our throats with a feather.

On September 16, 1907 he came here and paid me my wages, $1,717.00, for work at Price Dam, also saying that within sixty days he would have everything settled and cleared up so that we would be safe to go and come as we pleased, and all the time his hirelings have been sneaking around the field looking for a sure shot at us...

Two weeks before Moses paid me my wages he scattered a lot of money on our table saying there is $1,720.00 for your wages if you will sign a contract that removes all bones of contention. I told Moses that I couldn't accept any wages by selling my birthright and that his company owed me $8,000.00 for sluicing according to law ...

For four long years myself and my family have been the targets for conspiracy, blackmail and bullets of the land pirates and timber wolves ... If such a state of affairs is allowed to continue, the stars and stripes should be hung at half mast to mourn the death of our nation, for the grasping tentacles of the corporation has liberty by the throat."

"Sounds good, Pa," Leslie said. He was puzzled and hesitant over the dual meaning, the acceptance and denial of John's capitulation. "You didn't back down an inch."

"Good. That's the main thing people should know."

Again the family grew silent. Hattie sat with her darning needle. John reread his letter. Clarence lay on the floor with Stanley and Johnny and helped them connect the three cars from a hand-carved train he'd made. Leslie lay on his bunk and watched. Myra and Helen sat at the table opposite John and paged through a catalogue.

"I'm going to have a dress like that some day," Helen said. It did not occur to ask her mother, because they'd never had money for extras in the past. "And wear a big bonnet just like that Sara. Which dress do you want? Ma said we could choose any dress we like." Helen was excited. Leslie peered over her shoulder as Myra made her choice.

"Why would you get that?" he said in a shrill voice. "You trying to be fancy? You don't have anyplace to wear it anyhow."

"Didn't I tell you you talk too much, Leslie?" Clarence said. He rose from the floor and peered over Myra's shoulder. He rested his hands on her shoulders. "That's a pretty dress, Myra. And with you wearing it, it would be prettier yet."

Myra placed her hand over Clarence's and leaned her head back on his chest. "Yes, but Leslie's right. Where would I go?"

"You kids want to go some place, just speak up and we'll go," John said. "Osseo, Bangor, Rice Lake. We'll go tomorrow morning. Your mother can stay here and tend the farm."

"Yeah," Leslie said. He was enthusiastic, trying to make amends. "You should order that dress and then we could go to town, really show those people how to dress."

"I don't want to show people how to dress," Myra said. "I just want to wear nice things."

Hattie struggled to her feet. She was bent forward, hand massaging her back. "I swear, every day this rheumatism gets worse. Time for bed. We're low on kerosene and I don't want to run out." She gently closed the catalogue in front of Myra. "Tomorrow we'll make out a big order. The boys and John can have new Sunday suits. Helen and Myra can each order a new dress."

"Two dresses," John suggested.

"One," Hattie snapped. "We don't want to spend our money all at once."

"Will you order something, Ma?" Myra asked.

Hattie shrugged. "Maybe. I need some new underwear."

"And a dress," Myra said. "You deserve at least one new dress."

"Maybe," Hattie allowed. "It must be ten years since I've had a completely new dress." She turned and trailed John and Johnny into their tiny bedroom. In a few minutes their light went out and the caustic odor of kerosene smoke drifted into the room.

"Everything seems the same," Myra said.

"It'll be all right," Clarence replied.

"I thought the settlement would change things," Myra said.

"You shouldn't have thought that, Myra. Pa's the same now as he was before." He patted her arm. "Go to bed. I'll turn out the lamp."

"That's all?" Myra asked. "Just turn out the lamp and go to bed? Tomorrow will be the same as today, except no one will visit."

"There's nothing anyone can do," Clarence said. "We're lucky we got this money. Although I don't think we'll see Uncle Will for a long, long time. We just have to bide our time. Try to make things out for the best."

The two briefly squeezed hands, a sign of mutual affection. Really, Myra thought, it was all they had. She paused and kissed Stanley's forehead and then patted Leslie's cheek. "What are you doing?" Leslie protested and pulled back.

"Just saying good night, Les."

Myra went to the attached school room where Helen was already in bed. She undressed without a light. In a few weeks, the teacher would arrive and then she and Helen would have to move back into the living room with the boys. And then the snows would fly. And darkness would fall early. And they'd lie for long hours in bed and wait for the night to pass.

Myra crawled into bed beside Helen. She patted Helen's side. "Good night, Sis." Helen did not stir. Myra turned away. She closed her eyes and cried.

**PRESIDENT TAKES HAND
IN OIL FIGHT
Roosevelt is Determined
That all the Facts
Shall be Made Public -
His Action is
Independent of the House
AFTER THE TRUSTS**

**JOHN DIETZ BLOWED UP
BY DYNAMITE
Injuries Not Severe**

THIRD PASTURE

Now we come to a frisky lot, the "Labor Union" editors. You know down in Texas a weed called "Loco" is sometimes eaten by a steer and produces derangement of the brain that makes the steer "batty" or crazy.

Many of these editors are "Locoed" from hate of anyone who will not instantly obey the demands of a labor union, and it is the universal habit of such writers to go straight into a system of personal vilifications, manufacturing any sort of falsehood through which to vent their spleen...

When they go far enough with their libels, is it harsh for us to get judgment against them and have our lawyers watch for a chance to attach money due them from others? (For they are usually irresponsible.)

Keep your eye out for the "Locoed" editor.

CHAPTER XI

Relative to prior years, 1908 started out to be a very good year for the Dietz family. They had carry-over supplies from Roese's donations; money from guiding and an upswing in local markets for their produce and beef; money donated by sympathizers; and of course the sizeable settlement from Moses. They purchased new clothes, a springboard, horses, additional beef cows. They took occasional train trips to visit relatives and friends in Rice Lake, Cameron, Osseo and even members of the Hunt Club in Bangor. Mill agents and sheriff posses no longer trekked out to the farm. Moses, always careful to be friendly and generous, brought in a Phoenix steel-tracked steam hauler and crew and began hauling the logs. Visitors were more frequent, their lives a little less isolated than they had been before. While the settlement with Moses brought a feeling of triumph, in reality little had changed. The year's deadly conclusion made that abundantly clear.

Jay Gates was the first Dietz family school teacher John did not suspect of being an agent for the mills — at least not at first. Jay arrived from Rice Lake in the fall of 1907. He was a tall, dark-haired man with dark eyes and moustache. He received $40.00 a month for teaching the Dietz children. He seemed not at all frightened of John and was quick to wield the edge of a ruler if Stanley, Helen or Johnny acted up in class. "Jay could jerk a boy out of his boots faster than Pa can dynamite a stump," Myra said. She was taken by Jay's handsome looks.

"Did you ever feel that life is passing you by?" Myra once asked Jay. Her voice quavered with nervousness that she dared to be so personal. "It's out there, the big cities, theaters, all those department stores and restaurants. People carry on and here we are way out on the Thornapple River. I just keep getting older. Sometimes I could burst."

Jay stood, towering over Myra. She backed away. "Why don't you move away?" Jay asked softly. "The only way you're going to get life is reach out."

Myra stood her ground. He loomed. She felt terribly warm. His hands touched her shoulders. His face bent to hers, bringing his musky smell of manliness and lips that were surprisingly soft and warm. Her heart raced. In truth Jay was the first man she'd ever really kissed.

Someone entered the outer cabin, or at least so Myra imagined. She jerked away. "I have to go," she gasped and fled. Whatever would Pa say, she thought? And Leslie and Clarence? After that she was very careful she and Jay were never alone.

Washing clothes during winter was the one task Hattie disliked the most. Myra and the boys carried bucket after bucket of water from the spring, along with which she melted snow in the number three galvanized tub that covered the entire top of the Monarch wood cook stove. Once the water was hot, she'd wear her knuckles raw scouring the clothes against the metal-ribbed washboard. Then she and Myra would twist the garment over the grey wash water and then swirl it in a second tub of rinse water and then twist again, squeezing out as much water as they could before Myra and Helen took the wicker basket of wet clothes and hung them in the frozen outdoors.

Eight people to wash for, Hattie thought. The rheumatoid pain gnawed at her knuckles and shoulders and in the lower reaches of her back. Hattie rested her weight on the washboard and tub. Johnny, Helen and Stanley were yelling and squealing as they chased each other in and under the boys' bunk beds. Stars flashed. Hattie closed her eyes.

"Ma, are you all right?" Myra asked as she entered the cabin with an empty wicker basket.

"This rheumatism," Hattie started to complain. She held her side. "I think I have appendicitis also."

"Jay's pulling more stumps," Myra said, ignoring her mother's familiar complaints. She swirled a mound of dark clothes in the now grey rinse water. The children squealed. They had so little privacy.

"Jay's so good at it," Myra continued without looking at Hattie. "He knows exactly how to line them up."

Hattie paused. She'd noticed Myra's attraction and could see her hesitancy, her uncertainty when dealing with girls and boys her own age. She was still young. Hattie prayed there would be time. "Mr. Gates is your teacher."

"Yes. I know," Myra said in a meek voice. "I think he found a girlfriend in Winter. That's why he walks all the way back and forth to town every weekend."

"He's only been gone the last two," Hattie pointed out. "He's a very friendly man."

"Yes, I know," Myra said with deep sadness.

"What is wrong with you? You have no ties on Mr. Gates," Hattie scolded. "You never showed an interest when he showed an interest in you. Here, grab an end," Hattie ordered.

Myra twisted a pair of wool pants, unwilling to play the game of trying to be stronger than her mother. Besides, she could see Hattie wince as if pain shot up her arms. Myra took another basket of clothes outside to hang up and dry. Or freeze, Hattie thought. Later she'd have to hang frozen clothes all over the cabin to complete the arduous washing task. She slumped into a wooden chair, driven down by the gnawing pain of gout, rheumatism and who knew what else was eating her alive. The old refrain returned — a man can work from sun to sun, a woman's work is never done.

A few weeks later, without saying a word, Hattie began her fast. For breakfast she drank two cups of Postum. The others were half done eating before they noticed. Clarence was, of course, the first to notice her altered behavior.

"So you're going to diet," John groused after Hattie explained herself. The crinkling at the corners of his eyes alerted his children to a smile. "Might be a good thing. Bed was plenty warm last winter — although a mite more crowded than I like."

Jay Gates laughed uproariously, much louder than the others. The looks quickly reminded him he was not part of their group and he became red with embarrassment.

Newspaper editor Alfred E. Roese later pressed Hattie to write of her fast and then published Hattie's letter in the *Osceola Sun:*

> My sufferings became so terrible I could not sleep nights and I made up my mind that it was do or die, therefore, on the morning of May 18, 1908 I began fasting. For breakfast I drank two cups of Postum; for dinner and supper I drank tea and a generous quantity of milk therein. For the first ten days it was the hardest for me to go without food, and I drank several glasses of milk each day. Then milk became distasteful to me and the remainder of the time I lived on Postum and tea, with a little milk added to each cup. I ate no food for 56 days...
>
> When I was in Winter in March I weighed 220 pounds but as I have no way of being weighed I cannot give my exact weight but should say I have lost 50 to 60 pounds. My health is better than it has been for eight years, for which I thank God with all my heart.

Even the children noticed the change in Hattie. She was more energetic, more accessible, less given to complaints about her various aches and pains. "A regular queen of the Thornapple," John said on the first day Hattie again deigned to dine with the family. He took her shoulders and, before Hattie could withdraw, kissed her on the lips in front of the entire family. "I'd like to see any one of those fat corporation wives do what you just did. And all by yourself."

It was mid-July before Hattie decided to end her fast. Jay Gates had taken his leave. The men had the rutabagas, potatoes and onions in the ground and a new hay field under plow. The only contact with the mills had been Moses and his crew working on dragging out the cut logs. Newspaper articles had trickled down to the vehement opposition, the press bureau of the lumber mills who viewed John as an anarchist; and the stalwart supporters such as Roese in Osceola and Broughton in Fond du Lac. The talk within the Dietz household was directed towards dragging out their own logs, bringing in a portable sawmill and building themselves a large, two-story 30-foot-by-30-foot plank house. But that summer John never moved a log.

One day Leslie talked with Moses's teamster, Walter Bonk, who sometimes delivered hay and feed to the Dietz farm in Moses's ongoing efforts to maintain peace. Were there any job prospects, Leslie asked? "Sure," Walter told him. "Moses can always use another hand. Go talk to foreman Murphy."

Later Leslie and Clarence were working on the dirt turnpike just across the river from where they had hauled in rock in an effort to build a crossing they could utilize during high water. Myra carried out a sack of sandwiches and the three sat on a fallen log in the shade beside the narrow turnpike. A red-tailed hawk circled nearby searching for field mice. Clarence plucked at blackberries growing beside the road. Leslie mentioned the job prospect to Clarence and Myra. "What do you think Pa will say?"

"Everything's going so good," Myra said. "Why do you want to do this now?"

Leslie tossed a pebble across the road. He was as tall as Clarence now, only more stocky like his father. "I'm getting bored. I was thinking of moving south, down to Milwaukee."

"Moses contracted with Weyerhaeuser," Clarence said. "Pa doesn't trust either one." He was carefully noncommittal, for if Leslie stood against John, Clarence knew he'd have to stand at Leslie's side. "I'd be with you, Les, but not so hard Pa would force me out as well. It'd be unfair to leave Myra here alone."

"You better ask Ma before you ask Pa," Myra advised. Myra had been happy these past weeks. The editor of the nearby *Sawyer County Gazette* at Radisson was a Dietz sympathizer and had invited Myra to write a weekly column so people could get the facts about the goings-on at Cameron Dam. At first Myra had been excited, envisioning the prospects of her column expanding to papers throughout the Midwest.

Leslie picked up his hand-cranked phonograph he'd lugged out to the work site. He thumbed through a small stack of records he'd carried. "I counted my records the other day," he said. "I have a hundred and five."

"Pa catches you out here listening to music while you're supposed to work, he'll kick that apart," Clarence advised.

"I'll be careful," Leslie muttered with lack of real concern.

"You going to ask Pa about work?" Clarence asked.

"Nah," Leslie said. He'd already surrendered the idea. "He'd just get mad and I'd have to explain. And that would get him mad again." He set the record on the turntable and began to wind the crank.

The rustle of clothing drew their attention to two teenage boys and two girls gingerly walking down the isolated road. "What are they sneaking after?" Clarence asked.

"Hi there," Leslie said in a loud, gruff voice.

"It's the Dietzes," one of the boys yelled. One of the girls and the two boys whirled and fled as if being pursued by a bear. The remaining girl froze, her eyes wide, her face puffed and red with panic. One of the boys turned back and seized her arm. "Mary, quick before they get you." The girl ran then, holding her ankle-length skirt high, showing her bloomers.

Clarence, Myra and Leslie sat quietly. Long after the four adventurers were gone they could hear their laughter and loud talk of relief that they'd actually crept up on the Dietzes and then escaped.

"I should have scared the bastards really good," Leslie mumbled. He cranked his record player and tipped the needle in place. The tinny strains of *Camptown Races* wafted through the wilderness. The three children sat in silence, heads bowed.

* * *

That fall John blew himself up with dynamite. He'd lit the fuse to several sticks stuffed under a stump. A half-hour later the dynamite had yet to explode. John gingerly approached the stump. The dynamite exploded, tossing him ten feet into the air. He was dirty and had ringing in his ears and a trickle of blood from his nostrils.

That evening at supper John still talked about his escape. "If the Lord wanted me dead, He had His chance there. I bought that dynamite and fuse from Moses's bunch. I'll bet they fixed that fuse just trying to get me killed."

No one spoke or contradicted him. "That's the same as going against the Lord — going against what He desires."

Family member busied themselves with their food.

The early fall proceeded without other major incidents. After half a dozen tries, Myra stopped writing her newspaper column. "There's nothing to write about," she complained.

The family continued to work the scrub farm, pulling stumps, digging potatoes, gradually breaking more ground. Markets opened for their livestock and produce. John and the boys occasionally visited town. Visitors to the farm were fairly frequent. A cruiser named Bert Horel stopped for an hour. Elliot, a building contractor from Duluth and an ardent Dietz sympathizer, came in early November and stayed on for deer season. The new teacher, Asa Dewey arrived. The Bangor Hunt Club camped nearby for deer season and once invited the family and once joined the family for supper.

Hattie still carried more than two thousand dollars, the accumulation of many mailed donations and the payment from Moses, in a tin can concealed in her closet. Even though another deep-woods winter loomed and they had yet to saw logs for her house, she thought it had been a good year.

Next year, John had promised, she'd have herself a house, a mansion as big as any owned by the lumber barons.

And then the black diphtheria struck. It took Leslie down first with a fever, sore throat and a tightness in his chest.

"He just has a chest cold from all the wet and snow of deer season," Hattie said. She scurried about the cabin making an onion poultice to lay on Leslie's chest. She induced him to gargle with kerosene for his sore throat. He almost gagged. By morning Leslie was worse.

"Bad cold, he better stay home today," John declared in the predawn hours. He turned the kerosene lamp up high and gazed down on his son. "Couple days, he'll be back."

"I'll get you a big buck," Clarence said to his brother. He patted Leslie's shoulder, hefted his rifle and went out to join John and Elliot and walk over to the hunt club camp.

Leslie became worse. His hands fluttered nervously. His breathing became ragged and he complained of something clogging his throat. In midmorning Hattie moved Leslie into her and John's bed.

Toward noon, nine-year-old Stanley came down sick. Almost instantly, before the fever took hold and his throat became raw, Stanley could hardly breathe. Hattie used a spoon as a tongue depressant and peered in Stanley's throat. A filmy grey membrane at the back of his throat confirmed her worst suspicions. "Diphtheria," she breathed.

"Myra," Hattie called. "Run for your father. I think they're hunting the flats and that swamp south of the river." She pulled Myra into the outer room. "Tell him Leslie and Stanley have diphtheria. Tell him Stanley can hardly breathe."

By the time Myra could locate John and the men returned, it was late afternoon. Hattie had attempted to pack the two boys in towels filled with snow, but the snow melted and wet the bed and Leslie tossed the towels aside. John went into the room where the two boys lay side by side. He took Stanley's small hand in his. The lad was on fire and his chest heaved with each effort of drawing a rasping breath.

John knelt beside the bed. His eyes filled with tears. "I shot you a buck today, Stanley. A nice eight pointer. You get well now and your mother will make you that buckskin jacket just like she promised. "

Stanley managed to nod. He struggled to speak but could not. For some time John remained kneeling and stroking Stanley's hair. Eventually he stood and strode into the outer room.

The visiting G. E. Elliot had donned his winter coat. "I'll ride for a doctor," he said.

"You'll do no such thing," John said. "This is my family, my affair."

"John, please," Hattie begged. "Remember Harry? He was exactly the same." Hattie's eyes were red from crying.

"Yes, Pa," Myra added. "Please send for a doctor, please."

The lines of John's jaw worked as if under a strain. "How many times must I tell you, a doctor cannot change what's meant to be. Besides, do you honestly think a doctor is going to come out here to the Dietz farm? No." He shook his head with deep bitterness. "The boys are in God's hands. All we can do is pray."

Myra turned to Clarence, pleading with her eyes. Clarence

shook his head and grimaced as if about to cry. He was the oldest boy, the one suppose to take the lead. But against John he was as helpless as the others.

Young Helen came out of the bedroom and dipped another glass of water from the pail. A twelve-year-old girl, she stopped in front of John. Her eyes were clear, her voice firm.

"Father, can I walk to town to get a doctor?"

John patted his daughter's head. "You go stay by Stanley's side. He'll be all right. I'm sure."

Helen sighed with exasperation. "Yes, Father," she said politely.

As she had throughout the day, Helen remained constantly at Stanley's side. He was the sibling closest to her age, her friend, her constant companion in everything she did.

"If you get better, Stanley, I'll give you my sled. You can use it whenever you want. I promise."

Stanley's eyelids fluttered. They were caked with thick crystals of dried mucus. Helen took a damp cloth and gently wiped them clean. Even with her touch he strained for each breath with a gurgling effort like using a straw sucking the last drops of water out of the bottom of a glass. The heat of her brother's skin surprised her. Each time she touched him it was worse. He was burning inside, she thought with sudden terror. She could see the flames. As she'd seen Myra and Hattie do, Helen lay a damp cloth on his head. She took a glass of water from the cluttered bureau. Putting her hand behind his wet hair, she tried to hold him up while she forced water into his mouth.

"Stanley, please. Drink," she begged. "Put out the fire. Please." Her voice broke.

Leslie, lying tight at Stanley's side in his parent's bed, groaned. "Helen, he can't. He can barely breathe."

"He has to," Helen sobbed. "He's burning." She lay his head back down. His hand groped for hers. His eyes opened enough to show the black gleam of his pupils looking at her as his fingers tightened on hers. Stanley's breathing deepened and there was a croak as if he could not clear his throat. His thin chest heaved and then he seemed to sigh as if clearing all the air from his lungs. He lay still.

Helen stood silent, holding her brother's hand, still looking at the dark of his eyes. Something had changed. A terrible fear froze her mind as she stared at his face, realizing the fire inside Stanley's body had died.

The sour stench of feces filled the room. Leslie, lying at Stanley's side and blurry-eyed and barely conscious, looked at his brother then raised his head. "Maaaa," he wailed like a lost lamb crying for its ewe.

Hattie, exhausted after two days without sleep, rushed to the bedroom door. Her eyes were clear, seeing the world as it came. Only her shoulders sagged as if pressed by some unyielding weight. She reached for Helen but the little girl shrugged her away. "Pa said he'd be all right."

"The Lord giveth and the Lord taketh away," John muttered. "Don't you look at me with those eyes." But there were tears in his eyes. He tried to take Helen and hold her close but she pulled away and ran.

"No, John," Hattie pleaded when John made to move after Helen. John relented. His shoulders slumped as if in defeat.

That night John built a coffin for his son. Clarence, G. E. Elliot, and some men from the hunt club were over to help. One man rode to Winter to telegraph to Rice Lake for Minister Beaudette to come the next day on the morning train.

Hattie and Myra took care of the body, washing Stanley clean, the flesh of Hattie's flesh, running her weathered hands over his thin body, filled with images of two other children dead. They dressed the young boy in his Sunday best. Nine months a mother bore her child, then she fed him at her breast, changed him, bathed him, patched his cuts and scrapes and watched him grow. And now he lay dead, just as part of her lay dead, the taking of a woman's life, piece by piece.

And all the while Leslie remained the same, barely conscious, scarcely able to breathe.

At first light the next morning John trekked with pickax and shovel and broke the frozen ground and dug a small grave on the hillside behind the farm. On Sunday afternoon, November 22, 1908, Minister Beaudette and three other men drove in by wagon and they conducted a small ceremony and placed Stanley in the ground. John tossed in the first shovel of dirt.

After Stanley was buried on the hill behind the house, the

family and guests drifted back to the tiny cabin. The teacher, Dewey, had sat with Leslie, who had not improved. Myra and Hattie prepared hot coffee and a lunch for the guests crowded into the tiny, dark cabin. Helen disappeared, crawling in behind some boxes under one of the bunks. Myra tried to coax her out.

"Let her be," Hattie said. She turned and spoke to Minister Beaudette, "I never thought I'd face more disaster like this. I don't understand. What have I done wrong?" Her voice was dull, in a strange monotone without inflection. Her eyes were fixed, strangely lacking in focus.

"Stanley's death had nothing to do with you," Beaudette tried to comfort Hattie. He could see his words were not received. "It was God's will. Only He can understand. It's best for us not even to try."

Hattie did not respond.

Because the cabin was so crowded, most of the guests left that night, traveling by sleigh down the dark of a snow-covered road.

By the next morning Leslie was worse. Clarence worked in the frigid cold of the barn peeling the hide off the frozen carcass of one of John's bucks. The deer hung with five others from a rafter pole. He worked steadily, ignoring the numbness in his fingers. His breath billowed white in the freezing air. Myra came out to the barn. She took a knife and pitched in to help cut the attaching membrane and peel down the hide.

"Leslie's still crazy. He's thrashing and yelling. Ma and Pa can hardly hold him down. He acts like he doesn't even know who they are."

Clarence continued to work, using all his strength to pull down great chunks of hide before he had to cut attaching membrane.

"I think if Leslie dies Ma will have a nervous breakdown," Myra continued. "She feels Stanley's death was her fault."

Still Clarence did not reply. He worked harder, sweating in the freezing air. His fingers had lost all feeling.

"Do you think Leslie will die too?" Myra softly asked.

"I don't know," Clarence said.

"Why are you so curt? Do you think Pa should get a doctor?"

Clarence leaned on the deer. He clutched his hands for warmth. "What do you want of me, Sis? I've tried. I've stayed home. I try to help everyone. I'm not going anywhere. I'm not doing anything." He clenched his eyes. Tears of frustration leaked at the corners. "Did you want me to talk to Pa? All right. It won't do any good. Stanley died within one day. Leslie has been like this four days. Maybe a doctor wouldn't matter. Minister Beaudette, Elliot, the hunt club members, they couldn't move Pa. That's my job, huh? All right." He jammed his hunting knife between the deer ribs and stalked toward the cabin.

"Pa, I want to ride for a doctor," Clarence said as soon as he entered the cabin. He looked John directly in the face.

"Please, Father," Myra pleaded as she closed the door behind her. A freezing draft wafted into the room.

"Why would you do that?" John asked. His face was unshaven and drawn as if from great strain.

"Pa, he might die same as Stanley," Clarence pointed out. He was surprised at his complete lack of fear.

"That's God's will, not mine," John said softly.

"That's your belief," Clarence retorted. "A doctor might help."

They could all see the color rise in John's face. His blue eyes swung to Clarence with that hard, piercing look. Only this time Clarence held his ground.

"Are you insinuating something?" John's voice was hard. "Did I not go up there on that hillside and dig my own son's grave with these hands? Did I not build his coffin? Did I not lower the casket in the ground and throw in the dirt?" Tears welled in John's eyes. "Did I not love that boy? Would I not lay down my life if only he could live? I would gladly trade places with Lester. But of course that I cannot do. We can only accept what is our lot." He rose and clasped Clarence's shoulder. "You're the oldest. You set the example for the others. We're a family. We must stick together. I loved Stanley. I love Lester. I love all you kids. But even I cannot change what is foreordained. That is up to the Lord."

"We must do something," Clarence said. His shoulders sagged in acknowledgment of another defeat. He pleaded,

"Please, Pa."

"I'll walk to Bronsteads for whiskey," John said. "Maybe that will help clear the membrane in his throat."

Clarence nodded; at least he had won that.

Two days later G. E. Elliot informed John he was going for a doctor, ignored John's protests and left. But as John had warned, no doctor in Winter could or would make the trip to the Dietz farm. Elliot telegraphed to Rice Lake and two days later Dr. Helgeson arrived. But he was too late. By then Leslie was on the mend. His fever and the membrane clogging his throat broke. He was thin, drained and had lost almost fifteen pounds. He smiled weakly at his mother. "Next time I want to lose weight, Ma, I think I'd rather use your diet." The family laughed.

John knelt beside the bed.

"I suppose you want your bed back," Leslie said. He snuggled deeper. "Just when I was getting comfortable."

John tousled Leslie's hair. "You had us worried, Lester, putting your mother and I through that kind of hell. One more day of rest and then back to your own bunk and back to work."

"Yes, Pa. In the meantime could you bring the gramaphone in here and crank me out a song."

John shook his finger in Leslie's face. "Don't you take advantage, boy." He was mockingly severe. He carried in the gramaphone and cranked Leslie one song and then another, whatever the boy asked. After some time Hattie ushered them all out of the room. Leslie needed to sleep.

"I told you the boy didn't need a doctor," John said. He sat down at the table to write a letter to A. E. Roese:

> We could have got Stanley help, but no one would come from Winter and there wasn't time. They wouldn't come for Leslie either. The mills impede everything we do. It was because of them Stanley died.

He glared, small blue eyes as emotionless as frozen ice. One by one the family members turned away, even Hattie, who felt as worn and exhausted as Leslie appeared. Three children lay dead, Leslie almost. With stiff, wooden movements Hattie laid a blanket and pillow on the floor beside Leslie. She shook off

John's offer to sleep in Leslie's bunk. She pulled the wool blanket up over her shoulders. In the morning there would be work, housecleaning, return to normalcy. Leslie could return to his bunk. She could change the coarse linen on her and John's bed. Tomorrow night she'd lie where Leslie had almost died — and Stanley had.

She stared at the dark. Despite the presence of her family she'd never felt so alone. Her eyes squeezed tightly but there were no more tears. Mercifully, Hattie's mind ceased functioning and she slept, her first sound sleep in eight days, her mind going under the exhaustion as if she had died.

NOT BARRED
FROM SALOONS

Women Can Visit Them as Well as Men, Says Chippewa Falls Judge

---

SHOOTING BY JOHN F. DIETZ
Story Told by Special Wire From Hayward to the Leader Blame is Put Upon the Tough Man, "Hero of Cameron Dam"

FRAGRANT BATHS THAT WILL REMOVE THE SURPLUS TISSUE

In these days when every woman longs to be thin, it is comforting to know that there are baths that reduce the weight and take the flesh off just where you want it taken off. There is a beauty bath which reduces the weight. It is prepared by taking some squares of ammonia and covering them with oil of rose geranium. The whole is now placed in a tub and the hot water is turned on.

The too fleshy beauty seeker is soaked in this hot, sweet, aromatic bath, after which she takes a dip in benzoinated water to tighten the skin and keep it from falling in folds as the fat drifts away.

There is also a very cheap reduction bath which is second to none in the matter of efficiency. Common soap made into a lather and used with lots of hot water has the faculty of washing off the fat. It may be bad for the complexion, but when vigorously used it takes off flesh.

CHAPTER XII

B y September of 1910 the oldest Dietz children, as they were still referred to in the press, were fully grown, young adults. Clarence was 23, Myra 21, and Leslie 20. And yet they all remained bound to the farm and to one another. They visited and vacationed, going for as long as a week to the house of their oldest sister, Florence May, in Rice Lake. And they occasionally journeyed into Winter and stopped at the few reclusive and private neighbors who chose to live in the isolation of the deep North Woods. But they hung there, trapped, issues unresolved. They could not take up permanent jobs, or relations with outsiders and pursue lives of their own.

The years 1909 and the first half of 1910 brought few changes to the Dietz household. Moses and his men continued to work the huge jam of pine logs. No matter how cantankerous John would be, Moses refused to argue, acting as if he was John's friend, even bringing in documents to show the mills had dropped all civil complaints and injunctions placed against the farm. There were several reports that Moses, on behalf of the mills, even offered John ten thousand dollars if he would sell the mills the farm and move his entire family to Canada.

Ten thousand dollars for an isolated 160-acre scrub farm they'd purchased for $280! To the family members it seemed a fortune.

"You think I'd accept a mill check and let them run me out of my country?" John said.

A week later Moses returned with ten thousand dollars in cash. John did not even look at the money. "Do you actually think I'd sell my birthright down the river for ten thousand dollars? With the gold hoard the mills have from stealing the people's trees and land, that's equivalent to five dollars to me. It's a mere pittance of the money mills have stolen."

Moses looked at Hattie and shook his head in exasperation. But he would not argue with John. He knew better than that.

"I wouldn't even consider it for less than twenty-five thousand," John said as Moses departed.

Moses did not reply. The mills never offered to settle again.

The months faded one into another, one harsh winter followed by another. John slammed his ax into a green widow maker, one half-fallen tree held aloft by the bent back of another. At the first blow of the ax the bent tree snapped and slammed into John's shoulder.

"Broke the son of a bitch," he declared. Hattie wrapped the shoulder and arm in a sling. John refused to see a doctor.

On July 5, 1909, John was hired to speak before a large crowd at Chetek's Lake Chautauqua. "There were six thousand people there," he declared. "Came just to see me." He'd told them of his fight with the mills. "When I got done they stood and applauded," he said. His voice became choked that people would honor him so. Tears welled in his eyes. "Someone has to stand up for the common man. There can be no higher calling for a man." His family did not disagree.

In October 1909, John T. Howe hauled in a portable sawmill and sawed rough cut planks out of the large pine logs that had been left on the Dietz farm by Moses. The cut lumber was stacked in large piles on the hill behind the barn.

"We'll build a nice house," John again told Hattie after the boards were stacked. He hugged her around the waist. "You just wait."

A year later the lumber lay as it had been stacked. "Needs time to properly cure," John responded when Hattie mentioned her house. "We'll dig the footings in the spring."

In July 1910, John, Hattie and all the family, except for Leslie who was left behind to tend the farm, traveled to visit Florence May on her farm south of Rice Lake. With the exception of John's brother William, other Dietz family members joined for a large family picnic and celebration of the Fourth of July. The men had a shooting contest which John easily won.

That night John, flush from his triumph at the shoot, became amorous. Naturally Hattie complied. A month later she realized she'd become pregnant for the tenth time. She informed John with some sadness. There had been so many years, so much work. The children were older now, easier to manage. She'd thought her childbearing days were past.

"It'll work out," John said to Hattie's grumblings that she didn't know how she'd manage. "Myra isn't going anywhere. She can help." John sat on his rocker paging through a scrapbook of old press clippings. It had been more than a year since the last reporter called. He'd even stopped communicating with editor A.E. Roese, even going so far in one of his later communications to kiddingly threaten to take Roese by hand if he did not settle a note Roese had given to John some years previous. Over time old friendship and sympathies had died.

"Let Roese write me first," John said. Sure he and Alfred had been friends, but that was in the past when Roese was part of his cause. Over the months, John grew morose. He was forty-nine years old. He'd stood up to the lumber mills and their hired agents and sheriff posses sent by U.S. marshals and the county. Criminal warrants for his, Hattie's, Clarence's, Myra's, and Leslie's arrest still lay collecting dust in some back drawer where no one could see the painful reminder of the failure of the law. He paged through the clippings in his scrapbook: "The people's champion..." "One of the greatest heroes the State had ever known."

Now no one visited, no one wrote of his fight. The press clippings rapidly yellowed with age. John tossed the tattered scrapbook on top of a bureau. He bellowed with the force of old: "Clarence, Leslie, hook up the team. Let's go to town and vote, see what rascals we can turn away from the public coffers."

Clarence and Leslie hitched the two young colts to the new springboard. Going to town had become a normal part of their lives and they had no thoughts of trepidation.

It was September 6, 1910, Wisconsin's first primary election day. Blue sky shone in bright strips between white puffs of cumulus clouds. The clean briskness of early fall filled the air. Select maple trees had turned bright yellow and red and low level fauna had started to shed and turn yellow and brown. As usual when heading for town, John carried a Luger pistol in a holster strapped high around his waist.

For the first five miles the two colts were a fistful for Clarence to handle. But they were his trainees and he refused to surrender the reins. After they'd worked out some of their feed they were more manageable, but still prone to shy at the thundering eruption of a partridge or simply the sinister shape of a strange-appearing stump jutting from beside the road.

Leslie laughed as the horses shied at a tree limb lying half on the dirt tote road. "Remember what they say about a runaway, Clarence — hold on tight, keep your mouth shut so you don't spook them more, and pray to the Lord."

Clarence smiled. "Notice how I vary the pressure on the reins, Les. You don't keep it steady or they just get used to pulling against that. Although you have to be certain you never lose contact. Anticipation, that's the key. You have to correct what they're going to do before they do it."

"Too much work for me," Leslie said and settled down in the back with a piece of grass between his lips.

The day began to weigh on Clarence. He brooded. For years now he'd tried to take life one day at a time, to stay out on the farm with the others and do what he could. But lately he'd been thinking. He couldn't stop himself. He was 23, life was passing him by. If he was ever going to move... He could not get the refrain to stop.

"This going to vote is a waste of time," John groused. "The mills will get their man in anyhow."

"That's what I say," Leslie agreed from the back. "It doesn't matter to us who's in office. Nothing changes anyhow."

John whirled on the narrow seat. The colts startled and jumped ahead but Clarence immediately reined them back. "You think grafters and corrupters are the same as honest men?"

Clarence immediately sought to intercede. "Leslie's just saying whoever is in office doesn't affect us out on the farm."

"Loss of liberty affects everyone, Leslie, whether you see it or not," John screamed. His face turned ruddy with the force of his shouts.

"Yes sir," Leslie said quietly. He moved to the back of the wagon. Lately John would not even accept his jokes.

"We haven't heard about getting a teacher for this year," Clarence said in hopes of cooling his father's passions. "If I see O'Hare I'll ask him. Johnny and Helen surely want their chance to learn. Helen hasn't missed a day in three years."

"That bastard still owes us board for Dewey," John grunted. "If I see him I'll give him more than a piece of my mind."

Clarence glanced back at Leslie and pursed his lips in warning to watch what he said. As Leslie well understood, John was in one of his moods.

The trio of Dietz men reached Winter in the early afternoon. In less than six years an entire one-street mill town had emerged out of the Wisconsin forest. For the most part the buildings were square front, two-story plank structures that included hotels, general and dry goods stores, a number of saloons, churches, and built just the past year and dedicated in a ceremony attended by the Dietzes, a proper public school. The streets were still dirt, but board sidewalks could keep ladies' ankle-length dresses and men's shined leather boots relatively free of mud and dust. The town was serviced by railroad as the primary means of inter-town transportation, although many people rode horseback and others were resigned to walking long distances on foot. Daily mail and telegraph were still the primary means of outside communications, however, the general store possessed the town's first and, in September 1910, the only public telephone.

The boys and John separated, going their separate ways in the small town. John made his way to the town hall where 83 other men voted in Winter for the primary. People watched John and nodded and, if not physically, at least mentally tried to maintain a distance. John Dietz stories still made the rounds with strangers, but the old fear of the locals had ebbed with the passage of time. After all, John, Winter's most famous celebrity, had stood up to those rascals up at the county seat in Hayward. John was actually one of them, Winter's own.

"Hello, John," a cruiser by the name of Bert Horel said.

"Bert," John grunted as he strode steadily on his way. There had been a time or two Horel had called at the farm.

Sometime later that afternoon, Clarence noticed Charles O'Hare, a school board member engaged in a heated argument with a man from Draper. For some minutes Clarence stood beside Seller's ice house, hesitating, not willing to interrupt. After some time O'Hare glanced at him and spoke sharply, "Yes, Dietz, what is it you want?"

"I wanted to see about a teacher for my brother and sister for this year," Clarence said evenly. John had long taught him to never let others intimidate.

"What the hell business is that of yours?" O'Hare was in short temper. "They're not your children."

"They're my brother and sister and I'm responsible," Clarence said. He returned O'Hare's hard tone. "It's only right they get a fair education like everyone else." He could feel the eyes of several onlookers as several people slowed their passage. "You haven't paid us all our board due for last year."

"And I'll be damned if we will," O'Hare yelled. He shook his finger in Clarence's face, scant inches from striking him. "You Dietzes have been taking advantage of this district too long. Using teachers to do your chores around the farm. If your brother and sister want to go to school, you can find them someplace in town here to board like other people do. Either that or they can walk back and forth."

"It's eleven miles one way," Clarence protested.

A burly figure forced himself between Clarence and O'Hare. "You get your hand out of my boy's face," John declared in his rough gravel voice. "You're getting out of line, Charles."

"You're out of line, John." O'Hare, much smaller than John, nevertheless argued shrilly. The years of fear and deference to John and his demands had exacted too much of O'Hare's pride. He was damned if he'd take anymore. "If you want your children to go to school, they can board here in town just like the children from other country people."

"What about our back board? A bargain is a bargain."

"You've taken advantage of this district for too many years."

O'Hare sputtered with the force of his speech. "You won't see any more help from me, John. We're tired of giving in to you."

"You haven't changed, have you, Charles? You're against me now and you've always been against me. I used to think you were a friend. Some friend," he roared in a voice that made the onlookers jump. "You have a grudge?" John squinted suspiciously, "Or are you just fronting so someone higher up like that snake Stinson can get me?" John spoke of Charles Stinson, a walking boss for Kaiser Lumber Company operations in Sawyer County.

"Goddamnit, John, you're out of line here," a third voice roared into the argument. The man was Bert Horel, village president of Winter and a Stinson-hired employee. Bert was as solidly built as John, but younger. He had a reputation as a fighter, having twice been arrested for fighting in Augusta, Wisconsin and Argyle, Minnesota.

Allegedly he'd once been dismissed from a driving camp for decking a blacksmith with an iron rod.

"You," John shouted. His face turned a ruddy complexion. Spittle flew as he spoke. "You're against me too — same as the others."

John swung, or at least pushed to move Horel back. Other figures moved in close. John turned from Horel back to face O'Hare. Horel swung, taking John on the back of the neck. Even as John fell to the dirt in the gutter beside the street, Horel was at his back, driving John facedown in the dirt, half standing and kneeling on his back and sending blow after blow at the back of John's head.

The movement of the fight swirled so quickly across the alley and into the street, Clarence could scarcely comprehend. Suddenly John went down, his father. He moved as if in a doze, thrusting himself between the gathering bodies. He seized Horel's arm. Horel turned and pushed while others pulled Clarence back.

"Stay out of this young fellow, or you'll get the same," Horel snapped. His face was twisted like a mean, wild dog.

When Horel turned at Clarence, a stunned John crawled to his feet. Bodies pressed in at him from all sides. The alarm buzzed, a mill trap, setting him up to be jumped from all sides.

His first thought was to escape the surrounding bodies, to work into the clear where he could operate. He pushed out between the bodies.

But then Horel, flushed with success, went at John again. "You've had your way with this town too long, Dietz. No more." Horel swung, catching John alongside the head.

The onlookers pressed in closer. Several seized Clarence as he again jumped for Horel. A couple of men, including Town Chairman Buckwheat, grabbed for John. Town Constable Pomerlo stepped in front of Horel, arms outstretched, trying to hold the two powerful adversaries apart.

"You won't get me," John yelled. He bucked and heaved against the weight of the attacking mob. He clawed frantically, struggling against the weight of the mill trap.

Somehow one hand worked free. With arms and bodies blocking his every move he still managed to pull his Luger. He thrust the pistol past the constable towards where Horel leaned forward, looking to press the attack. The crack of the shot sent people scattering like wheat chaff on a strong wind.

The bullet grazed Horel's jaw, creased his neck and penetrated into his shoulder and shattered the bone. He staggered back as if in a daze. He blinked, grunted in surprise and meekly turned and staggered away like a drunk going home from a saloon.

John, Luger still in hand, turned in a circle. Those who hadn't run at the sound of the shot were slowly backing away, giving John wider and wider berth. "Clarence, get Leslie and hitch up the team."

"Leslie already has the wagon over across the street," Clarence said softly. A part of his mind was still trying to comprehend what had taken place. He moved in at John's side and the two walked across the dusty street, watching up and down in both directions in the event of ambush. Only a few men stood in the open. But at almost every corner and almost every window they could see heads peeking out, giving them the eye as if they were some monstrous attraction at the fair, Clarence thought. Just like in the old days.

As they reached the wagon, Dick Phelan of the Hotel Winter stepped out. "I just shot one of your prominent citizens," John said.

"I hope not without cause," Phelan replied in a frightened voice.

"There was plenty of cause," John said. "Ask Horel, he's the one that found out the results." He ordered Leslie and Clarence into the wagon. "Grab those rifles in case we get ambushed."

Leslie seized one rifle and sat in back. His eyes were wide, questioning Clarence as to exactly what had happened.

Clarence shook his head in warning not to talk. He clucked to the young colts and pulled them in a tight circle and put them into a trot heading out of town.

"If anyone wants to follow they can get the same medicine," John yelled at Joe Buckwheat and two other men.

And the Dietz gang rode south and out of town.

Joe Buckwheat turned to Charles O'Hare. "I think John's crazy. Going against the lumber mills is one thing. Shooting one of our own citizens is another. I don't know what it's going to take, but this time the bastard has to pay. If Madden wants a posse, he can get the men now. I'll swear out the complaint myself."

ASSETS OF STANDARD
$800,000,000
Statement filed at Washington - Estimate on other Investments Make Rocky a Billionaire
Known First Time in History

NO INITIATIVE FROM THE GOVERNOR
NOW UP TO SHERIFF MADDEN TO CAPTURE CRAZY OUTLAW ALIVE OR DEAD
AND HOW?
Dietz Defiantly Puts up Claim Shot Horel in Self Defense - Fears Arrest Would Result in Being Prosecuted For Resistance During the Dam Trouble - Puts Up Bluff for Concessions

TEST FOR SHERIFF'S NERVE AND WIT

Tyranny of Dietz Should be Stopped For Good and In a Way to Make Others of the Family Respect Civilized Law And Order — Is No Time for Cowardice Nor Rash Move — Sheriff Needs Public Support

---

CHAPTER XIII

Nightfall had taken firm hold by the time the Dietz men returned from Winter. Stars were bright overhead and the cool September night seeped in through their woolen clothes.

The eleven-mile ride had been long. Except for an occasional outburst from John justifying the shooting, the three were silent. Only the boys seemed cowed by the enormity of John's actions. But they did not talk. Clarence spoke low and soothing to the colts, working the reins to hold them back as they naturally tried to increase pace as they neared the farm. The two boys trailed John into the squat log cabin.

"Well, I shot one of Winter's Grand Dukes today," John informed Hattie without preamble. "Bert Horel jumped me and I shot him in the shoulder. "

Hattie turned from the wood cooking stove. Jars of beets, her day's canning work, covered the entire counter at her elbow. For a long time she remained silent, the worn lines of her face seeking comprehension and searching John's face. Of course she knew he was telling the truth, it was just so hard to understand. Her hands cupped over her belly as if in a protective gesture for the developing fetus inside. Stanley's replacement, she'd lately been coming to think.

"O'Hare was snapping his finger in Clarence's face. So I took it up with him," John said bitterly. He took Hattie's silence as disapproval. "I mentioned our board was overdue. Next thing Horel hits me from behind, just like the coward he is."

"No," Hattie breathed. "Dear Lord no." The glazed look of her eyes came into focus. Her voice started low, wondering. "Why, John? We were getting along so well."

Unconsciously her hands kneaded her apron into a small ball. She shouted, "Why? For God's sake, why?"

"They had it figured to trap me, " John responded in kind. "What did you want me to do? They were lying in wait and came out from every direction. Must have been fifty of them. A number of them grabbed me, Buckwheat, Pomerlo. Ganging up. I barely made it." He turned to his children as if playing to their audience. "You should have seen the varmints scatter when my pea shooter barked." John grinned at the telling. "Isn't that right, boys?"

Clarence and Leslie both nodded. "Yes, Pa," Leslie said.

"They ran like the devil took a bite out of their tail."

"This is no time for jokes," Hattie snapped angrily.

Leslie flinched. It was so seldom his mother yelled in that tone of voice.

"There'll be more posses now," Hattie said. She leaned against the counter for support. "It won't be the mills this time, John. It'll be people we call our friends."

"We have no friends in Winter," John said.

Hattie rubbed at her stomach where there should be life. But she felt nothing and wondered if another part of her had died. She mumbled as if to herself, "Come unto me all ye that labor and are heavy laden and I will give you rest."

Clarence and Myra exchanged worried looks — it wasn't like their mother to be distracted like this.

"What are you yapping on? What?" John shouted as if trying to wake Hattie from a stupor. "Horel works for Stinsen. O'Hare did once, still does. He's an undercover agent. Always has been. What the hell addles you, Hattie? Those are mill agents. They aren't our friends. Remember that. Do you imagine those men would dare come out here and face me? They had their chance in town and didn't take it. No, Horel jumped me. I defended myself. It's the code of the wilderness. Madden can come. But he'll never get a posse to come at me."

Moved by force of passion, John took Hattie's arm in a powerful grip. "Don't you ever talk at me like that. Understand?" He viciously jerked her arm.

"Pa, please," Clarence yelled. He grabbed at John's shoulder. John whirled a sweeping blow with the back of his hand and knocked Clarence backwards. But Clarence had grown, was young, raw-boned and strong. The muscles of his face tightened and he moved forward as if to respond.

"No, stop this," Hattie yelled. She stepped in between her husband and son. She could see clearly now. What was done was done. Johnny and Helen had moved back into the shadows near the bunks. Myra seemed transfixed, Leslie uncertain. In one motion Hattie jerked free of John's grip.

Deep purple bruises marked the force of his fingers. She held out a hand to stop Clarence, but her attention was focused on John. "You shoot a man. You put the children at risk. Meanwhile I'm in a family way. We count also, John. Remember that."

As quick as he'd angered, John was mollified, even amused at Hattie's defiance. "Of course you count. All I think about is keeping us together as a family. Even if it kills me." John rubbed at the few thin strands of hair on top of his head. "I just can't understand why you insist on fighting me on this." He shook his head in sad lack of understanding. "Do I not have enough to face? Well," he shrugged, "I guess I'll have to bear this as well."

The argument ended. The family became silent. Hattie and Myra turned to kitchen chores, churning butter and tending the fire and an early season venison roast in the cooking stove. Helen was sent out into the dark to the spring to fetch a bucket of water. Johnny tagged along. Myra had taken care of the other livestock, but Clarence and Leslie took a kerosene lantern outside to complete care, feeding and watering of the two colts. John checked two Winchester rifles in the corner to be certain they were loaded. Then he sat down in his rocking chair to read his mail. In the pure black outside, stars shone brightly and in the deep woods across the clearing a lone owl hooted its low, haunting call.

The Dietz family ate a late supper, hooked the screen door and went to bed. They did not post a guard.

Two days later John slipped up beside what the papers referred to as a land looker standing on the edge of the clearing and apparently watching the farm. "You goddamn spy!" John grabbed the man's rifle and smashed it against a tree. The man turned to run but tripped over his own feet. Before he could rise, John was attacking, slamming, kicking and punching.

"Please," the terrified man begged. He clubbed ineffectually at his assailant. As the man turned and tried to crawl off, John kicked the man in the buttocks. "Git, you goddamn spy. I hate rats and I hate snakes and you look to me like a little bit of each. I am the truth and I am the light and what you're seeing here is the people's justice — less of the corporation law, but more justice. Understand?"

But by then the man had gained his feet and, without his hat and without his rifle, hastily made good his escape.

The following day the first of the reporters once again started to visit the Dietz farm. The first two were R.D. Jenkins of Chippewa Falls and A.C. Brokaw of the *Minneapolis Tribune*. The newspapermen reported they could not get anyone to drive them from Winter to the Dietz farm. After a great deal of searching they located a lumberjack who took them to within a mile of the farm, and then pointed the way for the two to continue on alone. When John strode out to greet the two men he was unarmed and cordial as if pleased to go back to the old days and meet with his allies in his stand against the mills.

Sheriff Madden had journeyed to Madison to ask for a company of militia, the reporters said. John shrugged. Whatever they sent he'd face. It made no difference to him. He then informed them he'd shot Horel in self-defense. He invited the two for supper and to spend the night. In the morning when they departed, he quietly informed them, "All I want is to be left alone."

The very next weekend after he shot Bert Horel, John ordered Clarence to hook up the team. The two of them were going to town.

"Give me some money out of your tin box," John ordered Hattie. "They might try to starve us out like they did in o-six. There was another spy out there this morning, but he got away."

"We've got supplies enough," Hattie said. "You're just tempting the devil by going to town, John."

"Get the box," John said. He grinned wickedly at his family. "Your mother tells me I'm tempting fate ... and then she talks to me in that tone of voice."

Hattie quietly walked into their tiny bedroom and retrieved twenty dollars for John. She touched Clarence's arm as he strapped a Luger pistol high on his pants belt.

The rent from the bullet high on his forehead glared its terrifying reminder of death so close at hand. John went outside. "Try to keep your father away from people," Hattie said. "Just buy your supplies and come back as soon as you can."

"Yes, Ma," Clarence said. He bussed his mother's cheek as if he was going away on a long trip. It was a mistake, for immediately tears gathered in her eyes.

"Goodbye, Clarence," Myra said and gave her brother a hug. She was as choked as her mother.

"It'll be all right," Clarence said with more conviction than he felt. "They won't try anything."

Leslie helped Clarence hook up the two colts. "Shouldn't have given them so much oats," Clarence said in a normal tone. He busily tended to hooking up the harness.

"If they open fire, are you firing back?" Leslie asked.

"I don't know," Clarence mumbled in response to a question he'd asked himself a hundred times. "If Pa's there, how can I not?"

The entire family gathered to watch as the two men rode off down through the flowage and across the Thornapple on the log and rock crossing John and the boys had built in the river. The colts bolted out the opposite side of the stream and in a few minutes the two were swallowed by the yellowing walls of the dense surrounding forest.

DIETZ WILL NOT BE TAKEN ALIVE
Fear grips the Countryside as a Battle With Outlaw
Appears Imminent — Old Acquaintance Says He is
"Gun Crazy"

For a radius of fifty miles from his cabin fear dominates the people. Dietz is a desperate man, they say and point to his record of a few years back, when, with his rifle and revolver he fought off hundreds of deputies.

Over a week has passed since John F. Dietz, the crazy anarchist outlaw terror of the town of Winter shot, apparently with little or no provocation, Bert Horel, president of the village of Winter, and without even an attempt being made to arrest him either by local or county officers, although Dietz Saturday went boldly into the village with one of his sons, and is reported to have been allowed to purchase provisions without interference.

Eau Claire Leader:
DIETZ PREPARES FOR LONG SIEGE

Saturday afternoon John F. Dietz and his eldest son, Clarence, suddenly appeared in the village of Winter, greatly to the astonishment of the natives. The unwelcome visitors came at one o'clock and remained until 4:30.

Village Marshal Talidean took to the jungles. Both Dietz and his son were each armed with two automatic eight-shooters, belted around their waists and each carried a Mauser rifle. Armed to the teeth is the proper expression.

Dietz had the entire village overawed. He began to interview citizens freely and to assert he was justified in shooting Bert Horel last Tuesday afternoon. He said Bert Horel had no business to butt into Dietz's quarrel with School President C.G. O'Hare.

Of course every citizen fully agreed with Dietz, and in fifteen minutes after word was passed around that Dietz was there, most of the male population of Winter was out of sight.

Dietz and his son were suspicious of everybody, and were constantly turning about to see that no one got the drop on them.

Indignation is intense against Dietz in the village of Winter, but no one dared openly resent his presence.

He loaded his wagon with numerous supplies to last for a month, and found the Winter storekeepers most obliging and courteous and ready to discount their prices.

The *Sawyer County Gazette,* published at Winter and Radisson replied to the accusations:

> Reports have been sent to every daily paper in the state about the shooting of Bert Horel by John F. Dietz, and they are so misleading and false that we hope people will not place any credence in them.
>
> It is true that John F. Dietz and his son Clarence were in this village last Saturday afternoon, but it is not true, as some of the papers have it, that every male citizen took to the woods on account of their being in town.
>
> They visited the Gazette office and remained more than one hour. They did not make any threats to shoot or kill us if we did not retract what we said last week, as has been reported...
>
> The biggest liar in the state is the fellow at Chippewa Falls who is sending the different papers the reports of the Dietz case. Old Ananias would dwindle into insignificance beside the lying poltroon.

The next week even more reporters visited the isolated homestead. John, leaning back in his rocking chair like in the old days, propped his feet up on a trunk and freely talked with every one. One reporter asked him about the veracity of a story from Chippewa Falls:

> Sheriff Mike Madden of Sawyer County, armed with a warrant to take John F. Dietz, dead or alive, arrived at Winter last evening and went south ten miles through the forest to Cameron Dam this afternoon, where he met Dietz and had a friendly chat with the outlaw.
>
> The sheriff told Dietz that he had a warrant for him but Dietz, armed with two .38 caliber automatic revolvers and a rifle, told Sheriff Madden to keep the paper in his pocket and if he took it out he was a dead man.

"You have no business here," said Dietz, "turn about," he commanded, pointing north, "take that road to Winter. Don't look around or you're a dead man."

Sheriff Madden faintly smiled and at once obeyed orders and did not stop until he got back to Winter.

John shook his head as if in sadness at the plight of the man. "The Chippewa Falls lying machine has been working without the benefit of light. If Sheriff Madden made a friendly call we would have greeted him with open arms. But the simple truth is the man has not been around. Or perhaps he visited the wrong farm." John winked at the reporters.

"See how freely they put words in my mouth. That's the same part of the trust bureau that called Horel fat and good-natured and failed to mention his arrests for fighting and the time he cold cocked a blacksmith with an iron bar. It's that same machine I've been fighting against all my life."

His mouth took a hard, bitter twist that made the reporters edge back. "I'm just a poor farmer out here, and they have their caches of gold, their lineups of judges and so-called officers of the law, with which they combine to try to beat me down." He looked them directly in the face, "Well this is one man who will not quit. They may get me, but I'll get a lot of them first."

Later that second week after the shooting of Bert Horel, as John walked from the house to the barn, a shot buzzed just past his head. He spotted movement in the distant wood line.

"You son of a bitch," John yelled. His nostrils flared. He sprinted to the house and grabbed his rifle. "Leslie, Clarence, grab your guns," he bellowed, then stepped outside and in a fusillade of thunder, emptied his rifle towards where the movement had been.

Myra, prompt to help, handed John a second rifle that was loaded. "Let's go," John yelled. He set out at a trot directly across the open field. His two boys trailed him, one on either side, rifles he'd cross arms and ready. "Come out of there, you son of a bitch!" John yelled. He bore directly in where the smoke had been. They found matted grass, a spent cartridge, but the would-be assassin had fled.

That weekend John and the two oldest boys again went into town. "C'mon, Leslie, grab your pistol," John ordered. "You can come along. Talidean and Madden and Davis proved last week they will not try anything. You can watch all those loud talkers disappear like cockroaches under wood bark. Maggots every one."

They had no real need of supplies, Hattie knew. But John insisted on going. She did not protest. News of the arrival of the Dietz gang once again swept the town. No sheriff or marshals were in sight. The men ate dinner at the Hotel Winter and then stopped at the express office for a heavy package, purportedly ammunition.

While they were at the depot, a young lady asked if they would pose for a picture, which the three men did.

In the following days newspapers blared the news:

DIETZ HOLDS OFFICERS COWARDS AND
DEFIES THEM - KEEPS WINTER AFRAID
Outlaw Shows His Contempt for Constable and Sheriff
By Going Into Village of Winter for Ammunition A
Second Time After The Shooting and
No Attempt Made to Interfere

SOMETHING WILL BE DOING SOON
End of Second Week Since Warrant Issued
Finds Anarchist Outlaw Still Stuffing
City Newspaper Men and Getting All
the Notoriety Possible - But There is Reason to Believe
Sheriff Has Plans for Capture

... Last Sunday Dietz was in Winter for the second time since the shooting and was allowed to take home with him a package of ammunition received by express, without any form of protest even being made. This fact and the sensational and widespread support Dietz is obtaining from the degenerate city newspapers is resulting in many questioning the courage of Sheriff Madden...

There is strong, popular feeling, however, that Dietz and his sons also if necessary, should be crippled into a harmless condition when they venture into town and then captured and put on trial. This, it is claimed, could be done by a good shot from the protection of some building without danger to anyone.

...Yet this lazy, selfish, anarchist tyrant demands special favors at the expense of the public and all under the dastardly plea that he only wants to be left in the peaceful possession of his rights. Such low down, contemptible people are the lowest form of undesirable citizens and should be put to work at hard labor for the public good.

John crumpled the paper and tossed it across the room at the feet of the three reporters from Minneapolis and St. Paul. "That's the corporation lying machine. They bring all their money, all their power to bear on my back. They expect I will break. They will be surprised."

The three reporters exchanged glances and a smile. It was the first hint of John's famous temper they'd been able to provoke.

"District Attorney Davis says he considers you a desperate outlaw. That you think no more of killing a man than you would clipping the head off a chicken," one of the reporters quoted from a Sawyer County newspaper.

But John had already mellowed, bringing his temper back under control. "A man's conscious is the highest law. Not the word of Attorney Davis who was sent here by the mills. I have always said that the inner voice cannot go far wrong. The worst criminal and the best man here hears it speak."

John rummaged through the newspapers the reporters had brought him. He laughed, "It says here with a big headline, Sheriff will get Dietz. Mike Madden not afraid of the bad man of Sawyer County. And then down below in the same paper a small headline reads, Sheriff Madden may resign." He slapped the side of his leg. "There's your proof of the ignorance of the lying machine. They say exactly the opposite thing on the same page. Those are the lies I have faced for the last six years."

John stood and walked outside. Two of the reporters trailed after to receive John's tour and listen to his stories of past incidents. One reporter remained in the small dark cabin with

Hattie and Myra. He showed them part of a story from one newspaper.

> ...It is said that in case a posse takes him (John) live the boys are to kill the officer or shoot him (John) if necessary. Failing in this the mother is to shoot the boys.

"Would you do that?" the reporter asked. Hattie whirled like a demon school teacher attacking a defiant pupil. "You would give credence to such wild speculation by repeating it in front of my children? You accept lies as they are told? What kind of man are you?" She was shrill, shouting so loud and bearing down on the young reporter he hastily apologized and rushed out to join the others.

Hattie turned with a stiffness as tight as a piano wire. She picked up a bowl of green beans and sat on one of their plain wooden chairs with the bowl between her knees and began to snip the ends. She spoke to Myra in an agitated voice. "Can you imagine anyone would say that... I would shoot my own young? What do they think we are? Is this where your father has brought us?" She trailed off. Her red, worn hands worked feverishly.

"Maybe Pa is right about the way the mills lie," Myra said. "Under that picture of the family and Jay Gates the paper said Jay was used as a general utility man about the place at the expense of the public. Pa never made him work, Jay just volunteered." She picked up a newspaper. "And here they say, 'Seated in the foreground is Clarence, the hero, and they have a question mark, of the dam wars, who is ever ready to exhibit with pride and self-esteem the scar left by the bullet that plowed a furrow across the top of his head.' How can they say that? Clarence never fired at anyone. He goes to town five or six times a year. He doesn't go to saloons. He doesn't smoke. He doesn't have friends in Winter. The scar is there for everyone to see — what can he do?"

Hattie stoically began to slice rutabagas as if she had not heard.

"It goes on," Myra continued. "I don't think it will ever end. Listen to this article: 'Judging from the most reliable information, the Dietz family, from Dietz down to the oldest girl are of the anarchistic stamp, and they are also genuine outlaws who have terrorized the people of their vicinity in a most domineering manner. That such lawlessness, tyranny and fear should exist in a civilized community is a shameful disgrace to Sawyer County, and it is time the Dietz gang rule is broken up.'"

Still Hattie did not respond. Myra turned and peered out the tiny window of what the papers referred to as their fort. She could see John escorting the three reporters about, pointing here and there and describing battles long past. "What's going to happen to us, Mama?" she asked in a small voice. "Do you think we're all really outlaws like they say?"

Hattie continued to cut the rutabagas. Her head rocked back and forth in rhythmic fashion as if vibrating on the end of a spring. It was only after a few seconds that Myra realized the motion was a trembling not part of Hattie's conscious control.

Leslie entered the cabin. He seemed as exuberant as John that they had more big city reporters visiting. "Pa says we should put on our Sunday best. The reporters want to take a picture in front of the cabin."

"No," Hattie yelled. The clay bowl dropped from between her knees and broke in two. "No more press. No."

"Pa just said..." Leslie paused. He looked puzzled then turned without further word and fled.

A few minutes later John poked his head inside the cabin door. "Hattie, Myra, c'mon outside. The reporters want a picture. We'll show them what we look like when we work, which of course is always."

Myra quietly took her mother's elbow as if assisting an invalid and the two women dutifully trailed John outside. They gathered in a small group beside the cabin with its peeling bark walls and the stars and stripes flying proudly from a crooked sapling stick nailed to one corner.

"Why don't you and your boys hold rifles," one reporter suggested. "Maybe Myra as well."

"No," John snapped in a voice that made the reporter quake. "We don't make trouble. We only take care of what comes to us, like Horel came to me in Winter." He took off his hat to show his white and balding head. "I know the way those men work; they're looking to put one in my back. But that they cannot do. Madden isn't the man."

* * *

Sawyer County Sheriff Mike Madden was not a happy man. He could not turn around or walk or talk without someone hounding him about how and when he was going to get John Dietz. But call for a man to join a posse and everyone turned his back. "No sir, Sheriff, that's your job. Not mine."

Madden was a former lumberjack and law enforcement officer from Aitkin, Minnesota. He'd been elected sheriff of Sawyer County in the November election of 1909. He was an Irishman with a corpulent physique, wore loose baggy pants held up by suspenders and wore a black derby. In truth he appeared more like a kindly barkeeper than a sheriff. He seldom carried firearms. Firearms aggravated men. Most situations could be brought under satisfactory control through physical presence and force of will. Although John Dietz was a case by himself.

Winter Town Chairman Joseph Buckwheat, a participant in the Horel-Dietz fracas, had sworn a complaint and a warrant had been issued by Judge John Riordan to the sheriff of any constable of Sawyer County:

> WHEREAS, Joseph Buckwheat has this day complained in writing to me on oath that John F. Dietz did on the 6th day of September, 1910, at the town of Winter, in said county, being then and there armed with a dangerous weapon, to wit; a certain pistol or revolver, then and loaded with powder and leaden bullets, made an assault on one Albert C. Horel, feloniously, wilfully and of his malice aforethought to kill and murder, and pray that said John F. Dietz might be arrested and dealt with according to law. Now, therefore, you are commanded forthwith to arrest and apprehend the said John F. Dietz and bring him before me to be dealt with according to law.

Sawyer County District Attorney J.C. Davis, a dapper-dressing and openly ambitious man, had handed Madden the warrant along with all the others against the entire family. But who could he get to go with him, Madden had asked. Hayward residents were reluctant. No militia could be called. The day after the shooting Madden had stopped in Winter to ascertain the prospects of raising a posse. But it seemed the people of Winter were as opposed to the authority emanating out of the county seat of Hayward as much as they were now opposed to Dietz. Dick Phelan of the Hotel Winter had told him, "Mike, I'm a good friend of yours. I'll tell you this much; don't go out there alone, because I know just what he's going to do to you."

So Madden had stayed away, even though a number of papers reported he'd been run off from the farm. It was not worth getting shot by some backwoods farmer for the likes of people in Winter. After all, the town marshal and constable of Winter hadn't seen fit to attempt to move on Dietz when the man and his boys boldly rode into town in broad daylight. He'd leave it lie, Madden once thought wistfully, but he'd never have any peace.

It was the press he hated the worst. They were like howling, slobbering dogs making Dietz into a hero or a monster bigger than life and then hounding the sheriff's office as if John Dietz was the only problem he had to deal with. Even in support the papers would not let him be:

> ... it is probable that the governor is of the opinion that it is up to the county authorities to first show what stuff they are made of, and that he cannot be expected to interfere himself in matters so long as civil affairs officers allow such a man as Dietz to come and go as he pleases unmolested.

> ... The return to Hayward of the sheriff, Monday, without Dietz, and the passing of the week without any apparent effort to effect the capture or to make announcement of his determination to get the outlaw, is resulting in considerable criticism.

> While Sheriff Madden is noncommittal on the question, the *Record* is inclined to credit him with having formed a plan of action which he may be quietly working out, and if this be so he should be encouraged rather than criticized. It is true that when a man accepts the office he accepts with it the chance of personal danger and its demand for courage and decision.

Madden lay the paper on his desk. He addressed District Attorney J.C. Davis. "I cannot gather a posse in this town. What would you suggest?"

"Use that one thousand dollar reward the county board voted on in o-seven. It's still available. There are a lot of people down there that don't like Dietz. Some of those swamp trash down there would shoot their mother for a dollar bill or a bottle of whiskey. Go talk to that Fred Thornbahn, that grocery store operator in Radisson you mentioned. Rumors are he's a crack shot and doesn't have much regard for life. Let him lead things down there. They're more likely to follow one of their own. You stay in the background."

"Dietz has a neighbor by the name of Roy Van Alstyne. They used to be friends but had a falling out, the way Dietz does with almost everyone he knows sooner or later. Van Alstyne knows the land. Claims he out-shot Dietz one time and that he's the best shot in town," Madden said. He sounded hopeful. "He seemed to oppose Dietz as well."

That afternoon Madden telegraphed an innocuous message and the next day the two men appeared in Hayward. They were informed about the one thousand dollar reward and both were sworn in as deputies, with Fred Thornbahn willingly taking

Photo courtesy of Malcolm Rosholt

Main Street in Winter, Wisconsin, probably about 1912.

the title as Chief Deputy. "It was not a secret," Madden later testified about swearing in the two men, "but we did not let everybody know."

"The best way would be to keep an eye on the farm and take Dietz by ambush," Thornbahn said. He was a solidly built man with thin, pinched features, a man given more to act than to talk. He did not conceal his distaste for Madden and Davis and his ill-regard for authority in general. "John Dietz is just a man. I don't know why all the fuss or why no one has seen fit to uphold the law before now."

Madden turned bright red but judiciously did not respond.

"The people of Winter don't seem to mind what kind of people walk around in their midst," J.C. Davis snapped. "Dietz has been going into Winter and strutting around for the benefit of the press the last two weekends. The law and men of Winter always disappear."

"Saturday seems to be his favorite day," Madden added in an effort to head off an argument.

"If we can't get him at the farm, we'll take him along the road going into town," Thornbahn said. "If I have to I'll take him myself."

Van Alstyne spoke up. He was a lean, gaunt-faced man with a buckskin coat and gnarled hands of a woodsman.

"You'll never get close to the farm with those dogs of Dietz. If you get upwind they'll howl if you're half a mile off. If John comes to town we might just as well shoot him and the boys right off. If all three of us held a gun on John, he's so crazy he'd still reach for his." Roy nodded with certainty. "That's the truth. I know the man. If John comes down that road we might as well kill him right off."

The other three men stared at Van Alstyne, digesting his words. There was a quietness of men facing an immense challenge. Even Thornbahn seemed ill at ease. No one ventured to dissent.

MAN AND BEAR FIGHT
Meet in the Woods
Unexpectedly and Bruin
Begins Hostilities -
Man Retires - Injured

DIETZ TELLS OF
HOREL'S SHOOTING

Cameron Dam
Defender is Genial Host
of Newspaper Men
Who Drive to Cabin

MIND DWELLS
ON THE PAST

Fugitive Thinks the
Man he Shot is Employed
by Lumber Companies
to Hound Him

TOBACCO IS HEALTHY
In the course of my asso-
ciation with tobacco, about
twenty-five years, I have
known men all this time, every working day, to be inhal-
ing tobacco dust or fumes
produced in the process of
manufacture. Uninterrupted
good health is the general
rule of all persons engaged
in tobacco proceedings of
every kind, and generally of
large consumers.

CHAPTER XIV

On October 1, 1910, three weeks after the shooting of Bert Horel, John instructed the boys to hook the colts up to the springboard. The three men were going into town. Hattie walked from their outhouse and paused beside the large pile of winter firewood John and the children had cut with crosscut and ax.

The dozen face cords appeared huge, but in fact she knew it would carry them to the thirty below temperatures of mid-January and that was all. Hunting and trapping seasons were coming on and the men would be too busy to cut. And now John took them off to town. Her mouth set in the thin, compressed line of a woman whose turmoil had too long been held inside.

They had no need of supplies. They had no packages waiting at the express office. No orders were due from the catalogue store.

"I make it a point to avoid crowds in order to stay out of trouble," John had told one reporter. "Tuesday, election day, I made that mistake. "

How she'd like to rub John's nose in that, Hattie thought. But she did not say a word. It had been three weeks since John had shot Bert Horel in self-defense. There had been that land looker John knocked to the ground, a few others he could not catch, and the sniper. But the sheriff had not tried a thing. Perhaps, she prayed, he never would.

Hattie peered to the deep blue of the brisk fall day. The forest all around glowed brilliant yellows and reds, her favorite time of the year. No bugs, cool days and nights, no sweltering heat and sleepless nights in the tiny cabin. In the fall a woman could breathe. She glanced towards the piled of lumber still drying on the hillside. Clarence had planked the inside of the living room wall and then he, John and Leslie had rolled on bright, flowered wallpaper. But the rest of the lumber still sat, who knew how many months or years away from transformation into her home. Hattie sighed.

She reached and massaged her lower back. On the days previous they had been digging potatoes. The work had taken its toll. Myra's dog, Tippy, exploded with furious barking. The two other dogs joined in. Young Johnny came running as fast as his short legs could carry him.

"Ma, Pa, there's a wagon coming across the river. There's a kid and a man in a suit. "

Johnny was growing so fast, Hattie thought, almost ten now. She was reminded of the life in her womb. A woman bears, a woman endures, there was nothing else she could do.

The boy on the wagon was Dick and Mary Phelan's boy from the Hotel Winter. The man was reporter Floyd Gibbons from the *St. Paul Dispatch*. He'd been unable to find any man who would drive or guide him to the Dietz homestead. So finally the Phelans had volunteered their boy and team of buckskin horses. In the fashion he usually met visitors, John walked out unarmed.

Clarence and Leslie stopped near the front of the house with the team of horses. "Should I unhook the wagon?" Clarence asked. He understood John would talk to the reporter; he always did.

"You boys can go to town if you want," John said. "Pick up our mail. A lot of people have been writing again. We want to keep up on what they're saying. Pick up the newspapers as well. Ask your mother and if you wink just right she'll give you some money and you can eat at the hotel — if that doesn't sour Hattie's feelings of course," he said in loud jest so Gibbons could hear.

"Can I go along, Pa?" Myra asked. "It's been so long since I've been in town. "

"You need Myra?" John asked Hattie.

Hattie looked at her daughter's hopeful face. "Do you think everything will be all right?"

"Nobody's going to try anything," John said. "Isn't that right, Mr. Gibbons?"

"Town looked mighty quiet to me," Gibbons replied. "I couldn't even get anyone to answer the door when I got into town last night. People say there's a posse around. But if there is, they're darn well hidden."

"Sure, go ahead," John said to Myra.

Myra clapped her hands with glee, just her and the boys going into town. When had that ever happened? Myra rushed to change then back outside. She carried a large cloth handbag and wore an ankle-length black dress with frills. Although her face was as brown as an Indian's, she carried a large bonnet she could put on once they got close to town. She'd read where the pale, white look was the fashion of the day.

Leslie and Clarence climbed up on the narrow, spring-balanced front seat. Despite her protests, Myra was confined to the back of the wagon.

"I'll bring you some hard rock candy," Clarence called to Johnny and Helen. He could see the set of their mouths, the longing in their eyes; they too wanted an escape. He clucked to the horses and they were off.

Just the three of them riding into town without the ever watchful eye of John was a rarity they had not experienced before. As soon as they were out of earshot of the cabin, Leslie whooped. The horses startled and Clarence eased them back.

"We could just keep right on going," Leslie said. He ignored Clarence's admonishing stare at making the horses bolt.

"If it wasn't for Ma and Helen and Johnny, I'd consider it," Clarence agreed.

"Where would we go?" Myra asked, picking up the game.

"Milwaukee? The three of us could live together."

"Some day I'd like to buy an automobile," Clarence said.

"I read where they can run thirty miles an hour without ever stopping. "

"How do you think the colts would act if they saw one of those devil wagons coming down the road?" Leslie asked.

"They could toot that horn and the horses would jump fifty feet into the tops of the trees." He chuckled at the thought. The papers were filled with frequent stories of runaways, of panicked horses running directly in front of loud, smoking trains and shying from small chugging automobiles.

"I'd like to go to one of those theaters and see a play," Myra said. "Get all dressed up and go see *The Girl of My Dreams.*"

"It's all just pretend," Clarence said.

"So what," Myra protested. "I like to pretend sometimes. " Abruptly she began to sing the ballad *Red Wing.*

The boys listened quietly while her pure, clear voice carried into the thick, vast forest reaching out over the narrow, dirt tote road. Clarence turned the horses half into the ditch to avoid the upper limbs of a deadfall that half covered the bumpy and rocky road.

After *Red Wing,* they sang some Stephen Foster songs in which Clarence and Leslie joined in loud and strong.

"I'm tired of standing back here by myself," Myra complained after several songs. "Why do I always have to sit in back. "

"You can sit up here," Clarence said. "We can squeeze in." Myra quickly clambered around and sat on the boys' laps, straddling one leg of Leslie and one of Clarence's. They continued to sing, the music binding them together. Once Myra wrapped her arms around her two brothers' shoulders and pulled them to her as would a mother her young.

"People in town have no idea, no idea at all what it's like for us. " She sounded close to tears.

"C'mon, Myra," Clarence cautioned. "We have each other. That's something. "

"Let's sing *She'll Be Coming Around the Mountain,*" Leslie suggested in order to buoy Myra's spirits. They sang the sound loud, lusty, not worrying about tone as much as getting into the spirit, pulling back with their hands to imitate pulling on the reins, pumping their hands in unison as if blowing the train whistle. The colts became perked, ears cocked forward as if ready to bolt.

In the midst of their singing a voice shouted, "Halt, there. " Almost simultaneously flame and smoke belched as rifles cracked a terrifying thunder out of the peaceful forest. The two colts shied in wild-eyed terror. Clarence struggled with the reins to hold the two powerful animals from running away. Out of the flurry of explosions, a bullet punched Myra low in the abdomen, smashing through her spleen, a kidney, and nicking her spinal column as the bullet blew a large hole of flesh out of her back. Myra moaned and slumped forward, fighting for balance. Beside her Leslie jumped from the wagon.

"Run," Myra moaned. She slipped to one side. Her voice faded. "Get Pa. "

Two men with blackened faces emerged from the foliage down the road from the wildly jerking wagon. A third, heavy-set man, trailed unsteadily behind the first two. The grey colt reared in its traces. The black colt crow-hopped to the right.

"Raise those hands or I'll shoot," one man called in a high-pitched voice to Clarence.

"I can't," Clarence grunted as he fought the rearing horses. "They'll run away. "

"You run, you're dead," one of the larger men with blackened faces shouted. He snapped a shot that tore through Clarence's arm.

"Whoa! Whoa!" Clarence called to the horses.

"For God's sake," Myra moaned. "Give up, Clarence. " Her eyes were closed against the heaviness forming in her stomach.

The third, heavy-set man, Sheriff Madden, panted up to the horses and tried to take their heads to calm them down.

"I didn't tell them to shoot," he protested amid the din.

The horses settled, still dancing somewhat. Clarence dropped the reins and started to turn to help Myra but was stopped by the hard thrust of a rifle in his face.

"Myra," he called in a strained voice. Myra could only moan.

Down the road behind the wagon Leslie scrambled madly through brush and briars. He tripped forward over a log, then scrambled, running on feet and hands and then rising up on his feet. He reached for his pistol but it had fallen. He paused and peered back down the road. Two men had the wagon stopped. Another man approached, Roy Van Alstyne, their traitor neighbor. Leslie raised his hands to surrender. Beyond Van Alstyne Clarence stood on the ground beside the wagon, hands raised. Myra was slumped on the seat as if dead. Leslie, his face twisted with torment and wet with sweat, sobbed. What was he to do?

Abruptly he turned and rushed back into the forest. Van Alstyne rained a flurry of shots in his wake. Leslie cried out, "Pa! Pa!"

"Get up there," Chief Deputy Fred Thorbahn ordered Clarence. He kept looking around as if expecting to be jumped. "Where's your old man?"

"He's not here," Clarence replied. "Myra's bad hurt. We have to..." his voice broke.

"Damn, I could have sworn..." Thornbahn trailed off. He shrugged as if to dismiss his assumptions and jumped up behind the seat. He pulled the oldest Dietz boy's hands, including the one streaming blood, behind his back and snapped on a pair of handcuffs. Clarence clenched his teeth against the pain but did not utter a sound. Thornbahn then turned to Myra and pulled her hands behind her back to where they rested just over the hole the bullet made exiting her body. He ignored her moans.

"She's bad hurt," Clarence pleaded. "You don't need to handcuff her. She needs a doctor. My God, man! Can't you see?"

"She's as bad as the rest of you," Thorbahn growled. "There's a warrant for her arrest same as there is for you."

Van Alstyne returned to the wagon. He wore buckskins, his face was blackened and he panted heavily. He grinned wickedly. "The boy Leslie got away. He's running for his pa. " His head jerked back as if expecting John Dietz himself would suddenly emerge from the forest.

Clarence glared at the man who'd been his neighbor and was now his assailant. "How can you do this, Roy? Did my mother and father not bring you groceries when you were sick? Did we not lend you our pony for your children to ride? And then you turn like... You shoot Myra like that?"

"You people have broken the law for too long. You give all

of us a bad name. " Roy spat to one side. He gazed back at the thickets of woods where Leslie had disappeared. He could shoot just as good, if not better, than John Dietz. The problem with Dietz was he didn't know how to quit. He just kept bearing in no matter what he faced.

"That kid's going to fetch his old man," Roy said. "We better get out of here. " Despite himself his voice broke.

"Yeah," Madden said. He was as intimidated by the thickets of the colorful fall forest as was Van Alstyne. Sweat streaked the caked mud covering his face and his eyes rolled back and forth like those of a white man playing a Negro in the theater.

"Yes, let's get out of here," he snapped. Madden heaved his bulk up on the wagon and knelt in the narrow space in front of the seat where Clarence and Myra were handcuffed. Van Alstyne and Thorbahn stood behind the two shot and handcuffed prisoners, rifles high and ready.

Madden whipped the grey and the black into startled motion. They bolted, jerking the wagon. Myra moaned.

"Please," Clarence begged. "Can't you give Myra water, take off her handcuffs? She's bad hurt." He could see her weakness, her head lolling sideways, a thin line of blood seeping out of lips that were compressed against crying out.

"Quiet or you'll get the same," Van Alstyne barked. He jabbed Clarence with the barrel of his gun.

Despite the fact Leslie had to go several miles on foot to reach John and then John would have many miles more to catch up, Madden, as he later told reporters, "pushed the team to the utmost, thinking that John Dietz would cut through the woods and ambush us. "

Meanwhile, Clarence could feel blood seeping down his handcuffed hands. After a mile Thorbahn removed the handcuffs from Myra. A large splotch of blood had stained her dress and formed a pool on the seat where she sat. She slumped forward and then leaned sideways against Clarence for support. Her chin slumped to her chest. Her eyes closed against the jolting pain caused by the racing wagon.

"Myra," Clarence said in a choked voice. His sister did not reply.

Fourteen-year-old Helen Dietz stood out near the barn with

Johnny Phelan. They both heard the flurry of shots, but they were so distant they did not seem cause for alarm. Nevertheless, Helen became nervous. They had come from the direction her bothers and sister had taken into town.

"My dad said one day they'll have to send out the militia and clean all you Dietzes out of here," the Phelan boy said. "What do you think you'll do then?" He was younger than Helen. He was not mean. He was not frightened. His question derived from simple curiosity.

"My daddy said we've done nothing wrong. If the corporations want to try to kill us, he said we can only stand and fight back. " Helen paused as if trying to fully understand exactly what she said. Unaccountably an image of Stanley on his deathbed came to her, and then the small gathering on the hillside and the men lowering the tiny pine box into the cold, frozen ground. Tears gathered in her eyes. "Daddy says he thinks God is on our side," she whispered as if divulging a secret.

The Phelan boy was puzzled, if not sympathetic. "I was the only one in town who would guide the reporter Gibbons out here. Dad was too busy. All of the other men were afraid. But I wasn't. "

"Afraid of what?" Helen asked.

Johnny Phelan laughed. "Why, you Dietzes of course."

A figure materialized at the edge of the forest. The man ran as if exhausted, one hand clutching at a sharp pain in his side. It was Leslie, his clothes torn and his face streaked with dirt, sweat and tears. He bolted into the house where John, Hattie and reporter Gibbons were sitting.

"Ambushed," Leslie gasped in a thick, incoherent voice. "They ambushed us. " His eyes rolled with the agony from his run. He gasped for breath. "They shot Myra. Bad, I think. I don't think she'll live. She may be dead right now. "

John jumped to his feet. "Where are they at?"

"No, land's sake, Lord, no," Hattie moaned in deep distress. But as quickly as she broke, she caught Gibbons watching eye and quickly regained an outward firm and stoic composure. Nine children, May married, three others dead, Clarence under arrest, another child in her womb, and now Myra unlikely to live. The refrain repeated itself over and over like the din of crickets on a summer night.

Hattie's eyes were dry as she watched John rage at Leslie. Why had the boy run? He should have stood strong and fought it out. Stood firm side by side with his brother and sister.

"What have I taught you all these years? There isn't a corporation weasel around that can stand up to a Dietz," John shouted. "And then you run like some craven coward." He roared his shame at his son.

Poor Leslie, a distant part of Hattie thought. She'd never imagined the boy could become this upset over anything — except of course Myra and Clarence. And now John bellowed such fire in his ears Leslie verged on tears. Hattie opened her mouth to interfere but she could not talk. Laryngitis, she thought. She moved back against the wall. Her shoulders still appeared broad and strong, the slight droop discernible only to those most aware. Only the inability to speak, the slight bobbing of her head and the uncontrolled trembling of her hands gave her secret away. She was consumed with shame, the Rock of Gibraltar reduced to a tiny balsam shaking in a storm.

"Please, God," she whispered her prayer. "Don't let Myra die."

Floyd Gibbons grabbed his hat. He had a story to file. And he had to get away from John raging at his son. The man was "put out" at Leslie's failure, he later wrote. But he could not describe the fear John's rage triggered in himself, the absolute conviction the man was insane, an uncontrollable, unstoppable wild bull. But fascinating.

Gibbons yelled out the door. "Boy, hitch up the wagon."

John picked up a rifle and levered it open to load a round in the chamber. His face was purple, his mouth a sneer. His blue eyes snapped with twinkles of wild sparks or light, Gibbons reported. If Dietz asked to ride along, he could be ambushed as well, Gibbons realized. What a story that would be.

"You get going, Gibbons," John ordered. "Get on ahead. You tell them John Dietz is coming in."

"Yes sir," Gibbons said. He could scarcely contain his excitement. He had to get into town, get his camera set. John Dietz was coming in. As soon as Gibbons departed, Hattie broke down and began to sob.

A number of reporters had been hovering in and around Winter since the shooting of Bert Horel. They came running as Sheriff Mike Madden, still kneeling in the front of the wagon, raced into town. They saw the two wounded Dietz children, the girl Myra all but unconscious as she sat slumped in a pool of blood on the seat. They observed the lathered horses. They could not help but see the two heavily armed deputies standing just behind the wounded Myra and the wounded and handcuffed Clarence, as if ready to shoot the children dead should they make one move. John Dietz was no where to be found.

The reporters looked at one another and shook their heads; this was the doing of the law of Sawyer County? Wait until the world heard of this. Word of the ambush spread through the town almost before the two wild-eyed colts could be pulled to a halt outside Doctor Burn's office.

"Be strong, Sis," Clarence called as several men lifted Myra from the wagon. Clarence strained to join his sister but brutal hands slammed him back in his seat. Myra's eyelids flickered at her brother's voice but she was too weak to reply. Clarence, still handcuffed and with blood drying on his hands, was manhandled over to the town jail. Every few minutes he called to his jailer, pleading for news of how Myra fared.

Crowds of people gathered everywhere. Women with ankle-length skirts and large bonnets talked to other women. Men talked to strange men, many of them fingering weapons they seldom carried in town. Small, uncontrolled groups of children ran hither and yon, watching the jail, the doctor's office, and eying the dusty road from the south leading into town. If John Dietz approached, he'd approach from over there.

Madden placed Chief Deputy Thorbahn in charge of the town and so informed Town Marshal Pomerlo. A dozen other men were sworn in as deputies and posted to watch for Dietz. Madden telegraphed District Attorney Davis at Hayward to send Doctor Grafton with an automobile. Saloons were closed.

Reporters were forbidden to visit Dietz on his farm. The post office and telegraph office were instructed that no messages should pass to the family. As soon as Myra's wounds had been covered with gauze and tape, she was carried to the second floor of the Hotel Winter where Mary Phelan and Janette

Dunster were employed to care for the girl. A guard was posted just outside the door with a rifle and revolver. Besides the attending women and the law, no visitors were allowed.

After some time Doctor Burns walked over to the jail and bandaged Clarence in his cell.

"Your sister is fine," Burns said dryly to Clarence's demands for news of his sister. "It's just a little scratch. You've got more to worry about than her."

A warning cry swept the town. A wagon was approaching from the south. Armed men rushed from every direction. A freight train switching cars on the side track blocked their view. Dick Phelan ran from the Hotel Winter.

"Don't shoot," he shouted. "Don't shoot. My boy Johnny went out to the Dietz place with a reporter. "

The cars separated. Two dozen guns were raised. The horses appeared, light buckskins. "That's Johnny," Phelan shouted and ran out in front of the armed men. Floyd Gibbons and his young guide drove across the tracks and into town.

Gibbons jumped to the ground, waiting expectantly as people turned to him for information. The trace of a smile played at his lips. When he had their undivided attention, he spoke, "Dietz says he's coming into town."

The news struck the town like a tornado down main street. People shouted and ran in every direction of the compass, each with some set purpose important only to him. Within minutes Madden declared martial law. Any willing man with two legs and a pair of pants was deputized and assigned a specific area to patrol. Deadlines were established and, as darkness fell, lanterns hung in black alleys and near covering piles of lumber at the local sawmill. Flasks of whiskey materialized. Eyes were slitted, watchful. Rifles were held ready, crossarmed. One minute the rookie deputies were consumed by excitement, the adventure of it all, the next moment they suspected movement, John Dietz out there in the dark — then their mouths went dry with fear.

Well after dark the automobile with its dim headlights brought the doctor from Hayward. Despite the hour, Madden wanted the two prisoners removed to Hayward. However, Grafton, the Hayward doctor, said a move now would be tantamount to signing Myra's death certificate. Reluctantly Madden agreed. He loaded Clarence into the automobile and took three men beside himself as guards and set out into the night on the dirt turnpike headed north.

"There goes the Sawyer County law," one deputy grumbled. "Getting clear of town before John Dietz comes in. "

Chief Deputy Fred Thorbahn shrugged. He'd been left in charge. The promised reward was one thousand dollars. In truth, he was heard to remark, Madden just got in the way.

The long night dragged. In the town of Winter, it was reported, no one slept.

The following day the denizens of the press gleefully jumped to the attack. Headlines screamed of the transgressions by the peace officers of Sawyer County. Hundreds of telegrams sympathetic to Dietz were sent to Governor Davidson. Even the mayor of St. Paul and other prominent Minnesota citizens immediately wired the Wisconsin Governor:

"We, citizens of St. Paul, respectfully urge that you order the cessation of hostilities against the Dietz family until cooler counsel can prevail. It seems to us in humanity's name that the shooting of an innocent woman or children would not be tribute exacted in the name of the law, and that the great state of Wisconsin can preserve her peace and dignity and at the same time earn the respect of her sister states by compelling her peace officers to adopt other and more humane methods than now proposed by Sheriff Madden."

John Dietz slept like an untroubled child. Hattie did not sleep at all. She lay and stared at the black of the ceiling and wondered about the fate of her children. As soon as Gibbons left, her laryngitis magically cured itself. At first she had pleaded, and then with the argumentative fire of old, she'd all but told John he should not go to town and leave her alone with Helen and Johnny.

"What do you expect me to do if they shoot you and Leslie also? How would I live?"

John had put his arm around his wife's shoulders. He was almost amused at her vehemence. "They won't get me, Hattie. They've tried before and haven't succeeded yet. That alone should tell you what the fates have in store. "

John peered across the open fields and the miles and miles of tangled forest separating him and his family from civilization. "I'd sure like to be there when Gibbons gets in town and tells them I'm coming in. They'll go berserk. Probably set Clarence and Myra free. That's why they took them, to trap me into coming into town. Nope, you watch, the kids will be back home tomorrow. "

Hattie turned away, tight-lipped and silent. She sat down at the organ and began to sing her favorite hymn. At first her voice was quiet, choked, but then it built in volume. *"When you walk through a storm hold your head up high and don't be afraid of the dark..."*

The tremulous, raw emotion of her voice filled the cabin. By the time she finished tears ran in heavy streaks down her cheeks.

John, also choked with emotion, stood behind Hattie and squeezed her shoulders. The three remaining of his brood watched; Helen and Johnny silent, pulled down by the emotional state of their mother and the gravity of the news Leslie had brought. For his part Leslie was silent, subdued, a broken boy who'd been shamed by his father for running while his brother and sister were being attacked.

"It will be all right," John said to Hattie. "We stay here. If they come we fight. They've tried before." He patted his wife's shoulders.

Later, with the rest of the family sunk within themselves and paying no attention, John took a new American flag from a trunk in the bedroom and, without assistance, strung it up on the sapling nailed to the side of the cabin. He hefted his rifle and stared at the tote road leading from town. He spat hard then gazed at the flag standing straight out in a firm breeze. A lump formed in his throat. Tears welled in his eyes.

"Clarence. Almyra," he muttered. His grip tightened on the rifle. "With liberty and justice for all... by God!"

* * *

For two days Myra lay in the hotel room. There was never a moment without an armed guard standing at the door. Treatment of Myra's wounds consisted of simple bandage coverings on the front of her abdomen and the middle of her back. Interior damage was not addressed. Constantly draining pus and blood stained new bandages as quickly as they were placed. For the most part Myra lay quietly, but at times she sobbed. She spoke only sparingly, maintaining her own counsel. She did not sleep.

On one visit Mary Phelan patted her head. It was one of the rare occasions Myra spoke, "You know, I feel so badly for my mother, because mother is pregnant. She's already had three children die. My brother Stanley died out there on the farm. "

"Rest now, child," Mary said.

Shortly thereafter Mary bustled downstairs and confronted deputy Thorbahn. "You cannot leave that girl here. She has pains inside. She has got to have hospital care. "

Monday morning, October 3, 1910, the decision was made to ship Myra via train to a hospital. Fear that John Dietz might approach and attempt to rescue his daughter still ran high. More reporters and curiosity lookers had crowded into the tiny town. One correspondent described Myra's departure:

Most of the people were revolted by the spectacle of Myra Dietz's removal. She was carried out of her room at 7 o'clock and placed on a cot. One of the only two cries she allowed to escape her came then. The other was when she was shoved into a baggage car.

Aside from these cries, wrung from her in spite of herself, not a murmur or complaint came from beneath the cloth that covered her features.

The only part of her that was visible was her black hair lying across the pillow. The cot was picked up by men at the four corners and the longest way to the waiting baggage car was chosen, in spite of the fact that the direct route was down the main street.

Instead she was carried down an alley, ankle deep in the shovelings of stables, from which a nauseating odor arose. The men carrying the cot swore freely as they stumbled in the mire. The curses were half humorous, but they must have been none the less disgusting to the suffering girl.

Deputy Thorbahn stood in the middle of the wagon road alternately staring at the woods through field glasses and watching the group of deputies getting Myra into the car. Twenty deputies were on hand, and twenty rifles.

A dozen armed guards were placed on the baggage car for the first leg of the journey. No doctor was provided, however, Janette Dunster, who reportedly had sat with sick people in the past, was detailed to go along for the ride.

Sympathy for the Dietz children and outrage against the law enforcement officials of Sawyer County continued to build. A headline that day in the *St. Paul Dispatch* read:

CLUBWOMEN MAY AID MYRA DIETZ
Mrs. Hamlin is Trying to Get State Federations of
Minnesota and Wisconsin to Act
WOULD SEND NURSES TO GIRL
She Condemns Shooting and Subsequent Actions by
officials as Brutal in the Extreme

"Just to think," said Mrs. Hamlin, "of moving that young girl when she is dangerously injured, and, in addition denying her the care of women nurses and comradeship. It would be bad enough ordinarily for a young wounded girl to be surrounded by men when they are all friends, but to think of that poor girl staring from her bed of pain and seeing nothing but the grim putenances of armed men who have made it their business to shoot the members of her family, and who are planning ways to add her father to their list. "

Another article stated:

...As the train dwindled down the track, people were heard to declare that she (Myra) would never come back alive.

Six miles from their destination in Rice Lake the deputies on the train received news an angry mob had gathered in Rice Lake and were intent on freeing the girl. The decision to switch trains in Rice Lake and head for the hospital in Eau Claire was quickly changed. The entourage changed cars in Tuscobia and headed north for a hospital in Ashland.

Somehow during the switching, John's brother William, to whom John had not conversed for more than three years, boarded the train. Rifles were leveled as Bill was permitted to briefly speak with his niece. He patted her dark hair.

"How do you do, Almyra?"

Myra looked up in surprise. "Uncle Bill. "

"Are you in much pain?"

"Oh, yes. "

"It's a shame," Bill said. "They ought to take you to a hospital. "

"We are," Deputy Arneston responded.

"A hospital in Hayward?" Bill questioned, but Arneston would not reply. He motioned with his rifle and Bill departed. Arneston later asked Myra if she wanted to see her uncle again. Myra paused. Pa had been shouting at Uncle Bill, accusing him of siding with the mills because he had been present as a witness when Moses paid John the seventeen hundred dollars for his wages.

Myra looked at Arneston. "Do you think he wants to see me again?"

"I wouldn't know," Arneston said gruffly as if resenting his brief compassion. He then declined to go and ask. Myra was left alone, quiet, huddled down under her covers against her pain and humiliation.

Thus the ambush of the Dietz children lost the law enforcement officials the sympathy they had temporarily gained after John shot Bert Horel. One visitor to Winter wrote:

> ...Neither of these men (Dietz and Madden) is very popular in Winter at the present time. Fully nineteen out of every twenty men in Winter are against Dietz... Madden has nearly every one in Winter for his enemy. The shooting of the Dietz innocent children, in the opinion of residents of Winter, was one of the most dastardly acts ever committed by officers of the law.

In their defense, some officers claimed Clarence had pulled Myra in front of him as a shield. An editorial in the *St. Paul Dispatch* summed up much of the attitude against law enforcement methods and officials:

UNFOLDING OF THE TRAGEDY

It is intimated in the late news report from the seat of disgrace at Winter, Wisconsin, that the valorous sheriff has planned to train a siege gun, or mortar, or 13-inch rifle upon the Dietz home in vindication of the majesty of the law of Wisconsin. This would be in entire accordance with the methods which prevailed on Saturday.

When this heavy artillery shall have obtained the range of the log cabin of Dietz, it may be expected that diligence will be exercised by the sheriff in ascertaining that the wife and children of Dietz are within the walls before fire is opened. The cruel and scandalous tragedy would be incomplete, would be robbed of some of its spectacular features if the destruction of the Dietz home did not include the slaughter of its inmates, including the women and children.

It might be suggested to the law officers of Sawyer County, as something which should appeal to the instincts already made manifest, that dynamite is a very destructive agency and might be used very effectively in the clearing the Wisconsin landscape of every vestige of the Dietz house and household. Its use upon women and children may be expected to produce results of the most deadly. It might bring Dietz to time more quickly than gunpowder and failing that would certainly deprive him of power for harm and would dissipate the fear that has held the forty armed men of Winter in such abject terror.

There are only forty of them, while there is one Dietz and the fear which has robbed them of reason and humanity is a very rational one. No one will blame the sheriff for excluding the newspaper writers from Cameron Dam; the only wonder is that he has not exiled them from Winter and even from Wisconsin.

They have been telling the world what occurred at that ambuscade on the road to Winter last Saturday and the world has shuddered. They told of the heartless removal of the wounded and perhaps dying daughter of Dietz and no one has read of it without a malediction upon the responsible head. They will tell more as the amazing tragedy unfolds and the sheriff, if he is endeavoring to muzzle the news, if he hopes to keep from the world knowledge of the inhumanity of this case and the lamentable failure to uphold the laws which proceed it and made it possible, is showing a wisdom out of all fellowship with his previous conduct.

The story will be told and told fully and correctly. It will reach the world and will reach the ear of Governor Davidson of Wisconsin. The marvel has been that the chief magistrate of Wisconsin has permitted this travesty of law and order to reach its current stage.

The wonder now is what is he going to do about it.

**ADVOCATES DEATH FOR
ANARCHISTS**
Solitary Imprisonment
With Liberal Private
Application of Lash
Secretary Bonaparte Says
There is No Cure for the Evil
but He Would Inflict
Drastic Punishment on
Slayers of Officials

**DIETZ REJECTS TERMS
OFFERED BY FORELICH**
Call for Conference with
Colonel Munson, Governor
Davidson's Private
Secretary

**BLOODY BATTLE
IS LIKELY**
Cameron Dam Defender's
Cabin is Well Prepared for an
Attack by Armed Forces

**HAS REFUSED
TO SURRENDER**
Proposition Was that
Outlaw Yield on Promise of
Bail and Change of Venue
and Aid

**MADDEN INTIMATES
ASSAULT**

CHAPTER XV

Thus the war was joined, Socialists versus Capitalists, working men versus the monied forces, common citizens versus corrupters and grafters, Minnesotans versus Wisconsinites, country folk versus city folk, with Chief Deputy Thorbahn and Sheriff "Martial Law" Madden caught in the triple cross fire between citizens outraged at their brutal attack on the Dietz children, citizens angered at their failure to uphold the law, and, of course, John Dietz himself, who in turn was aligned against whatever forces the world chose to throw in his direction.

The tiny sawmill town of Winter was quickly overwhelmed. The combined forces of Thorbahn's hard rule, Madden's martial law, and the steady influx of big city reporters, sightseers, and photographers transformed the village beyond recognition:

...From civilization to this hole in the wild is only fifteen hours, but the difference is that of half a century. Isolated, save for two snail-like trains a day one lone telegraph wire and one lone telephone wire, with the nearest other point of communication fifty miles away, Winter swarms with newspaper correspondents, sent here from a dozen cities to send back to civilization the tidings of the famous war, termed by some the siege of Winter and by others the siege of the Dietz fortress.

Another article of October 5, 1910 read:

DRUNKEN TOWN AWAITS FIGHT

Winter, Wis. — This village, deprived of its garrison of deputy sheriffs by the beginning of the siege of John Dietz's home, and filled with Indians, lumberjacks and half-breeds, is growing drunker every hour, awaiting the conflict that seems to be impending.

A state of lawlessness prevails in the town. Armed sentries, left to guard the town while the posse advances through the woods toward the Dietz' home, patrol the streets staggering from the effects of drink and terrorizing residents with a careless display of Winchester rifles.

Many were seen on the streets of Winter late last night bearing bottles of liquor as they tramped their sentry posts.

The women servants at the Hotel Winter went on a strike early today and left town hurriedly after ineffectual attempts by the proprietor to quiet the most boisterous of the guards.

CORRESPONDENTS USE HANDCAR
TO REACH SCENE OF BATTLE

The correspondents who reached the seat of war here Sunday, got in after a consideration of every means of travel, including special engines, handcars, automobiles, and horses... Martial law is in effect and it is very martial. Only the band is lacking.

Reporters fought each other and fought the law. The Hotel Winter fed more than 300 people. The usual charges were the same, $1.50 per day for a room, 50 cents per meal for lumberjacks and 75 cents for all others, including reporters. Men who had started out one to a room soon teamed up and slept in shifts. After the women struck because of the loud and obnoxious behavior of the patrons, the reporters had to wait on themselves.

Reporter Floyd Gibbons, who had been visiting John when the children were ambushed, became angered at being jostled aside from the one telephone wire and hired an automobile to drive news flashes and photographs out of the isolated town.

Then, in order to thwart his press rivals, he climbed to the second story of a building and leaned out and cut the telephone wire. He was promptly reported, arrested and bundled into his own hired automobile and driven to Hayward where he posted $500 bail and quickly scurried back to the scene of the war.

Other reporters had their difficulties as well:

PHOTOGRAPHER SEIZED

The blockade of the Dietz farm is being rigorously upheld. A newspaper photographer, George Luxton of Minneapolis, who attempted to run it this morning, was arrested with a great flourish of "shooting irons" and "pump guns," driven back to town by a deputy who held a rifle between his knees and a cocked revolver in one hand, and thrown into the filthy jail with sundry prods from the business end of a rifle.

Deputy Thorbahn shortly elicited a promise Luxton would not again attempt to cross the blockade line and set the reporter free. Luxton immediately filed suit challenging Madden's martial law:

"Martial law is no law. It is an irresponsible tyranny. For a two-penny magistrate to establish martial no-law, without authority from the sovereign power, is an act of rebellion..."

Thorbahn, in reply to a question by a reporter, frankly admitted that Sheriff Madden had told him the soft pedal must be put on publicity so that Dietz would lose interest in the struggle.

Sheriff Madden, as he sat with a number of war correspondents said, "We will be able to dispense with the help of the newspaper men."

None of the reporters chose to heed Madden's advice. They were too involved in their war of words with the law and each other. An Eau Claire paper reported:

A lady from the seat of war... says the people of Hayward and Winter did not know much about the Dietz affair. ...They got their information from the Cock and Bull Story factory recently established in Winter, of which Baron Manchauson, a distinguished foreigner, was president and corresponding secretary.

She would not want to call this man a liar, but would intimate that he had a taste for amplification with an innate, an inveterate, and inexhaustible capacity for the falsification of the truth.

Copious reports, mostly apocryphal, were transmitted at all hours of the day and night to the Minneapolis Rowdy Journal, the St. Paul Private Listener, The Duluth Keyhole Reporter, the Superior Stabber, the Milwaukee Sewer, and the Eau Claire Family Spy. It was not amiss to have some source of information, such as it was.

Nothing could be obtained from the Sheriff, who was as dumb as a drum with a hole in it. Popular feeling was again in favor of Dietz since the shooting of his daughter.

Another editorial writer wrote:

It might be expected that anarchists and cranks would sympathize with, and uphold John Dietz in his murderous opposition to the law of the state and of the nation.

But that metropolitan dailies such as the St. Paul Dispatch and the Pioneer Press should inaugurate a propaganda of anarchy in their editorial columns, would be beyond belief were not the appeal to anarchy in cold print before the eyes of the world.

In the town of Winter more than a hundred letters and telegrams in support of John piled up at the telegraph office and post office. Sheriff Madden instructed there would be no mail deliveries in or out of the Dietz farm. In his turn, Madden received half as many letters as Dietz, the majority of which were abusive and threatening. John's mail was, of course, supportive.

Dr. George Kleinschmidt of Milwaukee wired John to "hold the fort, as reinforcements are coming." One paper reported:

Armed with repeating rifles and shotguns, prepared to battle for the liberty of John Dietz, Dr. George Kleinschmidt and a company of sharpshooters left Milwaukee last night on a train for Rice Lake, where they will proceed to Winter

Principals in the siege on the Dietz farm: Deputy Roy Van Alstyne, Chief Deputy Fred Thorbahn, Sheriff Mike Madden and Sawyer County District Attorney Davis.

and fight for freedom of Dietz.

St. Paul:

FORMING TROOP TO GUARD DIETZ

Veterans of Cuban War Ready to Rush with Rifles if
Sheriff is Inhuman
Volunteer Defenders of Dietz
Will go in Autos if Needed

One last telegram received in Winter read:

John F. Dietz, If you want help I stand ready with 25 cow-punchers, everyone a crack shot.
Bill the Wreck
Conder, Montana

One reporter willingly took it upon himself to set the stage for the great showdown:

Many times the deputies have said that the Dietz family are all that save him from an assault on his cabin. Now the taste for blood is on their lips and the sting of mortification is in their hides and Dietz must assuage the one and soothe

the other.

...Fred Thorbahn has brought in a man from some distance away who is said to be able to cut the tongue off a
whippoorwill at fifty yards... and his bullet may be the one
which will bring the long war to a finish and Dietz to his
resting place.

It may be said, however, that when Dietz goes the little
expanse will be enriched and ornamented by the headstones
of a number of well-known citizens hereabouts.

At present Dietz is not well fixed for defense. His rifle,
his wife's and his son Leslie's are all that can be depended
upon. Little Johnnie and Helen, 14 years old, may wing a
few deputies, but they are too young to count on.

The deputies here have an air of mystery which bodes ill
for peace and happiness hereabout. Winter is practically
left without deputies. The scene has shifted and the curtain
rising for the final act is showing the determined, square-
jawed, mustached face and figure of John Dietz, directly in
the foreground, with the deputies crowding the orchestra
pit and climbing across the footlights at him.

The thing has come to a pass where there is no going
back. All the determination that is in Dietz is going straight
up against all the power of the law that is Madden's and
something must break, and with the breaking of lives and
the breaking of hearts.

Hattie Dietz marched across the dirt yard from the squat log
cabin to the root cellar, the sunken building without windows
or shooting portholes that some city reporters had referred to
as a sunken fort. She took a brisket of corned beef from a
wooden keg of foamy brine. With a long-pronged fork she
extracted a bowl of good German sauerkraut from another
noxious-smelling keg. She tucked a jar of canned carrots under her arm and, thus laden, quickly went back across the yard
to the cabin. She did not linger, for John had informed her
there were two dozen men or more out there in those woods
watching their every move.

She ducked into the dark cabin and sighed. If she'd slept
these past few days she could not remember when. Keep busy,

keep working, she'd thought, it was a woman's only salvation.

Her eyes made an accidental swing over the organ and immediately she heard Myra's pure, clear voice. She then looked at Myra's picture on the wall and wondered if her daughter lay stiffened and dead.

"Dear Lord, give me strength to bear what I must bear," Hattie intoned. She quickly turned to preparation of supper.

She was bent, filled with the return of pain, lumbago she was certain, and perhaps a tumor growing side by side with her child. She should see a doctor, she thought. A stillborn would be the last straw she could possibly bear.

John ducked into the cabin. He kicked his boots at the side of the door to clear some of the dirt. The plank floor was covered with sand. Hattie wondered when the last time was she had swept the floor. She made a mental note to instruct Helen to sweep.

"I still see glimpses of them out there," John said. He did not sound overly worried. If anything he was pleased. "I walked within ten rods of a couple of them. They froze like rabbits and didn't even twitch their noses. They're holding Leslie and I up from getting enough firewood in to last the winter; what with deer season and all coming up."

John bent down and gazed out the thick and blurred glass of the small window facing across the flowage and Thornapple River fronting his land. Leslie herded their two milk cows into the barn.

"I thought Lester would stand up better than he did," John said with bitter disappointment.

"There were a number of them," Hattie said. "He dropped his gun. What was he to do?"

John responded angrily, "If he wouldn't have been scrambling like a frightened snowshoe he wouldn't have dropped his gun. When you get in a gunfight you don't run and hide behind a tree. For Christ's sake!"

"Clarence and Myra are gone; Myra maybe dead," Hattie yelled in a voice as shrill as if she'd lost control. "You'd have Leslie shot as well? What kind of father are you?"

"Was it I who fired? You squawk like a raven run off from meat it did not kill. " After some seconds a slow smile worked at John's lips, his usual amusement when he could goad Hattie into losing her temper. "I am not the Lord Jesus Christ, Hattie. I do not assign the fates. If Leslie had been meant to die, he already would be dead. In spite of that he ran. My son."

* * *

Hattie lay awake and in pain in the black of a cold autumn night. Complete silence filled the cabin. She could hear John breathe, she could hear the dog's low growl before the barking exploded from the front yard.

Immediately John leapt to his feet, banging Hattie beside the head and kneeing her in the stomach as he bolted across the bed. He completely ignored Hattie's moan and writhing and ran into the dark of the outer room and took a Luger pistol down off the wall. Leslie had also jumped out of his bunk bed and was feeling in the dark for his boots.

'I'm coming, Pa."

"You stay in the house with the women and children," John snapped curtly. He unlatched the tiny hook from the screen door of his fortress and padded out to where the dogs were tied. "Hush, hush, " John said softly. The dogs knew the tones of his voice, the warning and, with the exception of a few anxious whines over the wind blown scent carried to their noses, ceased to bark. John knelt down in their midst and peered in the direction the dogs faced.

John's teeth were clamped in a grim clench. The forces of the corporations and the monied interests were all being brought to bear, taking from him even the flesh of his flesh. But still he held them off. People didn't see or understand as clearly as did he; not even Hattie. But he knew the way they worked. Perhaps this time they would get him, he thought, the sheer numbers gave them the odds. But they'd be surprised at the cost. Newspapers would then tell his tale. Perhaps, he surmised, this was the way it was meant to be all along.

Myra's dog Tippy growled low in his throat. Then John thought he glimpsed approaching shadows below the cabin. He raised his pistol and fired several deliberate shots.

"It's Dietz!"

"Let's git out of here," a man yelled, his voice tinged with panic.

Not one of the approaching deputies returned fire. There were sounds of running, crashing in brush, the thud and grunt of falling bodies, splashing in the marsh grass, cursing. And then silence. John patted his dogs on the head.

He grinned at the cowardice of his adversaries. In truth he might just prevail. He ducked into the black of the root cellar and threw each dog a bone from venison scraps.

When John returned to the house Leslie was kneeling at a window with a rifle in his hands. "Put that gun up," John snapped.

Leslie lowered his head and quickly complied. He understood then, because of his failure when Myra and Clarence were captured, John would always be this way towards him. For Leslie well knew from John's reactions with Uncle Will — John never forgave.

John reloaded his pistol and hung it on the wall. He followed Hattie back into bed. "Two-legged scavengers coming after our fowl," he grunted with the hint of a smile. "I was forced to remind them the keeper of the castle was willing to defend his home." He settled deeper into the packed straw of their mattress. "You should have heard them squawk.."

He seemed satisfied, like after the time he'd informed a reporter how to enter a gunfight, "You never hide behind a tree. You keep your back to the tree and protect yourself from that quarter, and then you can face your adversary direct with a clear field of fire."

John returned to sleep and began snoring in surprisingly short time. Hattie lay awake and stared at the dark. In the first days after John shot Horel, she and John had been asked by a reporter why they remained in Wisconsin on the farm. Hattie recalled the exchange well:

"Has it occurred to you, that for the sake of your children, especially the younger ones, and the girls, who are being brought up in an atmosphere of danger and opposition and defense, and in daily prospect of encountering violence and sudden death, that it might be better to pull up stakes and go somewhere else?"

Dietz squared his shoulders and replied, "Where can I go? Everything I have is right here. And besides, I move on for no man. If I am to be a martyr, then I shall have to accept my destiny. But I shall continue about my business as I have done in the past, because I know that I am right."

SEES NO REASON TO MOVE

The correspondent turned to the mother for her answer. The sense of the question had been sinking into her, and she had turned from her mending to look thoughtfully out of the window. But her answer when she looked back was given with spirit. Then she exclaimed with a deal of pathos:

"Why we are no different from any other family. We come and go, and tend to our farm, and go into town for provisions, and molest nobody. Why should we have to give up our home and start all over again?"

The reporter had been warned by the people of Winter that the family would be pleasant to him and try to win him over by fair language. Perhaps that was what they were trying to do, but they seemed sincere. Also, they seemed well above the usual farmer's family in intelligence and native refinement. Their courtesy was genuine...

She'd tried, Hattie thought; but what good did it do?

At the first grey hints of dawn she rose and padded into the outer room and put a log on the smoldering coals in their wood stove. Only three children now lay in the room where once there had been six. Helen and Johnny were sound asleep. Leslie lay still, his back to the room. Hattie was certain by his stiffness the boy still lay awake. She turned and saw the picture of Myra with a scarf around her neck. A deep pain gripped her as forcefully as a heart attack. The question of Myra being living or dead consumed her every waking moment, so much so she even considered walking down to the wood line and asking one of those men if her daughter was still alive.

Hattie pulled on a long coat and walked outside to the outhouse. A heavy fog covered the river and farm, blocking a view from the shadow of the forest all around. Whistling wings turned her attention to four green-headed Mallard ducks winging down the river. It was a pretty morning with the sun shining silver rays through the obscuring fog.

Hattie blinked as if to force tears back inside. Myra was in the Lord's hands, dead or alive she was beyond her control. She sighed deeply as if trying to ease the weight on her chest. She'd fry corn bread this morning, she thought, Leslie's favorite. And warm some maple syrup. Perhaps the boy would be cheered.

* * *

The John Dietz family and Sawyer County officials were not the only beleaguered people in the state of Wisconsin that week. Solely because of the stubborn farmer from the deep woods north, Governor James Davidson faced his own special problems:

GOVERNOR DAVIDSON IS THREATENED

Letters, carrying skull and crossbones in red and black, threatening the life of Governor Davidson unless he instructs Sheriff Madden of Winter to discontinue the campaign to capture John Dietz, are being received at the executive office.

While Wisconsin's chief executive entertains no fear that these threats will be carried out, he is annoyed and perhaps a trifle nervous over the persistency of these violent letters, and last night Chief of Police Shaughnessy called at the executive department and was shown all of the threatening letters and telegrams that have been received. Chief Shaughnessy agrees with Governor Davidson that these messages are from cranks, and he does not think there is any great danger to the governor.

MAY NEED GUARD

In view of the fact that so many of these threatening epistles have been received and that they cover such a wide territory, including Chicago, where law defying organizations are strong, it may be deemed advisable by the local police to guard the executive mansion nights until the present Dietz wave subsides.

Governor Davidson feels that certain newspapers, particularly newspapers in Minneapolis, have thrown up a false sentiment in the Dietz case, making Dietz sort of a hero, and newspaper stories along this line have been taken as the facts in the case. Publicity of this character doubtless has stimulated a strong sentiment for Dietz, many people feeling that he has been abused and that he is in the right.

Governor Davidson is disposed to feel that these newspapers are entirely responsible for the existing division of opinion in this matter, and that in that way the newspapers are also responsible for the threatening messages received in Madison.

Despite the threats, Governor Davidson was moved by the large volume and sheer emotionalism of people's reactions. Everyone hungered for news of Dietz. It was an election year. He called for Attorney General Frank L. Gilbert and his personal secretary Colonel O.G. Munson. The time had arrived for the chief magistrate of the State of Wisconsin to weigh into the fray.

* * *

It was during those predawn hours, with the thick fog hanging over the river, that Hattie saw the first man standing on the narrow plank footbridge across the river. The man stood crouched, peering through the fog at her form. He carried a stick with a white flag tied on the end. A reporter, Hattie wondered? A man bearing news of Myra? A lump clogged her throat. "John, there's a man here to see you."

The first visitor that morning of October 6, 1910, was John W. Froelich of St. Paul, manager of Froelich Manufacturing Company and an avowed Dietz sympathizer. Mr. Froelich had been granted permission by Sheriff Madden to attempt to talk Dietz into surrendering. He had arrived at the surrounding cordon the evening before and made his approach on the cabin at six in the morning. He stayed with the dam defender almost three hours. When he walked out, he walked out alone.

PEACE AMBASSADOR TELLS OF HIS VISIT

If you take his word for it he won't surrender. If you take my judgment for it, he will.... He also said he would never go behind the bars, but I am sure that does not represent his present attitude. He showed plainly that he is considering the argument deeply, and expressed his wish that he might talk directly with the governor or a representative of the governor. I feel convinced that if he can receive assurance from the state authorities that he can be taken away without injury he will give himself up...

...Mrs. Dietz told Mr. Froelich that she would do what she could to persuade her husband to give up.

In mid-afternoon of the same day of his morning visit, Mr. Froelich escorted the attorney general for the state of Wisconsin, Frank L. Gilbert, and Colonel G.O. Munson, the personal secretary for the governor of the state of Wisconsin, up to the isolated log cabin beside the Thornapple River. John Dietz, unarmed, stepped out into the dusty yard. He doffed his hat to the state officials and held up his hands, palms outward.

"There, as you can see, I have no horns."

The two officials were invited inside the cabin where they met Hattie and the three remaining Dietz children. They were immediately offered chairs and refreshments. Attorney General Gilbert studied his adversary, this isolated farmer who had caused so much problem for the chief magistrate of the state. He later explained his first impression of John F. Dietz:

"There was nothing depraved, vicious or bulldog about him in appearance — except when he told us about those real or fancied wrongs. Then one could see bulldog determination in the man. He thought that everything that had been done was a move on the checkerboard in the interests of the lumber concerns, which he insisted were after his property. He stood about five feet nine inches, well built, powerfully built, I should say, with slightly stooped shoulders, a fair, florid complexion, sandy mustache and bald.

"His manners were pleasant and courteous. He had a winning smile, and I do not believe the man knew what it was to fear anything. He was perfectly calm and normal and unconcerned. One would think that the big circle of men, armed with rifles, about his little cabin on the hill, were there on nothing but a friendly and harmless mission. Everything in the Dietz house was going along in the usual way. They were waiting — just waiting. Mrs. Dietz was a motherly-appearing

woman, but it seemed to me that years of almost constant war-
fare had left lines of tragedy upon her face. Like her husband,
however, she thought her place was at home."

The conversation went easy. Attorney General Gilbert readily
recognized John was not a man to engage in heated argument.
"I have a letter from Governor Davidson, John. It's a promise
from the State of Wisconsin that if you willingly submit yourself to authorities your safety will be guaranteed, you will receive a change of venue to a nearby county and you will be
appointed competent legal counsel."

John regarded the state attorney general suspiciously. His
mouth was set, hard. "I cannot do that."

"You're surrounded," Colonel Munson pointed out. "There's
no place you can go."

"Since this conspiracy began, I've had hundreds of bullets
fired at me. I've had men come at me. I've been surrounded at
least nineteen times. One more time makes no difference to
me."

Munson and Gilbert exchanged glances. They'd been informed John was an educated man, but difficult. Nevertheless
they'd been cautiously optimistic. After all, they did carry with
them the weight of the authority of the State of Wisconsin.

"Mr. Froelich indicated you might consider submitting to
authorities but that you wanted to speak to us first," Gilbert
said carefully. They had to hold John's temper in check.

"Froelich," John barked as if he'd been slapped. "Another
hireling from the lumber trusts. One of Weyerhaeuser's agents.
I saw him snooping around here. Trying to subvert my family
against me." He glanced hard at Hattie who was busy peeling
potatoes. "He was looking to collect information, see what
kind of defenses we had."

"Mr. Froelich is sympathetic to your cause," Colonel Munson
said.

"I know how those reprobates work," John said heatedly.
"I've been deceived too many times in the past. I trust people
too much. They even hired my brother Bill against me. I presume right now they're shelling out their gold to Clarence and
Myra to turn them against me. They'll stoop to any low. Nothing is sacred. When they sent Jonas in here he gave me the

Masonic handshake with one hand and tried to wave a paper in my face with the other."

John leaned back in his rocking chair and smiled. "That's the last time he'll try that subterfuge."

"Is there anyone from Winter that I could bring out here to talk to you?" Gilbert asked.

"I have no friends in Winter," John snapped. "That's a saw-mill town. They tried to surround me that day Horel jumped me from behind. They've been against me from the start because I refused to submit. We moved out here as a pioneer family. We harmed no one. But the mills came after me. They've tried to pay my real estate taxes and claim my property as theirs. They've filed a twenty-thousand-dollar judgment against my wife, judgments that old liar Moses had promised had been quashed. That has been my history of experience with the lumber trusts, lies and then more lies. What chance would I have upon surrender? They control the legislature and the courts." John trailed off from his long tirade. He shook his head sadly, the image of one of the world's persecuted marking his every gesture.

Gilbert and Munson backed off then. The conversation was becoming too heated, leading nowhere in the direction of resolution. Gilbert commented he admired John's efforts at foraging a farm so far back in the wilderness. Presently John rose to show him around the farm. The two men, with John unarmed, walked within plain view of the surrounding posse. John showed Gilbert the sites of past battles, where Rogich had been shot, where other men had lain in ambush. The conversation was amiable, two neighbors out for an afternoon in the fall sunshine and bright colors of the surrounding forest.

Colonel Munson purposely remained behind to talk to Hattie. "Your husband's a hard man."

"He feels strongly when he's been wronged," Hattie said simply.

"Do you feel you've been wronged, Mrs. Dietz?"

"Myself and the children have harmed no one," Hattie said quickly, an almost automatic response. She'd learned from Froelich's visit that any hint of her opposition would somehow be reported back to John as if trying to drive a wedge between them. "Why did they shoot Clarence and Myra? They never fired on anyone. We are simply trying to live our lives. I do not understand why they keep coming after us as if they were trying to stamp us out."

The heavy features of her face became constricted, straining for control. She beseeched the governor's private secretary. "Have I or my children done that much wrong?"

Munson ignored the woman's emotionalism. He was hard. "Then you support your husband?"

Hattie understood there would be no sympathy from that quarter. The state's lack of understanding made her bitter.

"John and I have been married over twenty-five years. We've worked side by side with our children to build this farm."

She glanced out the window toward the lumber piles. "Some day we're going to put a nice home up here." Hattie suddenly turned. Her eyes gleamed as if damp. She held both hands across her lower abdomen. "I am in a family way, you understand."

"All the more reason you should consider our offer, Mrs. Dietz," Colonel Munson said. The woman did not reply.

Clearly her attitude was the same as her husband's, as it should be. He looked at Leslie, who'd been listening but scarcely said a word. "And how do you feel, son? Do you support your father?"

"Oh, yes sir," Leslie responded without hesitation. "My sister and brother have never fired a rifle at anyone. They had no right to gun them down like that without warning. Don't forget, Johnny and Helen are here. They and my mother have never committed any crime. None."

"Then you'd best convince your father. There'd be no charges against you or your mother if you give it up now."

Leslie looked down to the faded plank floor. No, he could not go against his Pa. It was not possible.

After two hours of fruitless talk, Attorney General Gilbert and Colonel Munson respectfully declined Hattie's invitation to stay to dinner. (The two later commented on how Hattie had worked every moment they were at the farm.)

Attorney General Gilbert handed John an envelope. "The letter from the governor. "

The two men then took their leave.

Mr. John F. Dietz
Winter, Wisconsin
Dear Sir:
You are no doubt aware that Sheriff Madden of Sawyer County has warrants for your arrest, charging you with assault and intent to kill. Some persons believe that your continued defiance of the law arises from the fear that you will not have a fair trial and furthermore that you have no means to employ counsel to defend yourself. As governor of the state, actuated by a desire to prevent further bloodshed I send Attorney General Gilbert and O.G. Munson, my private secretary, to represent me and promise you full personal protection, a fair trial and counsel to defend you. If you still refuse to peaceably submit to the orderly process of the law the responsibility of any bloodshed and loss of life must rest upon you alone.
I am very truly yours,
J.O. Davidson

Hattie laid the letter on the kitchen table. The last line hammered in her mind, "If you refuse to peaceably submit to the orderly process of the law the responsibility of any bloodshed and loss of life must rest upon you alone."

Her mouth was dry as if from fear. Words from the governor. A spasm of pain from her tumor almost knocked her to the floor. Yet she did her best not to show the pain. "What do you think they'll do, John?" She watched John closely, wondering if he understood exactly what it was they faced.

"I don't know," John said. He was unconcerned. "They can stay out in that woods as long as they like. We'll see what happens when the snow flies. The other night when they approached I ran them off easily enough. Besides, it doesn't matter what they do. Whatever they do, they do. I have no control over that."

Hattie nodded mutely. Yes, John was right. He had no more

The tote road to Winter and the site of the ambush of Clarence, Myra and Leslie.

control over them than she had over John. Not anymore.

The following afternoon Attorney General Gilbert and Colonel Munson made an unannounced visit and one more effort to talk John into surrendering. John stood silhouetted against the sun with a rifle upon his shoulder and the sun in the eyes of his adversaries. After a few seconds he walked back to the cabin and looked at the two men through field glasses. As the representatives of the State of Wisconsin approached, John stepped out onto the porch. He was unarmed.

"I've come one last time to try to avert bloodshed," Gilbert said. He stood in the worn dirt of the yard, soil too poor and beaten to even hold grass. He tried desperately for understanding. "The offer of yesterday still stands. Colonel Munson and myself will escort you out of here so you have nothing to fear."

"The two of you aren't big enough to stop an assassin's bullet," John replied.

"We could have all the deputies come out of the woods and stand in the open field," Munson said.

"How would I know they were all there?" John objected. "One sharpshooter could lie in wait." He smiled, surely the two officials could understand his clear logic.

"What would it take to make you submit to authority, John?" Gilbert asked. He was harder now. Time was short. He saw no purpose in avoiding confrontation. "If I had every criminal complaint against members of your family dropped? Including those against Clarence and Myra who are already in custody. And, with the one exception of the Horel shooting, all those against you dismissed and nullified, would you then submit?"

"No, I cannot," John responded with equal emphasis. State attorney general or not, it made no difference to him. "The state must clean up the other dirt first."

"What do you mean?" Gilbert asked with some exasperation. Every time he made an offer, John simply demanded more.

"The civil suits against my wife and her property. We want clear and guaranteed title to our property that we paid for in full. The trusts must pay for those logs they ran through on my dam before they blew it up."

"Neither I nor the governor have the authority to dismiss civil complaints, John. That's the law," Gilbert pointed out.

"Then I cannot possibly submit," John said in his lecturing voice. "I know your game. The government wants to deliver me into the hands of the assassins. As long as the American flag floats over my cabin, I'll fight for Cameron Dam and for my family."

"Sheriff Madden will send in his posse," Gilbert said. "My, God, man, do you understand what that means?"

The muscles of John's face twitched. He would accept condescension from no man. "You want surrender. I'd prefer to die in the defense of my home and family. What more righteous deed might a man do than to defend his wife and family? I suppose that'll make me another John Brown. Undoubtedly that will be the start of another revolution that will finally put a stop to these trials and injustices that have surrounded me all these years."

Gilbert sighed. He realized the cause was hopeless. "Would you permit Mrs. Dietz and the two younger children to come to safety with us? Surely you understand that if you persist there is going to be serious trouble here?"

"There are dozens of men out there with rifles," Colonel Munson added. He looked to Hattie. "Surely you must think of your children. "

"My wife and children are in their home," John said.

"What good would it do for me to surrender?" Hattie said. "I have done nothing wrong. If John went away the crowd around Winter would find a way to get rid of me and my children. No, Mr. Munson, this is our home."

"Would you at least permit us to carry young Helen and Johnny out of harm's way?" Gilbert pleaded.

John looked puzzled by the request. "This is the children's home. I see no reason why they should be compelled to leave their home. A proper place for children is in their home."

For several minutes more Attorney General Gilbert and Colonel Munson pleaded with John at least to let the children go to safety. It was all to no avail. They turned to small talk, an almost nervous passing of time. John presented Gilbert with a large set of antlers he had been admiring. John smiled and held out his hand to say goodbye and the two emissaries took their leave.

As the men walked away, John walked a few steps after them and shouted as if speaking to the deputies concealed in the forest. "I will hold my home against you all." He pointed at the American flag hanging from the sapling nailed to the cabin wall. "Until that flag is shot to pieces there on top of my house, I will guard the lives of my wife and children. When the governor of Wisconsin is ready to enforce the law and the constitution as he swore to do when he was inaugurated, then and not until then will I take chances with the horse thieves and murderers that are hunting me."

That same evening John and Leslie and Helen did chores around the barn and walked out to the spring in clear view of the deputies to fetch pails of water. In late afternoon, John dispatched young Johnnie to nail a message to a tree near the edge of the clearing:

"I know your game. The government wants to deliver me into the hands of the assassins. As long as the American flag floats over my cabin, I'll fight for Cameron Dam and for my family."

In response Thorbahn informed reporters, "I will get Dietz without killing other members of his family. Leslie will quit when the old man is shot. The shot that hits Dietz must be true."

Meanwhile Attorney General Gilbert and Colonel Munson met with Sheriff Madden. "He will not submit. He trusts no one," Gilbert said. "Do your duty."

The two state officials then drove back to Winter where they met with reporters before boarding a train for Madison:

"John Dietz will die fighting," said Mr. Gilbert to an interview... "The family awaits the end calmly."

"Do you think that if he sees there is no escape that Dietz may kill his wife and children and then shoot himself rather than be captured?"

"That is possible," answered Mr. Gilbert. "What is more, I think if Dietz told them to stand up in a line to be shot down by his hand they would do it, feeling, because they are fatalists, that it was to be that way."

PRESIDENT ROOSEVELT DECLARES CONDITION IN CHICAGO STOCK YARDS ARE REVOLTING

Sends Strong Message to Congress with Reynolds-Neill Report - Drastic Inspection of Meat Urged - Serious Charges Against Packers Are Substantiated in Document

---

REPORT HAS IT THAT JOHN DIETZ' CABIN BLOWN UP ENTIRE FAMILY MAY BE WIPED OUT OF EXISTENCE BY CHARGE DIETZ PUT UNDER HOME

Over 1,000 Shots are Fired in the Bombardment of Dietz Cabin, Riddling the Cabin and Making it Untenable - Leslie Shot in Groin

DIETZ THREATENED TO BLOW HIS HOME UP WITH DYNAMITE IF CROWDED

Last Chapter in the Romantic History of Man Who Refused to Surrender, and Fought to the Bitter End - Deputies Opened Fire Early in the Morning When Dietz Appeared in the open - Wounded him at the Time, But Not Fatally - Believed to Have Been Fatally Hurt in Rain of Bullets on Cabin. Wife and Children Thought Safe.

CHAPTER XVI

SLAUGHTER OF WHOLE FAMILY THREATENED

If the assault upon the cabin and John Dietz at Cameron Dam is not going on at this moment, it will probably take place either some time today or at the first light tomorrow. It has come to the Dispatch correspondent on the best authority obtainable that all plans for an arrest with the least possible bloodshed have been abandoned by Sheriff Mike Madden and that a determination has been reached to take the cabin by storm without further waiting for the outlaw to expose himself alone away from other members of the family.

RUMORS FLY THICK IN VILLAGE

When it became known in Winter that Fred Thorbahn intended to attempt the capture of Dietz at first light this morning, the town of Winter stood back aghast at the full realization of what that intention meant. When word came back from Cameron Dam that Thorbahn and Van Alstyne had crept close upon the cabin to get Dietz in the morning the excitement passed all reason.

THE JOURNEY TO CAMERON DAM

At two o'clock this morning, led by Father J.A. Pilon, the lone priest of the village, a cavalcade of carriages, an automobile or two, one bicycle and several on foot left for

Cameron Dam...

Silently through the night the teams passed out of the town across the railroad tracks and out upon the long stretch which lies between here and Cameron Dam.

Here and there in the slowly moving cavalcade a lighted lantern threw weird flickers of radiance in and out among distorted shadows by the roadside.

It is a long road and the going at night was not fast. The stars were completely concealed by heavy banks of clouds. The slender crescent of the moon showed only at intervals. Most of the time the road was as black as a pocket...

... The correspondents distributed themselves close to the edge of the trees, selecting positions from which they could see anything that went on without exposing their bodies to bullets if the firing should commence.

If men were turned back into gorillas they could not have shown a more sinuous, animal-like stealthiness than the deputies on guard at the edge of the clearing... The carelessness of the day before had disappeared. This was a locking of horns, a fight to the finish between civilized men, conducted with all the cunning of aborigines.

The deputies knew they had crossed the Rubicon with Dietz and that there was now no turning back, no giving or taking of quarter, no argument for safety except concealment and bulletproof self-protection. Here and there they were visible, shaggy figures, unkempt from their long watch, lying stomach down at full length on the wet foam which the sun never touches under the hemlocks.

EVERY RIFLE LEVELED AT DIETZ CABIN

Every man of them squinted along the black barrel of his rifle and every black barrel was pointed at the door of the little Dietz cabin... Every nerve in their bodies was stretched taut against the supreme moment for which every one of them was waiting when Dietz should expose himself to surrender and the premeditated consequences of his refusal...

During the early morning hours of October 8, 1910, three men walked into the men's shanty of Kaiser Lumber Company Camp Four. The camp was located near the John Dietz farm. The lumberjacks were informed a posse was being organized to get John Dietz once and for all. Foreman Charlie Stinson had given his permission to go ahead. Pay would be almost double pay, five dollars for the day and all the whiskey they could drink. Forty men volunteered and were sworn in as a group.

Ammunition and rifles, set on a nearby railroad flatcar, were provided. Each man was given six boxes, 120 rounds of ammunition. The posse was led through the woods and spread out in a half-moon covering one side of the farm. No reporters saw their approach, nor even learned of their presence. Only a few of the jacks were aware there were more than thirty other deputies covering other points around the farm. They lay down in the forest, rifles ready, waiting.

Leslie came awake with a start. He lay in the barn loft, wrapped in a wool blanket over which he'd pulled swaths of loose hay. The first grey of light showed through the loft door but fixtures inside the barn were still cloaked in black. He wrapped his hands on the reassuring stock of a Winchester rifle at his side. He listened carefully, wondering if any posse members had slipped into the barn while he slept. Here they could lie in wait, Pa had said, and shoot him down as he stepped out the door.

"I'll go stand watch," Leslie had volunteered. John shrugged. "Whatever you think you should do." He was still curt.

Leslie blinked against the cobwebs in his mind. Slowly, careful not to make a sound, he moved his stiffened limbs and crawled to the loft ladder. He peered down, probing the shadows. His stomach churned with fear. His shoulders ached across his back and neck as if he'd been hammered with an ax handle. He could not help but recall the fusillade of shots whistling past his head when the men from Milwaukee had shot Clarence in the head; and then again when Clarence and Myra were captured and he had run. He hunched his shoulders against their tightness. He could not stand firm as could Pa. He'd lain side by side with Stanley. He knew the finality of death.

The horses shuffled in their slip stalls. A chicken clucked. And then silence. At long last Leslie convinced himself the area was safe and he turned his back and climbed down the ladder. He reached ground safely.

He gathered half a dozen eggs in his hat then gingerly walked through the grey, fog-shrouded yard to the cabin. Hattie was up and starting a fire.

"Morning, Ma," Leslie said. He was seized by an unusual sense of affection, a desire to hug his mother. But of course he did not.

"Brush that hay off by the door," Hattie snapped. She immediately caught herself. Her eyes met Leslie's, a brief acknowledgment between mother and son of shared trials. She spoke softly as if trying to atone for her sins. "What do you want for breakfast?"

"Eggs and potatoes are fine," Leslie said. He quickly turned from his mother's strange stare. Helen and Johnny lay under their covers waiting for the house to warm. Uncharacteristically they were both wide awake and staring. Leslie winked at his brother and clucked a greeting to Helen.

"Cows are down pasture," he said to his mother in explanation of his failure to bring in milk.

John padded barefoot into the living quarters and sat on the rocking chair beside the potbellied stove. He pulled on wool socks and began to lace his boots.

"No one tried to come to the barn. It's foggy out but it looks okay from what I can see," Leslie said. "The dogs did cut loose once, but if anyone was out there I think they scared them off."

John did not reply. He pulled on his coat and hat and picked a rifle from the corner. He spoke at Hattie as if Leslie did not exist. "I'll check the barn and lumber piles and make sure no one crept close. Although I didn't hear the set-gun go, nor anyone step in a bear trap either." He opened the door and stepped outside.

Newspapers reported in detail John's next steps:

...Crowds had come out from Winter in every available rig and had halted on the edge of the clearing with the conviction that they had come to witness an execution...

As the morning gradually wore on and no sign of Dietz or his family was seen, the townspeople began to speculate as to what the reason was. Some thought that Dietz and his family had managed to get through the lines in the night to make a sortie upon the deputies from the rear.

At 7:35 a figure appeared at the door. "It's old John himself," announced Deputy Louis Lambert after gazing through field glasses for a moment.

John stood at the door of the house gazing intently about him. He looked down the hill toward the spring and into the woods to the north and east of his home but apparently failed to notice anything out of the ordinary, for he started out on a more thorough inspection of the place.

He walked to the northeast, passing the barn and continued toward the lumber piles. Having heard from Deputy Thorbahn, who laid out the plan of attack, that four deputies were to be stationed in the lumber piles, people watched every moment, expected to hear the crack of a rifle and see Dietz topple over dead. But nothing of the kind appeared.

Dietz continued until within a short distance of the lumber piles, where he halted with his hands in his pockets and coolly looked them over. Failing to find anything wrong, he walked back to the house and down the hill to the west and to the spring.

At this time it was not known that Paulson, the deputy detailed to shoot Dietz in case he walked out on his path, had deserted.

Dietz walked on and then walked back again, slowly, with his back slightly bent and his head drooping forward.

Slowly and deliberately Dietz walked on and into the house.

Then for two hours nothing occurred. No one came out of the house and it began to look as though the well-laid plans of the sheriff and his deputies, Thorbahn and Van Alstyne, would fail. But at 9:35 members of the family came out of the house and started in to do their usual morning duties, having been satisfied that nothing was wrong.

Helen started for the cornfield to get the cows, little Johnny ran about helping feed the chickens and other minor chores, and Leslie went into the barn. Soon his sister returned and told him that the cows had gone the opposite direction.

"Help Helen get old White Face yonder," John said casually to Leslie.

"Yes, Pa," Leslie replied. Without outward hesitation, he plodded up the hill, unarmed, heading toward the cow and the rock pile he and the rest of the family had piled up while clearing the fields. Some day John planned to use that lumber to build Hattie a plank house on the high knoll. The rocks, the fortress or the stronghold some papers called the loose pile, could be used to build a fireplace.

Leslie paused. The autumn sun was burning away the fog. All that remained was a thin line hovering in a distinct line six feet above the Thornapple. It would be a great day for jump shooting ducks, Leslie thought distractedly. He looked around uneasily.

"Just go about your chores like normal," John had instructed. Helen circled off to one side so the cows could not escape that way. John was out near the lumber piles attending to his set gun and one of the bear traps he had covered with loose grass. Johnny was feeding the chickens. Hattie was feeding breakfast scraps to the dogs. Just another day, Leslie thought, and knew it was not.

He stopped. Every fiber of his being commanded him to run back to the cabin. He stared into the depths of the brightly colored forest that was still damp and gleaming under the morning sun. Wisps of fog still obscured details.

But they were there. His heart hammered in his ears. He hadn't realized he'd moved this far from the safety of the cabin. He moved one step back then saw his father looking in his direction. Leslie quickly moved ahead, further away from the cabin, drawing ever closer to the woods.

"...It was early," Deputy Colpitts told his tale, "and there was frost on the grass, you know. It was slippery. And the cows was out in the meadow, out in the field. We could see right from the forest. And Leslie came out to round up the cows. And this doggone Jack Britton, there was an outlaw if there ever was one... and he was a trigger happy bastard... and so Leslie came out and rounded up the cows. He didn't see us you know... wasn't looking for anything like that... and by God this doggone Britton threw up his gun and fired a shot and the shot run in the grass alongside of him and, I'll never forget that boy. I bet he jumped fifty feet!

"And he hit that frosty grass and he went down and he slid another twenty feet before he got to his feet. And holy Jesus if you ever see a guy run. Oh, boy, oh, boy. Well, laugh. We had to laugh."

October 8, 1910, *St. Paul Dispatch:*

JOHN DIETZ, WOUNDED IN FIGHT WITH DEPUTIES, STILL DEFIES HIS FOES
THE DAM DEFENDER IS AMBUSCADED
Walks Right Into Squads of Armed Men Concealed
About His Clearing and is Target for 100 Rifles
GETS BACK TO CABIN AND FIRES
FIVE SHOTS AT ATTACKERS
Leslie Dietz Also Believed to Have Been Wounded in Gun Fire — Dog killed by Stray Bullet — Mrs. Dietz has Narrow Escape
LEADING EVENTS OF A THRILLING DAY

Winter, Wis. — Mike Madden's crack shots got old man John Dietz this morning as Fred Thorbahn said they would. That is, they shot him, and they think he is seriously wounded, but he is lying behind the logs of his cabin on the Thornapple River and no man dares beard the lion in his den for fear he can still shoot.

... John and Leslie Dietz were greeted by a fusillade of shots from every point of the compass when they exposed themselves outside the cabin at 9:45 o'clock this morning. In racing for the cabin, John Dietz suddenly went down to his knees... The deputies think the wounds are serious. It is believed at least two of the shots took effect in his back as he ran ... He lay prostrate a moment, then scrambled up and made the shack.

Leslie had a longer run to make ... For 200 feet he was a large target. He weakened perceptibly and staggered slightly before he reached the cabin, but whether he was hit cannot be told...

NO DEPUTIES INJURED

...The war is now on and further developments may come momentarily. None of the deputies were hit by Dietz's fire. They were all carefully concealed among the stumps and underbrush on the clearing. But they have a wholesome regard for Dietz's marksmanship, even if he is severely wounded, and, while they are now attempting to draw up closer to the cabin, they are exercising the greatest care, for they know "Old Man Dietz" is lying behind those logs, furious and suffering, and with a murderous Winchester in his hands simply aching to get his revenge.

Leslie ran as fast as he could, passing back and forth in an effort to avoid the fusillade of bullets that seemed to roar from every point of the compass. The angry whine of passing bullets buzzed in the air. Pulsating blood drummed in his ears and his breath came in great gasps. Several times he slipped on the wet grass and staggered with the efforts of his frantic exertions. In the blur of his running he saw young Helen running as fast as her thin legs could tear. His mother seized Johnny and ducked into the cabin. John suddenly dropped and lay still.

"Pa!" Leslie cried. He thought his heart would break. But then, magically, John arose and continued toward the cabin as rapidly as his 50-year-old legs could take him.

As Leslie rushed into the cabin, John rushed out with a Winchester rifle and levered five shots into the deputies hiding in the swamp grass and burnt-out stumps along the river. Then John returned to the cabin.

Sporadic firing continued, some taking effect in the cabin, blasting through the rot and mud between logs and exploding fist-sized showers of wood slivers into the cabin.

"The cheating bastards are using exploding bullets," John declared. He was tight-lipped, determined.

A bullet exploded through a log inches from Helen's face and the brave little girl let out a scream.

"Down, get down!" Hattie shrieked. She forcefully pushed Helen and Johnny to the floor. "Oh, dear mother of God. Stay down!" She seized a dresser, and without asking assistance, began manhandling it over to one corner. Leslie jumped to give her a hand. The two then pulled a large wooden trunk over beside the dresser and herded Helen and Johnny down behind the makeshift barricade.

"You get down," Hattie ordered Leslie. She tried to force

him to the floor.

"Please, Ma," Leslie protested. He dropped to his knees and peered toward his father for guidance.

The firing had lessened. Occasionally a bullet smacked the cabin walls, occasionally one found the chink between the logs and exploded through and inside the cabin with a shower of mud and splinters of wood and a crashing of glass.

"You hit, Pa?" Leslie asked.

"Of course not," John said. "I dropped to the ground there pretending to be hit and to throw them off. Maybe they think I was hit," he said with amused bitterness that his trickery had worked so well.

Leslie, on hands and knees and clutching a rifle, looked to where John stood just back from a window and peered out with his field glasses as if looking for deer. Leslie despaired at John's lack of fear. He could feel a quivering in his loins, a tightness in his bowels. One bullet had cut through his pants leg in his dash across the field. Even as he watched, another round exploded into the cabin and centered itself in the top of a family portrait hanging on the wall. There had been eight of them then, now three were gone, Stanley, Clarence and Myra.

"You get down!" Hattie yelled. She rose up from her shelter and tried to force Leslie to the floor. "This is your father's fight. Not yours." Her voice was shrill, her eyes fixed with a troubled, wild stare that made Leslie draw back. But the look also gave him strength. After all, he was now the oldest.

"Why don't you give up, Pa? Please. For the sake of Ma and the kids. For God's sake, at least spare them. What do Helen and Johnny have to do with any of this?"

"Get down like your mother says," John casually ordered.

He walked quickly from window to window, peering out with the field glasses, occasionally taking a shot. "You didn't stand when they took Myra and Clarence, no sense starting now."

Leslie sagged down upon the plank floor, down below the banked layer of insulating dirt that had been shoveled up against the lower part of the outside logs. He lay flat on his back like a dog submitting. His face was wet and dirty from his long run. His eyes were wide and staring at the bare sapling poles of their ceiling. He hadn't been touched and yet it seemed a part of him had died. He no longer sought to align himself with his father. His thoughts rambled, "How could they shoot at us like that? Even Helen. Don't they care?" he mumbled.

For some time the family lay quietly while John walked around the cabin and returned the sporadic fire. "They've got men all around," John once remarked as much to himself as the family. "There must be a hundred of them. Although it doesn't appear as if they're too eager to move in close. Must be mill poltroons, every one." He clucked grimly at that — they never would let him be.

"For God's sake, Pa, we can't continue this," Leslie repeated his lament. He'd become so tense, so outraged his fear had fled, like a cornered rabbit who has at long last realized his only option was to fight. And yet his voice lacked force, as if knowing he could not possibly succeed.

John turned his back and paid his oldest remaining son no heed.

"Damnit, Pa," Leslie suddenly shouted. "Think of Johnny and Helen. Ma's pregnant. She's sick. Think of them." He spoke more to the room than directly to John. He rolled as if distracted and turned to watch his father stalk around the cabin and checking each avenue of approach. Glass flew as a bullet splattered the last frame of the west window.

John did not flinch or even turn to look. Each bullet that broke through inside the cabin exploded as if into Hattie's brain. Little Johnny quivered and gripped his battered stuffed teddy bear with one hand and clung to his mother with the other. Helen's eyes were wide, darting around and watching her father, one moment filled with excitement, the next moment with fear. She and Johnny huddled close. A bullet smacked the dresser little more than a foot over their heads. Hattie jerked as if it had struck her. A sharp pain had worked like a knife into the small of her back and hip. Her stomach churned with nausea and for a moment she feared she would be ill in front of the children. Nevertheless she held her children close, keeping the life in her womb toward the open steel door of the stove and her back toward the wall so it would soak up any bullets before they struck her young. Her anguished face looked at Leslie as would one dying creature on another. She spoke in a dull monotone, "Therefore is the anger of the Lord kindled against His people and He hath stretched forth His hand against them and hath smitten them."

Leslie flopped back and looked at the ceiling. He did not know how to respond.

A shadow fell over them. Hattie looked up at John standing upright and looking down on his huddled brood. John said, "You look pretty well protected. You should be all right there. If they start using a field piece like Thorbahn threatened, Leslie might have to stack up more furniture."

For a moment Hattie stared without comprehension. A field piece? "John," her voice quavered. "John, please. We have to give it up. For the sake of the children, please. You cannot expect them to face this as do you. They mean business this time. They mean to kill us all."

John pursed his lips. He did not view himself as a mean or inconsiderate man. "That's exactly what those assassins want," he pointed out. He did not react as a bullet burst past his head. He casually checked the window. "I'll go out to the barn. It's a better view from there anyhow. That'll draw their fire. If they have a field piece they can train it there. You stay down."

"Pa, you can't," Leslie moaned. He'd surrendered all thought of helping John. There were too many of them. Too many bullets blasting through their walls and ringing in his ears. The house smelled of gunpowder. Window glass and broken dishes and cartridges were spread over the chaos on the floor. It was all beyond him, Leslie thought. John could stand alone.

John stuffed several boxes of ammunition into his coat pocket, hefted his rifle and stepped outside. He trotted up toward the barn, past where Myra's dog Tippy had been shot and now lay dead. The two remaining dogs were huddled deep inside their dog house. It seemed as if most of the deputies were keeping down and not looking, or if they observed him, they were not overly desirous of shooting him down, for as John made his trot the firing increased but little. In fact many deputies did not realize John went to the barn and continued with their firing on the cabin.

Once in the barn John climbed up into the hayloft. He

punched several of the wooden shingles out so he had viewing ports and firing holes in most directions. The remaining shingles shielded him from direct view, but they would not stop a bullet. That mattered little to John. He surveyed the battle lines then paused and simply watched. He spat to one side. They were out there all right, two or three hundred yards away most of them — and not too anxious to move in close.

In midmorning a bullet struck the cord holding the American flag to the sapling nailed to the cabin. The flag fluttered to the ground. Most deputies took this for a signal and firing ceased. But there was no further signal from the barn, and no movement whatsoever around the cabin.

In the cabin, as he did at almost every lull, Leslie checked his pocket watch. He'd taken a notebook from the dresser and was jotting disjointed impressions of the siege, a record for others in case they were all killed. Helen and Johnny had set, puffed-face expressions of incomprehension at the fury of all this. One minute Hattie was clear-eyed, protecting her young, the next minute she was mumbling and seemed glassy-eyed. Each time Leslie checked his watch he muttered, one time with fear, the next with anger and then resignation that reflected the sickness binding his guts.

"I wonder if they've killed Pa?" Hattie did not reply.

An hour or so after the flag dropped, one bored deputy fired a shot and firing again resumed, increasing markedly between eleven and one. Occasionally the defender of the dam fired back — just to let them know he was still there, still watching and waiting.

Despite huge numerical and firepower superiority, Chief Deputy Fred Thorbahn was faced with a significant problem: none of his volunteer deputies appeared anxious to risk their lives and move in closer and take the fight to Dietz. Those ordered to the lumber piles in the predawn darkness had failed to take their posts. Several men had deserted. With his big, high-top boots and twin Luger pistols, Thorbahn moved around the clearing and tried to urge others to move on up. Few of them complied.

Sometime during the midmorning shooting lull, Thorbahn returned to the chuck wagon where Sheriff Madden, who took no active part directing the siege, had located himself to maintain an overview of the situation and keep reporters and onlookers from interfering. Thorbahn gulped down a quick lunch, picked up some cartridges for resupply, a .35 Winchester carbine and started back on his rounds. Hadn't had his boots off for a week, he claimed. He cut down around the wood line and toward the river where Van Alstyne and Ackley were located. He paused and placed three shots into the manure hole in the north end of the barn then rose from his crouch and made his heavy-legged run. John immediately rattled several shots through the air where Thorbahn had been.

Other deputies described Chief Deputy Thorbahn's actions that day. Chester Colpitts said:

"So this Thorbahn came around, must have along about forenoon. So he says you fellows move on up. Move on up!... I'll never forget that big son-of-a-gun. He had his fingers off, four fingers off, I think, on his left hand. And he had two guns, and he had them big high shoes on, and he always wore them boots, and he come stumbling around there and givin' us orders to move up. And he had these guns and he was falling down and these guns would stick in the ground, then he'd raise himself up and, boy! He was a tough guy... and so after he went by and he went up to where Harp and Pomerlo and them fellows was, on the east side, they moved down, so we talked with Thorbahn a little while and laughed... and, by God, we ... we moved up."

Deputy Mont Wiley picked up the story: "Well, Thorbahn come in there and told us to go to the lumber piles, that everything was safe and that he thought Dietz was in the root house or in the house and he couldn't see us go in there. So we started, Walter Bonk, Johnny Pomerlo, Oscar Harp, Ernie Mewhorter. When we was crawling on our hands and knees all of us over the hill, John Pomerlo, I think was ahead and Harp was ahead of me. I was right behind him. He turned around to me and says, 'It's all right, Mont, we can make it all right.' He bent over and started to crawl and went about two steps and he dropped and there was two more shots fired just then and I thought they come pretty close to me. I could hear them whiz over my head and I turned and went back over the hill."

Oscar Harp, 31, married, no children, lay dead. The bullet tore off a piece of his lower jaw, three or four teeth of the lower jaw, shattered the jaw in four or five places, and passed underneath the tongue down through the neck, through the diaphragm and spleen, then to the bottom of the pelvis, about three quarters of an inch to the left of the anal opening and, turning at right angles to the left, lodging in the muscles of the femur.

Mont Wiley could see the dead man. Chester Colpitts, providing covering fire, had received one bullet through the ear. Pomerlo, Bonk, and Mewhorter had made it to the protection of the lumber piles. There they remained concealed, unwilling to raise their heads and risk returning fire least they receive what had happened to Oscar Harp who lay on the open ground they had just traversed.

John moved slowly around the soft hay in the barn loft. He had the viewing slots from missing shingles on two sides and a door and a board he'd removed from the two gable ends, all points of the compass secure and under his gun. After Deputy Thorbahn had made his ungainly run to the island down by the river, and those men had made their attempt to reach the lumber piles, the rest of them appeared content to lie behind cover and throw lead from a distance. Now that one of their own had fallen, John imagined the rest would be even more reluctant to move. He grimaced — mill agents, they gave a man no choice.

John checked the four sides then sat on a pile of loose hay and checked his pocket watch. It was getting on toward three o'clock. He had a powerful thirst. He'd already climbed down twice and drank from the horse barrel. The animals, of course, had fled, huddled with the terrified cows clear up against the woods. John, the old grizzled veteran as one paper fondly referred to him, wiped at parched lips. He had been under siege for more than six hours. One against a hundred, and he still held them off.

The little cabin on the Thornapple was almost completely surrounded, and guns belched forth their deadly missiles which all day had riddled the structure. It was the close of war, a war of lead and steel and powder and death; not such a proceeding as might be expected in Wisconsin. The floor of the house was covered with flattened bullets, the walls were filled with the holes through which they entered.

And still the war raged on. Waiting until nightfall before they closed, John surmised. The posse had fifty pounds of dynamite. They had fire. That was the reason they'd shot one dog. They'd kill the other two before it was dark. And then they would make their effort to close the noose.

He hefted his Winchester and climbed to his feet. Fifty years old but he'd still be ready, use his peashooter and send some lead whining and really test their courage under cover of the dark. He chuckled at that. He'd seen plenty of men run. Tonight he'd see more.

And yet within him there was a sadness, a sense of loneliness that made him bitter. When it came down to this last showdown he'd always expected his two boys would be on either side of him. What a fortress that would be.

But Clarence had opposed him from the start and then let himself be taken. Lester had actually run. And Hattie was on the verge of a breakdown — although she was in a family way.

A man had to allow for that. John spat hard. No — he was alone.

He stood confidently, bent forward to survey the open fields, one hand gripping a supporting log joist for maintaining his balance. Well then, if that was what the Lord decreed, he'd walk the valley alone. Other than the one attempt, they hadn't shown the stomach yet for moving in close.

All during the day John paid little heed to bullets passing through the barn. But this one struck the hand braced against the joist, exploding into fragments in the web of his left hand between thumb and forefinger.

"Son of a bitch!" John whirled, dropping his rifle and gripping his wrist against the searing agony of severed tendons and mangled muscles. Blood streamed down his hand, dripping off his fingertips and into the sweet smelling hay. He hissed angrily against the pain and peered out through an opening.

The firing remained sporadic. There was no movement close by that he could detect. It was unlikely they knew he was hit.

"Well, I still have one good hand," John said as if in warning. Still the nature of the wound put him in terrible agony, and he was bleeding severely.

After some time John tossed his rifle down on a pile of hay and used his good hand and struggled down the ladder to the lower part of the barn. He stepped out into the open and again half ran, half walked to the cabin. As there had been when he walked up to the barn, there was little increased firing.

Leslie whirled in surprise and fear when John pushed open the door. Hattie saw the blood and immediately sprang to her feet. Lines of pain were etched as if forever into the wrinkles around her eyes and mouth. "Oh, John! John! Please. I beg of you. I've prayed to God. We must surrender. We must!"

Leslie rose to Hattie's support. "For God's sake, Pa, spare us. Ma's been sick all day. Johnnie's shaking like a leaf. If we continue on Ma will die or surely have a miscarriage."

"They aren't getting any closer," John snapped. "They just got lucky." He walked through the debris of the living area and into the bedroom and sat on the bed. His hand pained him something furious. The fragments of wood and lead had so cut and wedged in his flesh, use and movement of his fingers was impossible.

Hattie scurried like a frenzied cow and found a towel and with unknown power ripped it in strips. She had difficulty focusing and her movements were unsteady as if her legs were about to fail. The pregnancy had taken its toll, John observed. Hattie was truly in poor health.

"Get that iodine," John instructed. Hattie seized the bottle from a cabinet and John poured the burning liquid over his hand. He sucked in his breath at the pain but did not utter a sound. He held the hand out for Hattie to bandage. She hovered close, her head just in front of his. Wisps of hair hung in every direction. Her eyes raised to his. There was a strange wildness and redness John had never before observed.

Her voice came faintly as if pleading weakly from the depths of a well. "Please, John. You've stood them off all day. Your hand is shot. The children are faint from fear. They cannot eat or drink." She clutched the slightly swelling mound of her lower abdomen. "Can we not give it up? I beg you."

Her strength had gone. Six days of siege and six hours of rifle fire exploding through her house had taken the final toll. Hattie trembled and wavered as if verging on collapse.

For a moment John felt tired himself, tired of always having to go it alone. He patted Hattie's shoulders in sympathy. She'd stood at his side a long, long time, rough times. His heart went out.

"Who would go?" he asked softly. "Whoever walks out they're going to shoot."

"I'll go, Pa," Leslie volunteered.

"And they'll give you exactly what they gave you this morning," John growled.

"I can go," Helen volunteered.

"No, she'll surely be shot just like Myra," John said. "They'll gun down a little girl just as fast as a man."

"Then I can only pray to God they will not shoot her," Hattie said solemnly. Before John could find reason for further protest, she handed Helen a graying white pillowcase. "Wave it as much as you can. Make sure they see it. Hattie escorted Helen to the door. She kept her arms around Helen's thin shoulders as they cautiously opened the door and waved the pillowcase outside. Silence reigned.

Helen stepped outside. She peered out at the distant wood line, the brilliant scarlets and oranges and yellows of falls. She could see no one. She walked a few paces and stopped.

"Wave the pillowcase. Wave the pillowcase, " Hattie urged.

Helen waved the pillowcase with both hands above her head. She ran forward a few paces. "Daddy gives up. Daddy gives up." Her thin voice seemed to be lost in the vastness of the forest. She ran halfway to the forest and then stopped. The line of trees and brush seemed so foreboding, a wall concealing men with guns she could not see. She looked back at the cabin, her home. Her mother waved an arm, urging her onward.

Abruptly, willing herself to not even think, Helen broke into a run towards the woods, waving the pillowcase above her head. "Daddy gives up! Daddy gives up!"

A man rose from behind a bush. "Over this way, little girl."

Another deputy rose and the two men escorted her back to where Sheriff Madden was located next to three buggies. The bulky sheriff stepped forward.

"Daddy gives up! Daddy gives up!" Helen repeated nervously.

Laying his hand on Helen's shoulder, Madden replied, "Tell your father that if he surrenders we will not harm him."

Meanwhile Father Pilon could no longer restrain himself. Without waiting he started running toward the cabin, waving a tiny white handkerchief as he went. Everyone stared, waiting for the priest to be shot dead. However, he reached the cabin safely and went inside. Meanwhile, Sully Heffelfinger of Radisson volunteered to return with Helen to arrange the surrender. No sooner had the two started for the cabin than Father Pilon passed them and hurried back to Sheriff Madden.

"Dietz will surrender," the angular priest said. He was panting and his movements were quick, exaggerated with nervousness in his efforts to prevent further bloodshed. "He wants a doctor to dress his wounds and he desires to talk with the newspaper men.

"He surrenders, I tell you," Father Pilon insisted. "If anything happens I'll stand personally responsible."

"Would your personal responsibility bring Oscar Harp back to life?" Fred Thorbahn said. He turned to Doctor Grafton, who was about to leave with the priest. "You tell Dietz I ain't going to wait much longer; if he is not going to surrender I want to know about it, and if he is I want him to come down this road with his hands up and no guns on him."

The group of men waited while the priest and doctor returned to the cabin. Meanwhile Helen and Sully Heffelfinger left the cabin to go to the root cellar to get food for a meal before the family had to depart. All around the clearing other men were standing, peering, shouting and wondering at the goings-on. The word passed, Dietz had surrendered.

"We better get up there," Thorbahn said to Van Alstyne. "If Dietz surrenders to someone else, they'll try to claim the reward." He started up the hill and several men followed.

Just then Helen and Sully Heffelfinger left the root cellar and were faced by half a dozen rifles. "Don't shoot, I'm one of you guys," Sully yelled.

John, his hand bandaged, calmly stepped out on the front porch. He still wore a belt with a Luger on the right side. He peered at the men confronting his daughter.

"Hold it there, Dietz," Thorbahn said. He raised his rifle.

"You men crazy?" he called to the approaching deputies. "Do you see that man with a gun on him?"

A dozen more rifles were raised and pointed at the porch. Hattie and Leslie peered out the door. "Take that gun away from your father," Thorbahn ordered Leslie, who stepped out of the door and circled behind his father and took the gun out of his holster.

The men closed in then, seizing Leslie and the pistol and quickly handcuffing him. Thorbahn took John and prepared a set of handcuffs.

"You don't need to put those on me," John said. He was amused at the extra precaution. "I give up, and you have got my word that we surrender. You have nothing to fear."

"I know you'll surrender when I get these on you," Thorbahn said.

"He gave his word he won't try to escape," Sully protested the treatment.

Thorbahn seized Sully's arm and handcuffed the helpful man to John's good arm. "There, now I know he won't escape," Thorbahn said.

"Watch out for that set gun up by the lumber piles," John called toward a group of deputies. He was calm, almost at ease. Before they departed the farm that day he posed for pictures with the sheriff and officials. When asked why he hadn't surrendered to the attorney general the day before, John replied, "They kept on changing plans. And I did not know what I could depend upon. Besides, we thought we could have lasted out and we could have but for the little baby we expected. I am not glad it's over — we have lived all right. You might go into the house though and see what we had to stand."

Hattie moved distractedly through her house. Johnny stayed close at her side. The damage cut Hattie as surely as if the bullets had cut her flesh. The bodies of men moved in, tramping over her floor. She began straightening, picking up bits of broken glass. A large man loomed at her side.

"I'm going to have to handcuff you, Mrs. Dietz," Thorbahn said.

Hattie shrank back. "No. Please! We didn't fire a shot from the house. There was not a shot fired from the house. Leslie and I did not shoot."

"Then why are all these cartridges here," Thorbahn replied. Despite Hattie's and then Helen's protests, he handcuffed Mrs. Dietz. A steady stream of tears unconsciously streaked Hattie's cheeks. Johnny and Helen clung to her side. They were all she had, all that remained.

In time Sheriff Madden reached the cabin. He ordered the Dietzes' handcuffs be removed and that they pack a few belongings for the journey to prison. John wanted to change into a good pair of pants, but Thorbahn said no. He could carry a pair along and change in prison. The big deputy did kneel down and place John's feet on his knee and change John's socks and then lace his boots.

Hattie knew not what to pack. Every minute more and more strange men crowded in, staring at her like she was a witch, checking over the contents of her home. Already the souvenir pickers were grabbing at cartridges they'd later sell for a dollar apiece, fingering her dishes, picking up pieces of glass like vultures picking at her still warm carcass. It was gone, a part of Hattie realized. All gone.

She wandered aimlessly, picking up articles and then discarding them as if undecided. How could she pack it all?

At the last minute she remembered her tin box with the fifteen hundred dollars in it. She dashed into the bedroom and took the box from the corner closet. A minute later she set it down in the living room and forgot it was there.

John's arm was placed in a sling and he and Leslie were again handcuffed and placed in one rig while Hattie and the children were escorted to another. Just after they crossed the river, Hattie again remembered the tin of money and Helen was sent scurrying back up the hill for all the stake the family had in life.

When they reached the smoother part of the dirt turnpike, Hattie, Helen and Johnny were transferred to a waiting automobile. In Winter Mrs. Dietz was given an opportunity to speak with reporters:

* * *

In the Hotel Winter, after the surrender, Mrs. Dietz, shaken by emotion and by the great strain, talked freely. She appeared a cultivated, reasonably well-educated woman; though her face was creased with lines of labor and of great care and worry. Tears streamed down her cheeks as with the little boy on one side and the fair-haired girl in the glow of health on the other, as she said, "I asked him in the name of God to give up. We pleaded with him all day."

As Mrs. Dietz told her story, she cried. People grasped her hand in sympathy, few with their own eyes dry...

"Oh, it was terrible, it was an awful agony — and they fired on the children and me when we were together too. None of us except Mr. Dietz fired a shot from the house. Later he went to the barn, hoping in that way to draw the fire away from us."

Helen and little Johnny talked of the terrible experience. There was a look of joy in the eyes of Helen.

"I am glad it's over," she said. "I am happy now." But the boy's face was somber beyond his years. He would not say he was happy. But he did crouch close in the arms of people around him, seeming to shrink away from the zing of bullets and the crash of exploding powder.

"Every window in our house was broken," the little chap said. "And once a bullet went right past my ear when they were firing at Leslie."

At the time the general public did not learn of the additional forty deputies that had been recruited from the nearby lumber camp. Fred Berlin, one of the logger-deputies that had crept through the woods the day of the siege, received his five dollars and a ride on the flatcar to Winter. The town was packed with strangers and wild with celebrating. Berlin said:

"Why-ah, it got so tough that I left town, to get out of that, them fighting and raisin' hell, you know. I thought somebody would get killed there. It was worse than the battle. You know, you could be in a saloon, you could go sit down in a chair and pay no attention to nothin' and one of them sons a guns would come and kick the chair from underneath you and say 'Here, why ain't you fighting with the rest of us?'"

* * *

Meanwhile, the Dietz family was not allowed to see each other in Winter. The large crowd and revelry caused Madden to order the wagon faced about and started at once for Hayward.

When John was taken to the Hayward jail, the streets of the town were filled with curiosity seekers. There was no show of violence, but there was pushing and determined efforts to see the man and his son. One story reported:

When Dietz arrived at Hayward he was placed in a cell beside his son Clarence but would not speak to him because the boy surrendered without shooting at Madden when shot at from ambush.

Within a few days of their arrest, Hattie Dietz, Leslie Dietz and John F. Dietz were formally charged with the murder of Oscar Harp.

DIETZ, WIFE AND LESLIE BOUND OVER FOR TRIAL

State Introduces Evidence to Warrant Judge Riordan Holding Them
to Circuit Court on Charge of Murder of Oscar Harp - Defense Threatens to Start Habeas Corpus Proceedings on Ground of Lack of Evidence

DIETZ SAYS DARROW IS ENGAGED

The first successful step in the effort of Sawyer County to bring the notorious Dietz family to justice for their continued outlaw acts was made by the capture of the offending members under tragic circumstances which have been heralded by the metropolitan press to every part of the continent.

...The hearing of the three on this charge of murder opened at 10 a. m.... the court room being packed almost to suffocation with many citizens of local prominence present.

EPILOGUE

Thus while the war with guns in the wilderness had at long last been brought to a close, the war of words between opposing elements of the press was only heightened. For a few days at the most, some previously sympathetic papers admonished John for his deeds:

> Dietz's refusal to treat with the governor's representatives caused a change in public sentiment that dragged Dietz from the pedestal upon which he had been placed and caused him to be looked upon by many as foolish or insane. That a sane man would refuse such offers when the refusal meant probable extermination of himself and destruction of his property, was hard to believe. He had everything to gain and nothing to lose in accepting the terms offered him.

However, condemnation was short-lived as the battle was joined in the courts and newspapers rushed to stake out their positions either backing or opposing the stalwart hero.

SOCIALISTS PLEDGE AID IN DEFENSE OF DIETZ
Vigorous backing of the Social Democratic administration of Milwaukee was promised early Saturday by Mayor Seidel to the John Dietz family in their fight for a fair trial

and freedom. The mayor offered to aid in a campaign for funds and gave his advice freely to Clarence Dietz and his uncle W. W. Dietz and brother-in-law Herman Voigt.

In addition to the shooting victims, other participants in the Dietz affair, paid a price. Despite his bravery and leadership during the capture of John Dietz, Chief Deputy Fred Thorbahn suffered his own independent tribulations.

BAD LUCK FOLLOWS MAN
WHO ASSISTED IN CAPTURE OF DIETZ

Fred Thorbahn, first he became an independent candidate for sheriff of Sawyer County... but despite all of his efforts he was defeated by a large majority.

About 10 days ago his store at Radisson was destroyed by fire. The loss was about $12,500 and while it was partially insured, Thorbahn was hard hit by the disaster.

Now it develops that Thorbahn and his wife are on the outs and he has started suit in the circuit court in Sawyer County asking that he be released from his marital ties. Thorbahn is the man who is generally supposed to be responsible for the shooting of Myra Dietz and her brother Clarence on October first.

Fred did receive the one thousand dollar reward for the capture of Dietz, a portion of which was divided with Roy Van Alstyne. But the pressure from Dietz sympathizers in Sawyer County was too great. After the rejection by the voting public, the loss of his store, and the dissolution of his marriage, Fred took his son and daughter and moved west to the even more sparsely settled wilds of Montana.

* * *

From the date of the arrest, John had been as put-out at Clarence's failure as he was at Leslie's. Clarence made little effort to mend the rift. But he could not and did not break from the family. After all, he and Myra still faced charges, and his mother and brother were charged with murder the same as was John.

As soon as Clarence was freed on one thousand dollars bond,

he set out to provide what help he could. After Clarence Darrow declined the case, William B. Rubin, one of the leading criminal lawyers in Milwaukee, was contacted and accepted the case. The initial retainer fee came from the savings Hattie had so carefully maintained in her small tin box.

Thus the Dietz family had counsel. They also had a great deal of other support. George Schultes, a Milwaukee saloon keeper, became chairman of the Dietz defense committee and spoke of a nationwide campaign to raise $25,000. Another Milwaukee citizen, Ludwig Berg, proposed making the Dietz land into a state park and erecting a monument to Mrs. Dietz for her loyalty to her husband. One by one the children and Hattie were released. On January 7, 1911, for a bond of $40,000, granted by the Illinois Surety Company of Chicago, even John was released on bond.

For some months members of the family traveled the state, attending fund-raising dinners, speaking in theaters and trying to gather funds for their defense. Leslie and Myra were given a desk in Rubin's Milwaukee office and assigned to record the gathering of contributions and act as custodians. Some papers did not take kindly to the public show of support:

> ...Judging from the numerous and various reports — many of them very probably circulated merely with the hope of encouraging contributions from misinformed sympathizers of Dietz, the leaders of the Dietz defense are making a desperate effort to induce the people to part liberally with their hard-earned cash in order that a few shysters may stow it away in their jeans.
>
> The whole defense scheme looks very much like a pure, unadulterated graft trick.

Other papers were convinced John would surely win:

WILL NEVER CONVICT DIETZ

> "I don't think the state has one chance in a thousand of convicting John F. Dietz or any members of his family of the murder of Deputy Sheriff Oscar Harp, whose body was found hours after the assault on the cabin at Winter Sunday," said Attorney Maurice McKenna, a law graduate of

the university now at Fond du Lac. "There were thousands of shots fired in the direction of the Dietz cabin, some score were probably returned. Bullets flew in all directions and to the four winds of heaven, such being the case how could the killing of Harp be fixed on any one individual. Harp was shot, but there is hardly an iota of evidence as to who shot him and there would always be the doubt in the minds of any unprejudiced juryman as to who shot him.

The friendly and hopeful articles gave Hattie little solace. The family split was worse than she feared, for with the children at long last free from John's domination, there'd be no returning to the fold. After an operation and 68 days in the hospital, Myra, resplendent in the latest bonnets and dresses, was up and traveling the state with Clarence and Leslie. The children were public figures now, people sought their company and public presence almost everywhere they went. Even Clarence soon lost his shyness.

Hattie withdrew, fearful and unwilling to face what she viewed as a hostile public alone. Because of her "delicate condition" her bail had been set at four thousand dollars. The bond money was raised by John's brothers, William and Henry. For a time she'd refused to leave the jail and go out on her own. Not until they also freed Leslie and John, she told the sheriff. Eventually Clarence and Myra talked Hattie into leaving. It was not abandoning John, they said. She did have to think of her health.

On March 7, 1911, attended by a Hayward doctor, Hattie gave birth to a son, Clifton Dietz. A birth of joy, a replacement for Stanley, Hattie thought. But the child was sickly. Two days later the boy died. Death caused by the battle of Cameron Dam, some papers quoted physicians as saying. Hattie's lips were set in a compressed line. Now she had lost four: Leanna, Harry, Stanley, and Clifton.

And she had yet to face trial for the murder of Oscar Harp.

Meanwhile, John and Attorney Rubin were having their difficulties. On motion of prejudice filed by Rubin, Circuit Judge James Wickham was disqualified and Judge Alexander H. Reid of the 16th Judicial Circuit Court from Wausau was appointed to the case. Legally the new judge constituted one change of venue. Motions for a second change of venue were denied. John, Hattie and Leslie would be tried before a jury of their peers in Sawyer County. The trial was set for May 2, 1911.

MYRA OFFERED BRIBE CHARGES

Hayward, Wis. May 2 — Openly charging a Milwaukee lawyer with offering Myra Dietz $500 to perjure herself and testify against her father, John F. Dietz informed the court at the opening of his trial today that he has no confidence in lawyers and had concluded to try his own case.

"That man, an attorney admitted to practice at the bar, was willing to promote perjury after he had trouble over the case," Dietz said. "We will have to fight the devil with fire in this case and do the best we can."

He told her the lumber company had 100 witnesses to impeach her testimony, and we would have to fight the devil with the devil's club.

Dietz then asked the court for permission to waive a trial by jury and that the court decide his case, but Judge Reid said he had no such power.

...The Illinois Surety Company, Milwaukee, at the opening of the trial before Judge Reid today, refused to carry the $40,000 bond for Dietz any longer.

After this statement by the company, the sheriff took Dietz into custody. He is no longer at liberty. Shortly after the afternoon session had started twelve jurors, evidently satisfactory to both the defendants and the prosecution, sat in the jurors box and were ready to listen to the testimony.

In his defense, Attorney W. B. Rubin made a statement on the reasons behind his breakdown with John:

"I am sorry for the whole Dietz family and for that matter I am sorry for John, himself. It looks as though it will go hard, later, with the rest of the family. John Dietz is very self-opinionated and self-confident and that is what caused all the trouble between the Dietzes and myself This I discovered shortly after I entered into the case and I could not get the family to see that it would be disastrous to let John have his own way further. To differ with John in a single idea that he entertained, was to become his sworn enemy, and to convince the family to the contrary after John had expressed his views, was like endeavoring to capture the Rock of Gibraltar...

Thus it was as it had been from the start, John thought — he'd take them on alone.

It was an ill-chosen jury John let sit in judgment. The majority of jury members were direct or indirect employees of the lumber mills. John faced them confidently as he made the opening statement upon which rested his family's fate:

"When justice falls so low that the state introduces false testimony to take away a person's life, I call it barbarism. The testimony the state says it will introduce is nearly all false. The whole trouble is over a piece of property coveted by the lumber trust which has tied up hundreds of acres in Sawyer County on which we all should be allowed to have homesteads. That is all I wish to say at this time."

On such a dubious note, John took his family into the trial for their lives. His efforts to thwart the introduction of his previous scrapes with law enforcement officials were repeatedly denied on grounds the State was justified in proving why such large force was needed to arrest John. The press continued to wash hot or cold either for or against John, one day stating how one-sided the case against John had become and how pathetic his defense, the next day headlines screamed:

DECISIVE POINT WON BY DIETZ -
MAY BE FREED

The case dragged on. The state introduced 57 witnesses, John 26. John asked most questions, Leslie and Hattie very few. The basis of John's case was that any one of the thousands of bullets fired that day could have struck Harp. However, witnesses who were with Harp contended they saw the shot come from the barn. Other witnesses testified they'd seen John run to the barn. The State introduced expert witnesses to testify they had fired John's rifle and then three other rifles into sawdust and were able to pick out the bullets that had been fired by John's rifle. However, they did not attempt to link the bullet from Oscar Harp to John's gun.

All the deputies that testified were those that had come out through Winter. No testimony was received and no mention was made of the forty loggers that had been hired and armed and spread out in a line along one side of the forest. John had been informed of rumors of the extra men He asked Sheriff Madden and then Deputy Ackley if the men of Kaiser Lumber Company, Camp 4 had been deputized. Both officials of the law calmly denied any knowledge of such an auxiliary force and the issue was dropped.

During the break after the prosecution rested their case, the state admitted to the press that if John had asked for dismissal of the charges against Hattie and Leslie on the grounds of lack of evidence to show complicity in the killing of Oscar Harp, the motion might have been granted by Judge Reid.

When asked by reporters, John hotly resented the imputation he was seeking protection behind his wife and son. He angrily replied, "We are either all guilty, or all not guilty of killing Oscar Harp and we will stand or fall together."

"That bastard," Clarence hissed to Myra. "He just won't quit."

John made the decision his family should not take the stand. After all, he informed reporters, "We don't know anything about the killing of Oscar Harp and our word without oath is better than the word of deputies given under oath who will shoot at women and children from ambush and behind ambuscades."

For her part Hattie said, "I wanted to take the stand and try out against the lies which have been told to convict us, but we thought it was best not to. I have prayed for our acquittal night and day. If John is convicted and I am freed, I'll follow him to prison."

The defense rested. Thirteen pages of instructions were given to the jury, after which they retired to the Giblin Hotel, where news reports spoke of heated arguments penetrating the walls. But when all was said and done, the verdict was received: John Dietz guilty of murder in the first degree. Hattie Dietz, not guilty. Leslie Dietz, not guilty. Charges against Myra and Clarence were dropped.

The *Milwaukee Journal* set out its front-page headlines:

DIETZ GETS LIFE SENTENCE:
OTHERS SET FREE
"I KNEW IT WAS COMING'
HE SAYS TO REPORTERS

The old smile with which the "old man" has always faced
the things that have happened to him did not desert him. He
smiled as the judge read the verdict handed up by the foreman of the jury. He made no demonstration.

...John Dietz' statement to reporters when leaving the
courtroom, "Shake hands all around, boys. I don't feel bad.
I knew it was coming. I was convicted before a witness took
the stand. There wasn't a man in Sawyer County who was
not out to get me. I am lucky that they were not fiendish
enough to send my wife and boy along with me. "

Mrs. Dietz said, weeping: "I knew they would do it. They
would have convicted John if the witnesses had testified he
was away from the farm when Harp was killed. My God! I
don't know what the future holds for us all."

The day after the verdict, John made a motion for a new
trial. The motion was denied. When Judge Reid asked John as
to why sentence should not be pronounced, John immediately
launched into a tirade against the lumber trusts.

His voice rose in uncontrollable madness, "Throughout the
trial I have seen the hand of the lumber trust. I consider it an
outrage that we were tried in Sawyer County. If any one deserved the peace of our home, it was us. We came here as pioneers when our place was forty miles from the nearest railroad. I have not been allowed to show anything of the conspiracy. The state had its inning and blackened our characters,
while we have had no opportunity to defend ourselves.

"It has been the policy of the lumber trust to rule or ruin. If
the lumber trust needs a victim no one can stand it better than
I. "

Judge Reid then handed down judgment by sentencing John
to... "imprisonment at hard labor... for the period of the balance of your natural life, and that on the 8th day of October, of
each year, you shall be kept in solitary confinement..."

John solemnly reiterated his defiance, "If the lumber trust

needs a victim, I can stand it."

On May 17, 1911, Sheriff Fred Clark, the same Fred Clark who as a deputy had visited John in 1904, accompanied John to the state prison on Waupun. More than 500 people crowded the depot in Chippewa Falls. John was taken to the county jail for a layover. There the sheriff permitted John to hold a reception for over an hour and shake hands with hundreds of people. The following day, before entering the prison at Waupun, the sheriff and his famous prisoner stopped in a saloon where the sheriff had a beer and John had a sarsaparilla and a cigar.

John was taken to prison. Almost immediately efforts were initiated to appeal John's case to the state Supreme Court. The court readily affirmed judgment.

Efforts to free John Dietz continued. Forty thousand petitioners, including a majority of the jurors who had convicted him, signed requests asking the governor to pardon Dietz.

Then Governor Francis E. McGovern, in his bid for a senate seat, was alleged to have lost thousands of labor union votes because of the Dietz matter. Nevertheless, as one of his last acts as governor, McGovern commuted Dietz's life sentence to twenty years.

Meanwhile the family had been broken apart. For a time they lived in a boarding house with another family of eight.

In 1913, a movie company from New York hired professional actors and journeyed out to the remnants of the ransacked Dietz farm and put together a movie of the brave woodman's stand against the powerful lumber mills. For a time Myra, Leslie and Clarence traveled the state to small towns where people flocked to see the movie and actually see and hear one of the original Dietz outlaws speak.

Eventually Myra married a member of the film crew. Clarence and Leslie also married and both went into the automobile business in the more populous southern part of the state. Hattie continued on her own, waiting for John, and raising Helen and Johnny.

On May 12, 1921, John was granted an absolute pardon from Governor Blaine. The report from the warden at Waupun stated Dietz had an excellent prison record and had helped save a guard from an attack by one of the inmates.

Myra and her husband took Hattie and drove up to Waupun to pick John up. The family gathered for a reunion in Leslie's apartment above the Dietz Motor Company in Milwaukee.

The reunion was short-lived. John's resentments of old had not faded. He even accused Hattie of having been "kept" by the lumber trust during his long years in jail.

Within days the children refused to visit or even speak with their father. Within three months, even Hattie could stand no more. "All these years I waited for you, John. You have not changed a bit. I've gone through hell with you, John... No more."

Hattie moved out on John to return to the peace and tranquility she'd found during the prison years living on her own. John took up residence in a variety of rented rooms and boarding houses. He journeyed north to Winter with one landlord with the idea of making his old farm into a mink ranch. The two men stopped in Lake Tomahawk and caught a mess of bass. During their stop in Winter John was greeted as a hero. One man reportedly said, "Dietz, him I'd like to see. "

On the journey out to the farm, John's landlord reported John chased a small bear up a tree. He then repeatedly jabbed the bear with a log until the bear climbed down the tree, at which point John clubbed the bear and knocked it unconscious. "I have a Luger pistol here," John disclosed and patted his pocket. "Warden gave it back to me. " He looked down on the bear. "I don't want to kill the critter. It'll soon revive and be on its way.

The two men journeyed on to John's old farm, the fortress. The cabin was rotting. It was too isolated, the landlord said. He declined any further thoughts of setting up a mink ranch in such desolate surroundings.

The men continued on and visited John's oldest daughter, Florence May, in Rice Lake. After two days they boarded the train and returned to Milwaukee.

While in prison John had become sickly and diseased. His unidentified illness took a turn for the worst and he was hospitalized. Family members were notified and once again united and gathered around his bed. On May 8, 1924, John passed away.

"Always a fighter, a man willing to give his all for what he thought right and I personally believe he was a victim of a great injustice," Pastor Frank Dunkley said in his eulogy at the funeral.

A large stream of mourners visited the funeral parlor and attended the services. Hattie, Helen and Johnny Jr. accompanied the body by railroad back to John's hometown of Rice Lake. The body was placed in the ground in the family plot. Not even a marker was placed.

After years of trial, at least for the family, John Dietz had died, but his legend lived on.